Social Democratic Party Policies in Contemporary Europe

The end of the twentieth century saw an unprecedented coincidence of electoral success for Social Democratic parties in western Europe leading to intensive discussion on the future of this new European left. The debates often centred on the notion of a 'Third Way' and generated major expectations for policy change among Social Democratic politicians and voters.

The authors collected here examine the recent social and employment policies of these progressive parties, looking for change in the guiding principles of policy and on actual policy decisions. They show how the maxims of demand management and egalitarianism have been replaced by social investment and equality of opportunity and demonstrate the full extent of convergence on policies such as employment maximization, the containment of social expenditure and a shift towards a social investment welfare state.

The book includes case studies on the Social Democratic parties of Austria, Belgium, France, Germany, the Netherlands, Portugal, Sweden and the UK as well as on the Party of European Socialists.

Giuliano Bonoli works at the Institute of Political Science at the University of Bern and the University of Fribourg, Switzerland. **Martin Powell** is Reader in Social Policy in the Department of Social and Policy Sciences, University of Bath, UK.

Routledge/ECPR Studies in European Political Science
Edited by Thomas Poguntke, *Keele University, UK* and Jan W. van Deth, *University of Mannheim, Germany on behalf of the European Consortium for Political Research*

The Routledge/ECPR Studies in European Political Science series is published in association with the European Consortium for Political Research – the leading organisation concerned with the growth and development of political science in Europe. The series presents high-quality edited volumes on topics at the leading edge of current interest in political science and related fields, with contributions from European scholars and others who have presented work at ECPR workshops or research groups.

1 **Regionalist Parties in Western Europe**
Edited by Lieven de Winter and Huri Türsan

2 **Comparing Party System Change**
Edited by Jan-Erik Lane and Paul Pennings

3 **Political Theory and European Union**
Edited by Albert Weale and Michael Nentwich

4 **Politics of Sexuality**
Edited by Terrell Carver and Véronique Mottier

5 **Autonomous Policy Making by International Organizations**
Edited by Bob Reinalda and Bertjan Verbeek

6 **Social Capital and European Democracy**
Edited by Jan van Deth, Marco Maraffi, Ken Newton and Paul Whiteley

7 **Party Elites in Divided Societies**
Edited by Kurt Richard Luther and Kris Deschouwer

8 **Citizenship and Welfare State Reform in Europe**
Edited by Jet Bussemaker

9 **Democratic Governance and New Technology**
Technologically mediated innovations in political practice in Western Europe
Edited by Ivan Horrocks, Jens Hoff and Pieter Tops

10 **Democracy without Borders**
Transnationalisation and conditionality in new democracies
Edited by Jean Grugel

11 **Cultural Theory as Political Science**
Edited by Michael Thompson, Gunnar Grendstad and Per Selle

12 **The Transformation of Governance in the European Union**
Edited by Beate Kohler-Koch and Rainer Eising

13 **Parliamentary Party Groups in European Democracies**
Political parties behind closed doors
Edited by Knut Heidar and Ruud Koole

14 **Survival of the European Welfare State**
Edited by Stein Kuhnle

15 **Private Organisations in Global Politics**
Edited by Karsten Ronit and Volker Schneider

16 **Federalism and Political Performance**
Edited by Ute Wachendorfer-Schmidt

17 **Democratic Innovation**
Deliberation, representation and association
Edited by Michael Saward

18 **Public Opinion and the International Use of Force**
Edited by Philip Everts and Pierangelo Isernia

19 **Religion and Mass Electoral Behaviour in Europe**
Edited by David Broughton and Hans-Martien ten Napel

20 **Estimating the Policy Position of Political Actors**
Edited by Michael Laver

21 **Democracy and Political Change in the 'Third World'**
Edited by Jeff Haynes

22 **Politicians, Bureaucrats and Administrative Reform**
Edited by B. Guy Peters and Jon Pierre

23 **Social Capital and Participation in Everyday Life**
Edited by Paul Dekker and Eric M. Uslaner

24 **Development and Democracy**
What do we know and how?
Edited by Ole Elgström and Goran Hyden

25 **Do Political Campaigns Matter?**
Campaign effects in elections and referendums
Edited by David M. Farrell and Rüdiger Schmitt-Beck

26 **Political Journalism**
New challenges, new practices
Edited by Raymond Kuhn and Erik Neveu

27 **Economic Voting**
Edited by Han Dorussen and Michaell Taylor

28 **Organized Crime and the Challenge to Democracy**
Edited by Felia Allum and Renate Siebert

29 **Understanding the European Union's External Relations**
Edited by Michèle Knodt and Sebastiaan Princen

30 **Social Democratic Party Policies in Contemporary Europe**
Edited by Giuliano Bonoli and Martin Powell

31 **Decision Making Within International Organisations**
Edited by Bob Reinalda and Bertjan Verbeek

32 **Comparative Biomedical Policy**
Governing assisted reproductive technologies
Edited by Ivar Bleiklie, Malcolm L. Goggin and Christine Rothmayr

Also available from Routledge in association with the ECPR:
Sex Equality Policy in Western Europe, *Edited by Frances Gardiner*; **Democracy and Green Poltical Thought,** *Edited by Brian Doherty and Marius de Geus*; **The New Politics of Unemployment**, *Edited by Hugh Compston*; **Citizenship, Democracy and Justice in the New Europe**, *Edited by Percy B. Lehning and Albert Weale*; **Private Groups and Public Life**, *Edited by Jan W. van Deth*; **The Political Context of Collective Action**, *Edited by Ricca Edmondson*; **Theories of Secession**, *Edited by Percy Lehning*; **Regionalism Across the North/South Divide**, *Edited by Jean Grugel and Wil Hout*

Social Democratic Party Policies in Contemporary Europe

Edited by Giuliano Bonoli
and Martin Powell

Routledge
Taylor & Francis Group
LONDON AND NEW YORK

ecpr

First published 2004
by Routledge
2 Park Square, Milton Park, Abingdon, Oxon OX14 4RN

Simultaneously published in the USA and Canada
by Routledge
270 Madison Ave, New York, NY 10016

Routledge is an imprint of the Taylor & Francis Group

Transferred to Digital Printing 2005

Typeset in Baskerville by Wearset Ltd, Boldon, Tyne and Wear

British Library Cataloguing in Publication Data
A catalogue record for this book is available from the British Library

Library of Congress Cataloging in Publication Data
Social democratic party policies : in contemporary Europe / Giuliano Bonoli and Martin Powell, (eds).
p. cm.
Includes bibliographical references and index.
1. Socialist parties–Europe, Western. 2. Europe, Western–Politics and government–1989– 3. Mixed economy–Europe, Western.
I. Bonoli, Giuliano. II. Powell, Martin A., 1961–
JN94.A979.S645 2003
324.2'172'094–dc21

2003004674

ISBN 0–415–30425–3

Contents

Illustrations

Figure

Tables

Contributors

Karen Anderson is Assistant Professor of Public Administration at Leiden University. She received her PhD in political science at the University of Washington (Seattle) and was previously a Post-Doctoral Researcher at the University of Twente, the Netherlands. Among her recent publications are 'The Politics of Retrenchment in a Social Democratic Welfare State. Reform of Swedish Pensions and Unemployment Insurance', *Comparative Political Studies* (2001); 'Wohlfahrtsstaat und Arbeitsmarkt in Schweden und den Niederlanden. Ergebnisse und Erfahrungen aktueller Reformen' (The Welfare State and the Labor Market in Sweden and the Netherlands: Recent Reform Experiences) *Zeitschrift für Sozialreform* (July/August 2001); and 'Europeanisation and Pension Policy', in Philippe Pochet and Caroline de la Porte (eds), *The Transposition of EU Soft Law into National Policy* (Brussels: Peter Lang, 2002).

Andreas Aust, is a researcher in the EU project 'Welfare Reform and the Management of Societal Change' at the Humboldt University Berlin. His publications include: 'Irlands Entwicklung im europäischen Binnenmarkt', Wiesbaden 1999; 'Konjunktur und Krise des Europäischen Sozialmodells. Ein Beitrag zur politischen Präexplantationsdiagnostik', *Politische Vierteljahresschrift* (43 (2002), 2: 272–301).

Giuliano Bonoli is Associate Professor at the Department of Social Policy and Social Work of the University of Fribourg and at the Institute of Political Science of the University of Bern, Switzerland. He has written several books and articles on the politics of welfare reforms, including *The Politics of Pension Reform. Institutions and Policy Change in Western Europe*, (Cambridge: Cambridge University Press, 2000); and 'Political Institutions, Veto Points and the Process of Welfare State Adaptation', in P. Pierson (ed.) *The New Politics of the Welfare State*, (Oxford: Oxford University Press, 2001).

Dietmar Braun has studied political sciences at the University of Amsterdam (PhD) before he worked as a research fellow at the Max-Planck-Institute for Societal Research in Germany. In 1996 he presented his habilitation thesis at the Institute for Political Science at the University of Heidelberg before he became, in October 1996, full professor for political science at the University of Lausanne in Switzerland. Dietmar Braun has published on labour market, higher education and research policies and federalism as well as on modern political theory.

Ben Clift is a Lecturer in International Political Economy at Warwick University. He is currently completing a book entitled '*French Socialism in a Global Era: the Political Economy of the New Social Democracy in France*' (London: Continuum, forthcoming 2004). He has written several articles on French politics and Social democracy, including 'New Labour's Second Term and European Social Democracy' in Steve Ludlam and Martin Smith (eds), *Governing as New Labour* (Basingstoke: Palgrave, 2003), and 'Social Democracy and Globalisation: the Cases of France and the UK', *Government and Opposition*, (Vol. 37, No. 4, October 2002).

Marina Costa Lobo is associate researcher at the Social Sciences Institute of the University of Lisbon, and Lecturer in Political Science at Coimbra University. At the moment she is co-director of a Project on Electoral Behaviour and Political Attitudes of the Portuguese in a Comparative Perspective. She has published articles on Portuguese party politics and elections in several journals, namely the *Journal of Southern Europe and the Balkans*, *Party Politics*, *Southern European Politics and Society*, *West European Politics*, *Análise Social* and *Política Internacional*. Her most recent publication is a co-authored volume on reforming the Portuguese Parliament entitled *O Parlamento Português: uma reforma necessária* (Lisbon: ICS, 2002).

Monika Feigl-Heihs is on the staff of the political party 'Die Grünen' in Austria and writes her PhD on the SPÖ, SPD and Labour Party at the University of Vienna. Her research areas include Social Democratic Parties, European Union, Social and Economic Policy. She is the author of the publication: 'Wie demokratisch ist die Europäische Forschungs – und Technologiepolitik?' (Wiesbaden: Nomos, 2002; with Susanne Pernicka, Alfred Gerstl and Peter Biegelbauer).

Olivier Giraud is a fellow researcher at the French CNRS (Curapp, Université de Picardie Jules Verne). His areas of interest relate principally to comparative public policy in vocational training, education and employment and to the interactions between industrial relations' systems and public policies. Recent publications include: 'Firms' Further Training Practices and Social Exclusion – Can Industrial Relations Systems Provide Greater Equality? Theoretical and Empirical Evidence from Germany and France', in Klaus Schöman and Philipp O'Connell (eds), *Education, Training and Employment Dynamics: Transitional Labour Markets in the European Union* (Cheltenham: Edward Elgar Publishing, 2002) and 'Une école allemande d'analyse des politiques publiques entre traditions étatiques et théoriques', *Revue Française de Science Politique* (vol. 52, 2002, pp. 5–21).

Martin Hering is a PhD candidate in Political Science at the Johns Hopkins University in Baltimore (USA). His work focuses on theories of institutional change. His dissertation explains why institutional path-departure occurs in 'frozen' welfare states. Other research interests include comparative political economy, comparative political parties and elections and European integration.

Renaat Hoop is a PhD candidate at the Law Faculty of the University of Utrecht (the Netherlands). He obtained a degree in Law (LLM) at the university of Ghent (Belgium) and a Diplôme d'ètudes approfondies (DEA) en relations internationales et politique européenne at the University of Liège (Belgium). His doctoral research is on 'Citizenship and the Obligation to Work', and aims to provide a critical analysis of the work obligation in the Dutch Social Assistance Act with regard to different perspectives on citizenship, work and social security in political philosophy.

Pedro C. Magalhães is associate researcher at the Social Sciences Institute of the University of Lisbon and director of the Centre for Opinion Polls and Surveys of the Portuguese Catholic University. He has published articles in journals such as *Southern European Politics and Society*, *Journal of Southern Europe and the Balkans*, *Comparative Politics*, *Análise Social* and others, on issues such as judicial politics, parliamentary behavior, electoral turnout, and political attitudes. His most recent publication is a co-authored volume on parliamentary reform in Portugal, 'O Parlamento Português: Uma Reforma Necessária' (Lisbon: ICS, 2002).

Traute Meyer is a Lecturer in Social Policy at the University of Southampton, having previously taught at the Free University of Berlin. Her research focuses on current changes of European welfare states, and she is a member of 'Private Pensions and Social Inclusion', a six-country comparative project funded by the European Union. She has recently published 'Path dependent or neo-classical? Lessons from the Dynamics of the British Welfare Sector' in Gottschall, K. and Pfau-Effinger, B. (eds), *Gender and the Future of Employment* (Opladen: Leske & Budrich 2002; in German).

Martin Powell is a Reader in Social Policy in the Department of Social and Policy Sciences, University of Bath, UK. He has published a number of articles and books on New Labour and the Third Way in the UK. He is the editor of *Evaluating New Labour's Welfare Reforms*, Bristol: Policy Press, 2002), and the joint author (with Martin Hewitt) of *Welfare State and Welfare Change* (Maidenhead: Open University Press, 2002).

Andrea Volkens, MA, is a senior research fellow at the Social Science Research Centre Berlin. Her research on parties, elections and governments in comparative perspective has been published in a number of academic articles. Her current work is particularly concerned with updating and expanding the data collection of the Manifesto Research Group.

Series editor's preface

To a high degree the story of European politics is the story of the rise and fall of Social Democracy. The development of the modern welfare state – guaranteeing a combination of democratic rights and social security for each citizen – is shaped by the revisionist and Keynesian programmes of Social Democratic parties in many countries. In the 1990s these parties seem to have attained everything they could dream of. Most of their traditional goals have been materialized in the era since the Second World War and after a period of severe political setbacks Social Democratic parties found their way back to the focal points of political power. In spite of the 'end of ideology' and the appeal of 'neo-liberalism' Social Democratic parties regained power and enjoyed an astonishing revival. At the end of the century they participated in government power in many countries in Western Europe and most cabinets were led by members of Social Democratic parties. Is this resurgence based on a distinctively new approach to the social and economic problems of stagnating welfare states confronted with almost unsolvable budgetary troubles and highly disputed reform efforts? Are Social Democratic policy programmes in various countries based on common Social Democratic concepts and objectives? And did Social Democratic parties appealed to new parts of the electorates by reformulating their traditional goals in more appropriate or even trendy terms?

Popular debates strongly suggest a renewal and a common understanding of Social Democratic policy programmes along more or less analogous lines in several countries. This joint approach has become celebrated under the label 'Third Way'. However, already Eduard Bernstein in his classic statement of democratic socialism presented to the German Social Democratic Party at the turn of the twentieth century, pointed out to the inevitability to adopt universal principles to national conditions. Looking into the far future he already anticipated clear distinctions between actual Social Democratic policies in different countries: '... one can probably set up general political principles of Social Democracy with a claim that they apply to all countries, but no programme of action applicable for all countries is possible' (Bernstein 1972 [1898]: 166). About a century later the leaders of European Social Democratic parties challenged this position by developing the idea of a 'Third Way'. The contributors to this volume differ clearly in their study designs, selected material, and the scope of their analyses, but they all cope with claims about the convergence and the uniqueness of Social Democratic policy programmes in various countries in the last decades.

Before specific treatments of these claims are presented Martin Powell offers an overview of the main approaches and contested conclusions in this area (Chapter 1), underlining the importance of using a policy process approach to disentangle the relevant elements (values, policy goals, policy mechanisms). On the basis of extensive analyses of party policy positions as contained in election programs in the period 1945–98 Andrea Volkens observes that, although Social Democratic parties move along the left-right dimension, there are no signs of a general conversion of the distances between most major political parties in this period (Chapter 2). The next eight contributions are based on reviews and comparisons of Social Democratic policies in various countries. Dietmar Braun and Olivier Giraud analyse the adaptation of party strategies concerning citizenship in The Netherlands and Sweden during a period of exceptional change (Chapter 3). Renaat Hoop compares recent policy reforms by the two 'purple coalitions' in The Netherlands and Belgium (Chapter 4), while Marina Costa Lobo and Pedro C. Magalhães pay attention to the development of the Portuguese Social Democratic party in the last decades, especially since the party took office in 1995 (Chapter 5). Dealing with a very different situation Martin Hering examines the implementation of the reform of Germany's pension policies, stressing the significance of political power and the notion that polarization might be more important than persuasion in reaching specific goals (Chapter 6). Ben Clift discusses a number of obstacles faced by the Jospin Government in attempts to realize its 'neo-Keynesian' goals, showing the impact of the permanent electoral frailty of the French Social Democrats on their prospects for long-term successes (Chapter 7). In a comparative analyses of the wrestle with welfare state reforms in Germany and Sweden, Karen Anderson and Traute Meyer demonstrate that Social Democratic politicians in these countries thoroughly avoided the use of concepts like the 'Third Way' in their disputes about pension policy reforms (Chapter 8). Monika Feigl-Heihs focuses on the importance of steady and cohesive party leadership for the explanation of changes in Social Democratic employment policies in Austria, Germany, and the United Kingdom (Chapter 9). In the next to last contribution Andreas Aust discusses the role and position of the Party of European Socialists confronted with (neo-liberal) European employment policy programmes and its strategy of adapting the institutional settings of the EU (Chapter 10). Finally, Giuliano Bonoli returns to the two central questions of this volume – is there a convergence among Social Democratic policies and is the new approach distinctive – in his extensive concluding contribution (Chapter 11).

There is no lack of fashionable opinions on the rise and fall of Social Democratic parties. The unique character of the contributions to this volume is that they offer a critical assessment of available approaches on the basis of extensive studies of policy programmes and policy-making processes in various countries. By focusing on policies instead of ideologies or political statements, the nature of the Social Democratic revival in the 1990s becomes clear. In the last decade Social Democratic governments have implemented policies that indicate a clear break with the past. In this sense a convergence of Social Democratic party policies can be observed in Europe. Yet these policies appear to be highly depended on the specific political circumstances and historical constellations in various countries. In other words: despite the common ideological and conceptual background of 'Third Way' politics, actual Social Democratic policies exhibit a number of characteristics that can be understood only if nation-specific aspects are taken into consideration. For Social Democratic policies, then, Bernstein's prediction is as relevant today as it was more than a century ago.

Jan W. van Deth, Series Editor
Mannheim, December 2002

Reference

Bernstein, Eduard (1972 [1898]) *Evolutionary Socialism. A Criticism and Affirmation.* New York: Schocken, 7th Edition.

Acknowledgements

We would like to thank the ECPR for supporting the workshop on 'Third Ways in Europe' at the Grenoble Joint Sessions of 2001, and all the participants who contributed to the workshop. We are especially grateful to Professors Hans Keman and Frank Castles who contributed their academic rigour and good humour throughout the workshop.

Giuliano Bonoli would like to thank the participants of a staff/graduate seminar in Bern, as the project greatly benefited from the comments made by colleagues, especially Klaus Armingeon, Wolf Linder, and Sandra Lavenex.

1 Social Democracy in Europe

Renewal or retreat?

Martin Powell

Introduction

Much has been written on the recent fortunes of Social Democracy. One strand is concerned with electoral results. After varying lengths of time in opposition, Social Democratic parties returned to government in the late 1990s. Blair and Schröder (1999: 1) open their text on the Third Way by stating that 'Social democrats are in government in almost all the countries of the Union'. As an editorial in the British *Daily Telegraph* (11 June 2002: 19) put it, in 1997 when New Labour was still new, the Left was ascendant everywhere, with socialists or Social Democrats in government in thirteen and a half of the 15 EU states (the exception was Spain, with the half in Ireland whose parties do not fit the classic Left–Right definitions). Dyson (1999: 195) claims that following the German election of 1998 West European Social Democracy found itself in a uniquely advantageous position. For the first time in the history of the European Union social-democratic-led governments were in power in Bonn, London and Paris; the Party of European Socialists (see Aust, Chapter 10, this volume) was represented in the leadership of 11 of the 15 governments. By August 2000, according to Green-Pedersen *et al.* (2001), they were in government in 10 out of 15 EU nations. This electoral dominance was termed by Cuperus and Kandel (1998) 'the magical return of Social Democracy'. However, as we entered the new millennium the magic seemed to be wearing off (see Bonoli, Chapter 11, this volume). The left lost power in countries such as Denmark, Italy, Portugal, Austria, the Netherlands and France. For a time, it appeared that only Britain was immune to the return of the right, where in 2001 New Labour secured another landslide electoral victory. More recently, Social Democratic governments have been (just) re-elected in Sweden and Germany, and the Dutch PvdA regained much of the support they lost some eight months earlier in an Election of January 2003. On the other hand, in the same month the German SDP lost regional elections and so the Christian Democrats now have the power to veto SDP legislation in the Bundersrat. The electoral prospects for Social Democracy, then, are very uncertain.

However, at the height of this parliamentary dominance, electoral optimism coexisted with pessimism. Critics argued that Social Democrats entered office only by moving to the right: 'Social Democratic governments' were, in effect, no longer Social Democratic. The main problem here is the seemingly endless debate about what constitutes 'Social Democracy'. For roughly a century, Social Democratic parties in different countries have shown marked variations, and accusations of moves to the right as old as the parties themselves (e.g. Berman 1998; Pierson 2001). Even the chronology of the 'golden age of Social Democracy' is not fully clear (see Hicks 1999: 110, fn). In short, the overarching question to be explored in this book concerns not Social Democratic governments per se, but Social Democratic party policies in Europe.

Recent debate on the future of Social Democracy is characterised by a great variety of positions. On the other hand, Social Democracy is in retreat or has ended (e.g. Callaghan 2000; Thomson 2000; Glyn 2001). As Pierson (2001: 1) summarises, there is a widespread consent that traditional Social Democracy is exhausted. On the other hand, other writers point to the 'the magical return of Social Democracy' (Cuperus and Kandel 1998) and 'new Social Democracy' (Gamble and Wright 1999). However, they are clear that 'new' Social Democracy is not the same as its 'golden age' version between the 1940s and the 1970s. In short, Social Democracy has been transformed (Kitschelt 1994). The obvious – but unresolved – issue is to what extent Social Democracy can be transformed before it ceases to be Social Democracy? In other words, what are the limits to Social Democracy?

Although there is a vast literature on Social Democratic renewal, it suffers from a number of problems and gaps. The first is that much of this literature was written in the period when Social Democratic parties were in opposition or newly elected to office. There is much less material – as yet – on the policies of Social Democratic parties in office. The second is that while there is general agreement that Social Democracy has changed in recent years, the parameters of change are less clear. Social democracy has often been vaguely defined, and rarely operationalised. This means that it is difficult to place changes in context. The different possible changes include variation from the 'ideal type'; variation from 'old' Social Democratic parties in office; convergence with other parties; and convergence between countries. What are the important variables? By how much have they changed? How far can they change before they break the limits of Social Democracy? The third, and linked, problem is that much of literature is at a fairly high level of abstraction. Some of it is concerned with causes and strategies (e.g. vote and office seeking). When there is a focus on policies, it is generally on economic (e.g. end of Keynesianism) rather than social policies. However, the 'fine print' of policy is important. For example, many analyses focus on 'supply side policies', but these may contain a large range (e.g. Boix 1998). Moreover, many Social Democratic parties in the past and present stress active labour market policy, but this may also see a large variation (Lodemel and Trickey 2000). There has also been a focus on certain countries such as the Netherlands, Germany, Sweden and the UK and on certain broad policy areas such as social security. Less attention has been paid to countries such as Austria and Belgium, and more specific policy areas such as pensions.

The debate on new Social Democracy is inextricably linked with the debate on the 'Third Way' (e.g. White 2001). This is associated with the writings of Giddens (1998, 2000, 2001, 2002) and the administrations of Clinton and Blair in the USA and the UK respectively. Proponents of the Third Way make two broad claims. First, the Third Way is a renewed or modernised Social Democracy: it is a left of centre project (Blair 1998, 2001; Giddens 1998, 2000, 2001, 2002). Second, the Third Way is a global model (Blair 2001; Giddens 2001, 2002). According to Blair (1998: 2):

> the left is not returning to the old politics of isolation, nationalisation, bureaucracy and 'tax and spend'. . . . Across Europe, Social Democratic governments are pioneering welfare state reform, tackling social exclusion, engaging business in new partnerships, and establishing a stable economic basis for long-term stability and investment.

Giddens (2001: 1–2) defines the Third Way as a generic series of endeavours, common to the majority of left parties and thinkers in Europe and elsewhere, to restructure leftish doctrines. In this wider sense, Giddens stresses that whether or not one uses 'Third Way' does not matter: 'modernizing Social Democracy' or 'the modernizing left' (or perhaps, Tonyism – after Blair and Giddens) can be used instead. The Third Way is not to be identified solely with the outlook and policies of the New Democrats, or indeed any other specific party, but is a broad ideological stream with several tributaries flowing into it. The changes made by left parties in Scandinavia, the Netherlands, France or Italy since the late 1980s are as much part of Third Way politics as those developed in Anglo-Saxon countries (Giddens 2001: 2). Interestingly, this is similar to Jospin's earlier view before he rejected the term: 'I believe that the Third Way is the national form that the effort to reshape theory and policy has taken in the UK, the same project as that has been embarked upon by all the socialist and Social Democratic parties in Europe (Jospin 1999: 4–5). According to Merkel (2001: 51), at the end of the 20th century the debate about the Third Way has become the most important reform discourse in the European party landscape. He claims that there are at least four different Third Way models in Europe (but see Callinicos 2001: 9). Etzioni (2000: 13–14) sees the countries of Continental Europe, the UK and the USA all as 'different Third Way societies'. While societies such as France and Italy drive more in the left lane with others such as the USA more on the right, 'the road they all travel is fully distinct from the one charted by totalitarian and libertarian approaches.' Moreover, 'while the various Third Way societies differ in their specific synthesis of the ways of the state and the market, they are pulling closer to one another.' Callinicos (2001: 1) writes that the Third Way has set the agenda for the moderate left on a European, and indeed a global, scale.

Both claims have been criticised. First, many critics argue that the Third Way has more in common with neoliberalism than Social Democracy (e.g. Hay 1999; Thomson 2000). Navarro (1999) writes that the Third Way is closer to Christian Democracy than Social Democracy (cf. Deacon 2000). Second, it is seen as an Anglo-Saxon model, and not exportable to Continental Europe (see Bonoli and Powell 2002; Powell and Barrientos, 2003).

The focus of this book is not on the Anglo-Saxon Third Way *per se.* However, it is a useful backcloth for two main reasons. First, the debate about the Third Way is relevant for new Social Democracy. The problems of defining the Third Way (e.g. *The Economist* 1998; White 1998; Powell 2000; Callinicos 2001; Pierson 2001; Powell and Barrientos 2003; but see Etzioni 2000: 13) parallel those of new Social Democracy (see below). As Clift (2001: 72) argues, it needs more rigourous definition before firm conclusions can be drawn about its compatibility with contemporary European Social Democracy. Second, the concept of *a* Third Way or trichotomy (rather than *the* Third Way) is useful to analyse whether new Social Democracy is different from the 'first' way of old Social Democracy and the 'second' way of neoliberalism. In the words of Przeworski (2001), how many ways can be third?

Our main aim in this book is to address the problems and fill the gaps identified above. In other words, a focus on Social Democratic party politics in Europe will complement existing studies. We examine policies for a broad range of countries and policy areas to critically examine welfare state trajectories in Europe. The welfare state has often been considered to be the jewel in the crown of Social Democracy. For Green-Pedersen *et al.* (2001), it is its heartland. However, the specification of the Social Democratic welfare state remains problematic (see below).

The remainder of this chapter provides a broad context for the contributions that follow. First, the rationale for the current study is justified by outlining the problems and gaps of existing studies. Second, a broad framework of analysis differentiates discourse, values, policy goals and policy mechanisms.

The long fall and rise of Social Democracy

As Pierson (2001: 20) notes, it is often the 'high water mark' of the 'golden age' of Social Democracy that critics have most frequently in mind when they think of Social Democracy's decline and fall (p. 20; cf. Callaghan 2000: 6). However, 'Social Democracy' has varied over time and space. Pierson (2001) begins his chronological discussion in the nineteenth century, viewing Social Democracy as a label that could be attached to the claims of both social ownership and democratisation. He progresses through Bernstein's revision of Marx at the turn of the twentieth century to 'classical' Social Democracy' of the 'golden age' after the Second World War. Other recent accounts have extended this chronology. For example, Stammers (2001) traces the evolution from traditional through modernising to globalising Social Democracy. Similar discussions of the 'global age' are given in Garrett (1998), Krieger (1999) and Tam (2001), but see Berman (1998) and Hicks (1999).

Much has been written about changes in Social Democracy since the end of the 'golden age' (e.g. Padgett and Paterson 1991; Piven 1991; Gillespie and Patterson 1993; Bell and Shaw 1994; Ladrech and Marliere 1998; Callaghan 2000; Pierson 2001). Much of this literature is pessimistic, focusing on problems, retreat, decline and periods of political opposition. This culminates in terms such as 'after Social Democracy' and 'the death of Social Democracy' (see Pierson 2001). However, a more optimistic literature (e.g. Boix 1998; Garrett 1998) suggests that partisan differences may still exist. Writing after the electoral successes of the late 1990s, Cuperus and Kandel (1998) write of the 'magical return of Social Democracy'. Critics argue that 'Social Democratic parties' have magically returned only by using a wand to make Social Democracy disappear (e.g. Krieger 1999; Hay 1999; Thomson 2000). This clearly relates to the problem of defining the limits of Social Democracy (below), but the point to note here is that much of the literature is anachronistic in that it could not focus on the record of Social Democratic parties in office.

The limits of Social Democracy

Pierson (2001: 19) argues that many existing typifications do very limited justice to the diversity and ambiguity of the Social Democratic tradition (cf. Berman 1998; Cuperus and Kandel 1998; Hicks 1999; Przeworski 2001). Indeed, it is really quite unclear when and what Social Democracy is or was. In practice Social Democratic parties and policies in few countries fitted their 'textbook' or 'ideal type' models. At times, Social Democratic strategies were pursued by governments that would never call themselves Social Democratic, and Social Democratic governments pursued non-Social Democratic programmes. This section uses two recent frameworks to analyse the limits of Social Democracy.

The first approach is given by Krieger (1999: ch 1) who aims to locate British Social Democracy in theoretical and comparative perspective. He presents three models of European Social Democracy: the institutional–collectivist model; analytical Social Democracy (Przeworki 1985) and the strategic adjustment model (Kitschelt 1994). Although they add important dimensions in some respects, Krieger finds major problems with the last two models. With narrow and fixed definitions of class and conceptions of party organisation, analytical Social Democracy is poorly equipped to ask important contemporary questions. On the other hand, the strategic adjustment model is too wide. There is a disconcerting vagueness in what might be called the political morality of Social Democracy. Strategic considerations take precedence over the traditional core egalitarian or redistributive values of parliamentary socialism. The strategic adjustment approach makes it very difficult to analyse Social Democracy in all its dimensions, as the term assumes a nominalism being applied *de facto* to any party that carries a labour, socialist or Social Democratic label. The institutional–collectivist model is a conceptual amalgam intended to represent base-line European Social Democracy. According to Krieger, this approach has dominated both the academic and the wider public discussion of Social Democracy in both the US and the UK. Using Keynesian economics, states intervened extensively to regulate economies, promote economic growth, and secure nearly full employment while expanding welfare provision. Indeed, 'its normative dimension is such standard fare of the center-left that it requires only brief comment here' (p. 6). The model covers quite a range of empirical variation. At the height of the postwar settlement, there was extensive variation in the empirical application of the model in different countries in a host of dimensions: adherence to Keynesian principles; expression of collectivist principles' labour movement dynamics and the level and institutional form of labour inclusion in economic and social policy; approach to economic governance and the degree of state planning; levels of spending, instituitionalisation, universality, range of provision, and comprehensiveness of the welfare state; and several more (pp. 6–7). The ends of the spectrum include Swedish Social Democracy and British Labourism. However, the most glaring weakness of this model, the 'classic base-line interpretation of European Social Democracy' (p. 11) lies in the fact that 'Social Democracy in the form theorized by the institutional–collectivist model ceased to exist in pure form (if it ever existed) early in the 1970s' (p. 10). Krieger considers that no 'off-the-rack' model of Social Democracy fits New Labour without significant alterations (p. 16), and so he proceeds to use directly a set of key variables of agency, policy approach, political morality, and institutional orientation (p. 20).

The second approach is given by Hay (1999: 54) who points out that the term 'Social Democracy' is frequently deployed in a great diversity of ways, but it is virtually never defined – it being assumed, falsely, that protagonists in the debate and readers alike share a common and largely intuitive sense of its essence.' Hay (1999: 56) presents three potential strategies. The first is to specify a number of Social Democratic parties and to argue that Social Democracy is, like the view of socialism of Herbert Morrison (a British Cabinet Minister in the 1945 Labour Government), simply 'what Social Democratic parties do'. This strategy, though frequently deployed, is seldom defended explicitly (but see Kitschelt 1994: 1). According to such a view, Social Democracy will persist almost indefinitely. The second, equally evasive, strategy is to define Social Democracy historically in terms of the practice of nominally (or self-proclaimed) Social Democratic parties at some point in their hey-day. According to such a view, Social Democracy is largely a thing of the past. The third is to extrapolate from the history of Social Democracy a series of (potentially) trans-historical premises and values. 'It is only this last strategy which offers us the possibility of any comparative historical analysis of Social Democracy' (p. 56). Hay (1999: 57–8) presents 'a rather more exacting definition: a commitment to redistribution, democratic economic governance, and social protectionism'. By such a definition, the Labour Party throughout the post-war period was Social Democratic in its stated aspirations and ideology, though far less frequently Social Democratic in practice. In the late 1970s, in government, it came to subordinate its, by that stage somewhat beleaguered, Social Democratic aspirations to the perceived (and, to some extent, externally imposed) imperatives of economic prudence. Elsewhere, Hay (1999: 12–14) differentiates novelty into three different senses: endogenous; comparative and contextual. The first relates to claims made about an institution or party with respect to its own immediate history or tradition. The second is judged with respect to contemporary conduct of other parties, either competitor parties, or parties in different political systems that traditionally share a common lineage or ethos (e.g. other Social Democratic or labour parties) – domestically or internationally. The third concerns the fit between the party and its changed external environment, which includes demographic and other socio-economic trends and the development of international or global political economy.

A recent attempt to develop a 'trait' model that appears to combine Krieger's institutional-collectivist model and Hay's trans-historical values approach is that of Stammers (2001: 28) who argues that Social Democracy has always been a moving target, so defining it is a difficult, contingent and contentious task. He presents six characteristics of Social Democracy (pp. 30–1). The first three- commitments to liberal democracy, capitalism and mitigation of some of the worst effects of capitalism – 'comprise the ideological terrain upon which the vast bulk of arguments for and against Social Democracy were contested during the twentieth century.' First, Social Democracy assumes that liberal democracy works. Second, it perceives capitalism as both inevitable and also inherently dynamic, accepts the logical and structural imperatives of a capitalist market economy. Third, it recognises that inequalities and deprivation are generated by a capitalist market economy but believes that these can be effectively mitigated by some (greater or lesser) forms of economic and/or social intervention and regulation. 'These points should be relatively uncontentious' (p. 30). However, the second set of three – elitism, statism and methodological nationalism – are required when thinking about global governance, and have rarely been given the attention they deserve either by proponents or critics. Fourth, Social Democracy is largely wedded to an elitist understanding of the potential relationship between people and political leadership and tends to assume a top-down, hierarchical model of governance. Fifth, it almost entirely is 'statist' both internally and externally. Sixth, it is both united and split by a commitment to methodological nationalism: a privileging of national levels of debate, analysis and policy over other possible levels, whether local, regional or global.

Giddens (1998) contrasts 'old-style' Social Democracy with the Third Way of renewed Social Democracy. The defining characteristics of old Social Democracy are: pervasive state involvement in social and economic life; state domination of civil society; collectivism; Keynesian demand management, plus corporatism; a confined role for markets; the mixed or social economy; full employment; strong egalitarianism; a comprehensive welfare state; linear modernisation; low ecological consciousness; internationalism; and belonging to bipolar world. In contrast, the key values of the Third Way are: equality; protection of the vulnerable; freedom as autonomy; no rights without responsibilities; no authority without democracy; cosmopolitan pluralism; and philosophic conservatism. The most important programmatic elements are: the radical centre; the new democratic state; active civil society; the democratic family; the new mixed economy; equality as inclusion; positive welfare; the social investment state; the cosmopolitan nation; and cosmopolitan democracy.

Thomson (2000) is one of the few other writers who has explicitly compared 'classic' and 'new' Social Democracy. He claims that the aims of the two can be presented as follows: equality versus fairness; collective rights versus individual rights; expansion of the state to counteract the ills of capitalism versus 'aid the market'; redistribution versus individual entitlement to achieve enhancement; the state as a provider versus the state as enabler; an ethic of cooperation versus community.

This is not the place for a comprehensive discussion of the characteristics of Social Democracy, nor an attempt to operationalise the term. However, it is sufficient to demonstrate a number of points. First, there is a considerable overlap between the authors discussed above. Second, many of the criteria are fairly vague. For example, Pierson (2001: 16) criticises Hay's criteria as too modest – all governments intervene to moderate initial market income – and too demanding – no government has attempted to secure full equality of outcome. Third, the list above appears to conflate values, policies and institutions. For example, some of Thomson's 'aims' may be best considered as 'means' (see below). Fourth, there have been few attempts to operationalise these criteria. Garrett (1998) develops an index of 'left-labour power' based on political power in cabinets and legislatures and labour market institutions. On the basis of rankings in the top five, middle four and bottom five respectively (p. 127), he finds that a Social Democratic corporatist regime (Austria, Denmark, Finland, Norway, Sweden); 'incoherent regime' (Belgium, Germany, Italy, Netherlands); and a market liberal regime (Canada, France, Japan; UK; USA). Similarly, there is an extensive literature on left-right scales for political parties (e.g. Budge *et al.* 2001; see Volkens, Chapter 2, this volume). However, it would be difficult to claim that either approach represents a direct measure of Social Democracy.

In search of the Social Democratic welfare state

In very general terms, there has not been much of an explicit focus on the criteria of the Social Democratic welfare state, and many of these sources tend to focus on economic policy (e.g. Boix 1998; Garrett 1998; Glyn 2001). In general terms political scientists have not been greatly concerned with the welfare state for its own sake. Rather they tend to use the welfare state as a dependent variable to test hypotheses (see Esping-Andersen 1990). Conversely, few social policy analysts have been greatly interested in the concepts of Social Democracy.

Although there are other accounts of the Social Democratic model of the welfare state (e.g. Shalev 1983; Huber and Stephens 1998, 2001a, b, 2002; Hicks 1999; Clasen 2002), the best known is that of Esping-Andersen (1985, 1990, 1999; see Anderson and Meyer, Chapter 8, this volume). This presents three worlds of welfare capitalism: Social Democratic, Continental and liberal regimes. The Social Democratic world consists mainly of the Nordic countries. Its essential characteristics are being comprehensive and inclusive, universal, redistributive, service heavy, gender egalitarian, and active or labour mobilizing (cf. Huber and Stephens 2001a,b). To sum up with the original term of Esping-Andersen, the Social Democratic regime decommodifies: it provides income that is not related to market worth. A cottage industry has developed to provide a critique of this thesis. For the moment, three points will be mentioned. First, Esping-Andersen is clear that 'welfare effort' or state welfare expenditure is not a particularly good indicator of a welfare state (cf. Bonoli 1997; Powell and Hewitt 2002). However, second, his definition of a welfare state is not clear. It is implicitly based on the Swedish model (Ikea worship?), and concentrates on cash income rather than service benefits. Third, there is a potential paradox in that Swedish active labour market policy exists to reintegrate people into the labour market, or *re*-commodify. Indeed, as Kolberg and Esping-Andersen (1992: 9) put it, 'The Beveridge model of the UK, or the People's Home model of Sweden, was not meant to stimulate exit from the market; on the contrary, it was designed to encourage maximum labour market dependence.'

Bearing these points in mind, much of the writing on the Social Democratic welfare state suffers from a number of problems. First, definitions of the welfare state are absent or at best fairly thin (e.g. Garrett 1998; Callaghan 2000). Second, there is much reliance on the index of welfare effort (e.g. Garrett 1998). Third, there is a concentration on unconditional social rights as an index of Social Democracy. However, it has been argued that the aims of social citizenship were best characterised as 'softer' than the conventional 'hard' accounts suggest (Powell 2002). Marshallian social citizenship was more compatible with 'equality as inclusion' (Giddens 1998) than equality of outcome. As Pierson (2001: 122) argues, the idea that Social Democratic conceptions of citizenship ever underwrote unconditional access for citizens to extensive societal resources is some way wide of the mark (cf. Kleinman 2002). In particular, work has always been central to the Social Democratic welfare state. Fourth, there is a great emphasis on the 'Keynesian welfare state'. However, as Pierson (2001: 60–1) puts it, Social Democrats used a range of tools to achieve their economic goals, and 'Social Democracy cannot be reduced to the Keynesian welfare state'. Keynes was, after all, a political liberal. If some version of Social Democracy existed before Keynesianism (see Berman 1998), then some version may exist after it. Not all Social Democratic welfare states made extensive use of Keynesianism, and some countries such as the USA and Japan – surely not Keynesian welfare states – made extensive use of it. Fifth, accounts of social policy are often fairly thin and brief. For example, Krieger (1999) discusses social policy in under four pages (pp. 25–9) and in his key table (p. 172) the policy approach of institutional–collectivist Social Democracy – 'postwar settlement, Keynesianism, and welfare state' – is contrasted with that of New Labour – 'Third Way, Keynesianism, and business partnership. Similarly, Hay (1999: 117–23) examines welfare reform and social policy in terms of pensions, family policy, NHS reform, and workfare. However, his selection of eight criteria and the evidence used to justify his conclusions cannot do justice to a much more complex story. This 'keyword' or 'key phrase' approach is a useful starting point for setting the framework of the debate (see below), but it must be followed by more detailed accounts that aim to place empirical flesh on the analytical bones.

Pierson (2001: 60) concludes that in practice welfare states, even those that have been subclassified as Social Democratic, have varied significantly in size, structure and intent and we need to attend to these important differences if we are to avoid the trap of generalising, as some have been tempted to do, about the past and present of the 'Social Democratic welfare state'. In particular, it is important to sharpen up the criteria of change, and to provide more detail rather than rely on keywords, criteria based on mythical histories, and measurement of problematic variables. The next section introduces the framework that informs the choice of criteria, while the remaining chapters fill in some of the policy details.

The essence of Social Democracy

The problem in examining the debate on the renewal of Social Democracy is that the terms of new Social Democracy and the Third Way is used in very different senses. A number of commentators have suggested broad characteristics or themes. Giddens (1998: 70) suggests a 'Third Way programme' including the new democratic state, active civil society, the democratic family, the new mixed economy, equality as inclusion, positive welfare, and the social investment state. White's (1998) themes include the state as guarantor, not necessarily provider; receptivity to forms of mutualism; new thinking about public finance, including increased use of environmental taxes, hypothecation at the margin, new consultative procedures on tax, and community fund; and asset-based egalitarianism. Vandenbrouke (1998) offers what Cuperus and Kandel (1998: 25) term 'the nine commandments of a post-pessimistic Social Democracy'. These are full employment for men and women, attention to new risks for the welfare state, an 'intelligent' welfare state, a revalorisation of active labour market policies, subsidising low-skilled labour as a new redistribution target, preventing poverty traps, developing a competitive private service sector, finding non-dogmatic approaches to a fair distribution of burdens and benefits, and maintaining discipline with regard to growth of average wage levels. Blair and Schröder (1999) suggest a 'new programme for changed realities' that include a new supply-side agenda for the left, a robust and competitive market framework, a tax policy to promote sustainable growth, adaptability and flexibility, a active government that invests in human and social capital, and sound public finance (see Green-Pedersen *et al.* 2001). Ferrera *et al.* (2001) list 'elements of an optimal policy mix' that consist of a robust macroeconomic strategy; wage moderation; employer-friendly and efficient tax and social policy; labour market flexibility and 'flexicurity'; investment in education, training and mobility; and new forms of fighting poverty and social exclusion. Thomson (2000: 159) contrasts six 'aims' of classic and new Social Democracy. However, these aims are not policy goals in our terms, and are best considered as broad themes: fairness; individual rights; aid the market; individual initiative to achieve enhancement; state as enabler; and community. Finally, Bresser-Pereira (2001: 368) distinguishes the new left from the old left and the new right from the perspective of developing countries or 'the view from the south'. These characteristics are party control by the new middle class; a complementary role of the state; managerial state reform; basic social services executed by public non-state organisations; financing of basic social services by the state; state assured basic state security; neo Keynesian macroeconomic policy; and globalisation seen as a challenge.

The positions of the commentators are expanded in their original sources. Clearly such a brief listing cannot do justice to the variety of arguments advanced. However, it does illustrate the problem of constructing a composite model of new Social Democracy. In particular, different dimensions such as aims and mechanisms are conflated. In other words, it is difficult to specify clearly the form of the 'dependent variables' of the new Social Democracy.

The next section aims to explore the different ways of defining new Social Democracy as a Third Way, differentiating it from first and second ways of old Social Democracy and neoliberalism. This may be found in discourse, values, policy goals or policy mechanisms (Bonoli and Powell 2002; Powell and Barrientos 2003).

Discourse

A significant degree of recent attention has been directed towards political discourse (e.g. Fairclough 2000; Schmidt 2000, 2001). The most sustained analysis is Fairclough's analysis of New Labour in Britain. According to Fairclough (2000) the Third Way is a political discourse built out of elements from other political discourses, of the left and of the right. For example, 'enterprise' belongs to the right, while social justice belongs to the left. The language of the Third Way is a rhetoric of reconciliation such as 'economic dynamism as well as social justice', 'enterprise as well as fairness'. While the old politics suggests that you had to choose between the economic competence associated with the right and the social justice of the left, the Third Way declares that these are not antagonistic. It follows that it is important not just to identify the keywords of new Social Democracy such as 'new', 'tough', 'deal', 'reform' and 'partnership', but also their relationship with the rest of the discourse. The discourse contains a mix of 'old left' words such as welfare, new right words such as enterprise and words that attempt to stamp a Third Way identity such as partnership.

Values

Most Social Democratic parties insist that their values have not changed. However, analysing values is problematic for two main reasons. First, an adequate understanding of values requires more than one word treatments. This links with an extensive ideology/ political philosophy literature (see George and Wilding (1985) for an application to social policy). There is general agreement that equality is a key value for Social Democrats (e.g. Crosland 1964; George and Wilding 1985; Thomson 2000). Similarly, freedom, individualism and inequality are the fundamental social values of the anti-collectivists (e.g. George and Wilding 1985: 19). However, terms such as 'equality' as essentially contestable concepts, meaning different things to different people. More specificity is needed to explain more precise meanings. For example, neo-liberals emphasise some dimensions of equality such as equality before the law and basic ('starting gate') equality of opportunity. It follows that values must be more clearly defined and linked with goals (see below).

Second, and linked, it is not clear whether new Social Democracy is concerned with 'old' values, new or redefined meanings of old values, or new values. The best known accounts argue the first position. Blair (1998, 2001) and Blair and Schröder (1999) claim that the Third Way is concerned with linking traditional values with modern means. According to Blair (1998) these traditional values are equal worth, opportunity for all, responsibility and community. Blair and Schröder (1999) write that fairness and social justice, liberty and equality of opportunity, solidarity and responsibility to others – these values are timeless. Social democracy will never sacrifice them. Moreover, there is certainly not complete agreement. To some extent, different values draw on different traditions of socialism (e.g. Crosland 1964), and some terms have been more prominent than others. 'Responsibility to others, equality of opportunity and equal worth' hardly fits on flags as easily as 'liberty, equality, fraternity'. In particular, equality of opportunity has often been dismissed as insufficient (e.g. Crosland 1964; George and Wilding 1985).

Critics point out that some terms have been redefined. Moreover, a few 'new' values appear to have been smuggled in. Positive mentions of terms such as entrepreneurship (e.g. Blair 1998, Blair and Schröder 1999) were rarely part of the vocabulary of traditional Social Democracy.

Goals

Goals or objectives may be seen as a more specific operationalisation of values. For example, 'equality' is often referred to as a value, but this may result in very different policy objectives such as equality of inputs or equality of outcomes. As seen above, the Third Way is sometimes viewed as moving from equality of outcome to equality of opportunity (e.g. Lister 2000).

Policy mechanisms

The discussion of policy themes (above) includes some mechanisms, but they often tend to be rather vague. New Social Democracy emphasises conditional or contractarian welfare. Rights are not 'dutiless' but tend to be given to those who have fulfilled their obligations, which are largely associated with work. Services are largely financed by the state, but may be delivered by private or voluntary bodies in a 'purchaser/ provider split'. Rather than hierarchies or markets, co-ordination and collaboration through 'partnerships' or networks is stressed. Work is central to new Social Democracy. Full male and female employment is to be achieved more by the 'supply-side' than by 'old' style Keynesian demand management. Blair and Schröder (1999) emphasise a new supply side for the left, including active labour market policy. Although this will have both carrots and sticks, it will emphasise advice from case workers and investment in human capital rather than 'starving the poor back into work' through low or time-limited benefits. The slogan of 'making work pay' includes a national minimum wage, in-work benefits of tax credits (or fiscal welfare) and making high quality, affordable child care available.

There are some clear policy suggestions in a 'new programme for changed realities', although 'we are presenting our ideas as an outline, not a finalised programme' (Blair and Schröder 1999; see Green-Pedersen *et al.* 2001). There are positive references to a welfare system that promotes work; education, training, lifelong learning, and employability; and active labour market policy. They claim that the balance between the state and the market needs to change. Although both supply and demand-side policies, 'macro-economic stability and micro-economic flexibility', are viewed as important, there is a clear message that the latter has been neglected, and there is a need for 'a new supply-side agenda for the left'.

New Social Democracy as a Third Way

As suggested earlier, a brief keyword approach is necessarily rather stylised at best, and inaccurate at worst (cf Bresser-Pereira 2001). Clearly, the same concepts and policies cannot be expected across Europe. Just as 'old' Social Democracy and neo-liberalism in practice varied from their textbook characteristics, there is unlikely to be a uniform 'new' Social Democracy given the different national contexts, with different histories, polities, and economies (e.g. Cuperus and Kandel 1998; Leonard 2000; Clift 2001; Bonoli and Powell 2002). To this end, the Table 1.1 should be seen as a broad framework that will inform the analysis in the following chapters.

Table 1.1 sets out the broad themes of new Social Democracy in terms of discourse, values, goals and policy instruments. This framework is applied to the material presented by the contributors in subsequent chapters in Table 1.2.

It can be seen that while the contributors cover a wide range of sectors and countries there is some measure of agreement on the basic themes (see Bonoli, Chapter 11, this volume). Although few countries use the term 'Third Way', there is a general commitment to a new pragmatic approach that reconciles previously antagonistic themes. It is generally claimed that old values remain, but will be achieved by new means. However, while most governments stress 'social justice', this may have been redefined with greater emphasis placed on linked concepts such as duties and obligations. Goals generally included high levels of male and female employment; equality of opportunity and solidarity; constraints on public expenditure and limited and often redefined redistribution. Policy

Table 1.1 Dimensions of the Third Way in social policy

Dimension	*Old Social Democracy*	*New Social Democracy*	*Neoliberalism*
Discourse	rights	rights *and* responsibilities	responsibilities
	equity	equity *and* efficiency	efficiency
	market failure	market *and* state failure	state failure
Values	equality of outcome	inclusion	equality of opportunity
	security	positive welfare	insecurity
Policy goals	equality of outcome full employment	minimum opportunities employability	equality of opportunity low inflation
Policy means	rights state state finance and delivery security	conditionality civil society/market state/private finance and delivery flexicurity	responsibilities market/civil society private/state finance and delivery insecurity
	hierarchy	network	market
	high tax and spend	pragmatic tax to invest	low tax and spend
	high services and benefits	high services and low benefits	low services and benefits
	high cash redistribution	high asset redistribution	low redistribution
	universalism	pragmatic mix of universalism and selectivity	selectivity
	high wages	National Minimum Wage/tax credits	low wages

mechanisms tend to include activation; labour market flexibility; privatisation; a greater tolerance of means-testing; fiscal welfare; and investing in human capital.

Conclusions

Our 'policy process' approach suggests that it is conceptually important to disentangle the different elements of discourse, values, policy goals and policy mechanisms. A country that 'talks' a Third Way may not have Third Way policies in place. Conversely, a country that does not use or even rejects the label may have been practising the Third Way for many years (cf Green-Pedersen *et al.* 2001). Similarly, there may be some policy drift between values and goals, or between goals and policies.

From this brief macro-level analysis, it is easy to detect similarities between countries, but differences will also become apparent from the

Table 1.2 Dimensions of new Social Democracy in Europe

Author	*Sector/country*	*Discourse*	*Values*	*Goals*	*Policy instruments*
Braun & Giraud	Citizenship				
	Netherlands	pragmatic consensual	more market & less government	jobs, jobs, jobs	workfare/ALMP
	Sweden	third road; adapted Social Democratic model	efficiency; weakened egalitarianism and paternalism	growth > redistribution	supply side; ALMP; less universalistic pensions
Hoop	Netherlands	Flexibility & security; Polder model	social justice; responsibility	jobs, jobs, jobs	fiscal welfare; ALMP; Labour market flexibility; activation; rights and duties
	Belgium	active welfare state	positive welfare	employment	fiscal welfare; ALMP; activation
Lobo & Magalhaes	Portugal	pragmatism; reject TW, new way	equity > equality; pragmatic liberalism	redefine equality as inclusion;	employment centred–social policy; responsibility; privatisation; state as regulator; investment in human capital
Hering	Pensions				
	Germany	pragmatism	individual responsibility	fiscal discipline;	supply side agenda; decrease tax and expenditure; partial pension privatisation

Clift	France	realism de gauche; pragmatic realism	values and ends same, but different means	employment creation and protection; universal health coverage; means-testing	35 hour week; interventionist employment policy; fiscal redistribution; partial privatisation; chastened Keynesianism
Anderson & Meyer	pensions Sweden	Social Democratic renewal; adaptation; new social risks; active welfare state	reduced de-commodification	inclusion; protection for vulnerable groups	work incentives; publicly-regulated privatisation; enhanced role for market; less redistribution
	Germany	modernisation	limited de-commodification	individualisation of risk	partial privatisation
Feigl-Heihs	employment Austria	(all) supply-side	(all) move towards pragmatic liberalism	(all) increased conditionality; flexibility	(all) flexibility privatisation; ALMP mix of supply and demand supply side
	Germany				
	UK				
Aust	employment PES	modernised European Social Model; new European way; new social contract	reconciling economic efficiency and social progress, (but) increased neo-liberalism	competitiveness; social investment state; reform of welfare state	investing in people; increasing human capital; market intervention; supply side policies
Bonoli		few use Third Way	Equality of opportunity	maximise employment; Contain public expenditure; social investment	

micro-level analyses of the contributors in subsequent chapters. Put another way, the scale of the map is important (cf. Powell and Barrientos 2003). Pitched at the large scale, many previous analyses – like this chapter – tend to stress similarities, but important differences are also clear from the smaller scale study of countries and sectors in subsequent chapters. Both perspectives are essential ingredients to the study of Social Democratic party policies in Europe.

References

Bell, S. and Shaw, E. (eds) (1994) *Conflict and Cohesion in Western European Social Democratic Parties*, London: Pinter.

Blair, T. (1998) *The Third Way*, London: Fabian Society.

Blair, T. (2001) 'Third way, phase two', *Prospect*, March.

Blair. T. and Schröder, G. (1999) *Europe: the Third Way/Die Neue Mitte*, London: Labour Party.

Berman, S. (1998) *The Social Democratic Moment*, Cambridge, Mass.: Harvard University Press.

Boix, C. (1998) *Political Parties, Growth and Equality*, Cambridge: Cambridge University Press.

Bonoli, G. (1997) 'Classifying welfare states: a two dimensional approach', *Journal of Social Policy* 26(3): 351–72.

Bonoli, G. and Powell, M. (2002) Third ways in Europe?, *Social Policy and Society* 1(1): 59–66.

Bresser-Pereira, L. (2001) The new left viewed from the South, in A. Giddens (ed.), *The Global Third Way Debate*, Cambridge: Polity Press.

Budge, I., Klingemann, H.-D., Volkens, A., Bara, J. and Tanerbaum, E. with Fording, R. C., Hearl, D. J., Kim, H. M., McDonald, M. D. and Mendez, S. (2001) *Mapping Policy Preferences. Estimates for Parties, Electors, and Governments 1945–1998*, Oxford: Oxford University Press.

Callaghan, J. (2000) *The Retreat of Social Democracy*, Manchester: Manchester University Press.

Callinicos, A. (2001) *Against the Third Way*, Cambridge: Polity Press.

Clasen, J. (2002) 'Modern Social Democracy and European welfare state reform', *Social Policy and Society* 1(1): 67–76.

Clift, B. (2001) 'New Labour's Third Way and European Social Democracy', in S. Ludlam and M. Smith (eds), *New Labour in Government*, Basingstoke: Macmillan, 55–72.

Crosland, C. A. R (1964, revised edn) *The Future of Socialism*, London: Jonathan Cape.

Cuperus, R. and Kandel, J. (1998, eds) *European Social Democracy*, Freudenberg/Amsterdam: Friedrich Ebert Siftung/Wiardi Beckman Stiching.

Deacon, A. (2000) 'Learning from the US?', *Policy and Politics* 28(1): 5–18.

Dyson, K. (1999) 'Benign or malevolent Leviathan?: Social democratic governments in a neo-liberal Euro area', *Political Quarterly* 70(2): 195–209.

Economist, The (1998) 'Goldilock politics', *The Economist*, 19 December, 47–9.

Esping-Andersen, G. (1985) *Politics Against Markets*, Princeton, NJ: Princeton University Press.

Esping-Andersen, G. (1990) *The Three Worlds of Welfare Capitalism*, Cambridge: Polity Press.

Esping-Andersen, G. (1999) *Social Foundations of Post-industrial Economies*, Oxford: Oxford University Press.

Etzioni, A. (2000) *The Third Way to a Good Society*, London: Demos.

Fairclough, N. (2000) *New Labour, New Language?*, London: Routledge.

Ferrera, M., Hemerijck, A. and Rhodes, M. (2001) 'Recasting European welfare states for the 21st century', in S. Leibfried (ed.), *Welfare State Futures*, Cambridge: Cambridge University Press, 151–70.

Gamble, A. and Wright, A. (eds) (1999) *The New Social Democracy*, Oxford: Blackwell.

Garrett, G. (1998) *Partisan Politics in the Global Economy*, Cambridge: Cambridge University Press.

George, V. and Wilding, P. (1985) *Ideology and Social Welfare*, London: Routledge and Kegan Paul.

Giddens, A. (1998) *The Third Way*, Cambridge: Polity Press.

Giddens, A. (2000) *The Third Way and Its Critics*, Cambridge: Polity Press.

Giddens, A. (ed.) (2001) *The Global Third Way Debate*, Cambridge: Polity Press.

Giddens, A. (2002) *Where Now for New Labour?*, London: Fabian Society.

Gillespie, R. and Paterson, W. (eds) (1993) *Rethinking Social Democracy in Western Europe*, London: Frank Cass.

Glyn. A. (ed.) (2001) *Social Democracy in Neoliberal Times. The Left and Economic Policy since 1980*, Oxford: Oxford University Press.

Green-Pedersen, C., Van Kersbergen, K. and Hemerijck, A. (2001) 'Neo-liberalism, the Third Way or what?', *Journal of European Public Policy* 8(2): 307–25.

Hay, C. (1999) *The Political Economy of New Labour*, Manchester: Manchester University Press.

Hicks, A. (1999) *Social Democracy and Welfare Capitalism*, Ithica: Cornell University Press.

Huber, E. and Stephens, J. (1998) 'Internationalisation and the social democratatic model', *Comparative Political Studies* 31: 353–97.

Huber, E. and Stephens, J. (2001a) *Development and Crisis of the Welfare State*, Chicago, Il: University of Chicago Press.

Huber. E. and Stephens, J. (2001b) 'The Social Democratic welfare state', in A. Glyn (ed.), *Social Democracy in Neoliberal Times*, Oxford: Oxford University Press, 276–311.

Huber, E. and Stephens, J. (2002) 'Globalisation, competitiveness and the Social Democratic model', *Social Policy and Society* 1(1): 47–58.

Jospin, L. (1999) *Modern Socialism*, London: Fabian Society.

Kitschelt, H. (1994) *The Transformation of European Social Democracy*, Cambridge: Cambridge University Press.

Kleinman, M (2002) *A European Welfare State?*, Basingstoke: Palgrave.

Kolberg, J. and Esping-Andersen, G. (1992) 'Welfare states and employment regimes', in J. Kolberg (ed.), *The Study of Welfare State Regimes*, New York: M. E. Sharpe: Amrouk, 3–36.

Kreiger, J. (1999) *British Politics in the Global Age*, Cambridge: Polity Press.

Ladrech, R. and Maliere, P. (1999) *Social Democratic Parties in the European Union*, Basingstoke: Macmillan.

Leonard, M. (2000) 'Introduction', in B. Hombach (ed.), *The New Centre*, Cambridge: Polity Press, xi–xxix.

Lister, R. (2000) 'To RIO via the Third Way', *Renewal* 8(4): 9–20.
Lodemel, I. and Trickey, H. (eds) (2000) *An Offer You Can't Refuse?*, Bristol: Policy Press.
Merkel, W. (2001) 'The third ways of Social Democracy', in A. Giddens (ed.), *The Global Third Way Debate*, Cambridge: Polity Press.
Navarro, V. (1999) 'Is there a Third Way?', *International Journal of Health Services* 29(4): 667–77.
Padgett, S. and Paterson, W. (1991) *A History of Social Democracy in Postwar Europe*, Harlow: Longman.
Pierson, C. (2001) *Hard Choices. Social Democracy in the Twenty First Century*, Cambridge: Polity Press.
Piven, F. F. (ed.) (1991) *Labor Parties in Postindustrial Societies*, Cambridge: Polity Press.
Powell, M. (ed.) (1999) *New Labour, New Welfare State?*, Bristol: Policy Press.
Powell, M. (2000) 'Something old, something new, something borrowed, something blue: the jackdaw politics of New Labour', *Renewal* 8(4): 21–31.
Powell, M. (2002) 'The hidden history of social citizenship', *Citizenship Studies*, 6(3): 229–44.
Powell, M. and Hewitt, M. (2002) *Welfare State and Welfare Change*, Buckingham: Open University Press.
Powell, M. and Barrientos, A. (2003, fc) 'The route map of the Third Way', in S. Hale, W. Leggett and S. Martell, (eds) *The Third Way*, Manchester: Manchester University Press.
Przeworski, A. (1985) *Capitalism and Social Democracy*, Cambridge: Cambridge University Press.
Przeworski, A. (2001) 'How many ways can be third?', in A. Glyn (ed.), *Social Democracy in Neoliberal Times*, Oxford: Oxford University Press.
Schmidt, V. (2000) 'Values and discourse in the politics of adjustment' in F. Scharpf and V. Schmidt (eds), *Welfare and Work in the Open Economy. Volume 1. From Vulnerability to Competitiveness*, Oxford: Oxford University Press, 229–309.
Schmidt, V. (2001) 'The politics of economic adjustment in France and Britain: when does discourse matter?' *Journal of European Public Policy* 8(2): 247–64.
Shalev, M. (1983) 'The Social Democratic model and beyond', *Comparative Social Research*, 6: 315–51.
Stammers, N. (2001) 'Social democracy and global governance' in L. Martell (ed.) *Social Democracy: Global and National Perspectives*. Basingstoke: Palgrave, 27–48.
Tam, H. (ed.) (2001) *Progressive Politics in the Global Age*, Cambridge: Polity Press.
Thomson, S. (2000) *The Social Democratic Dilemma*, Basingstoke: Macmillan.
Vandenbrouke, F. (1998) 'Globalization, inequality and Social Democracy', in R. Cuperus and J. Kandel (eds), *European Social Democracy*, Freudenberg/Amsterdam Friedrich Ebert Siftung/Wiardi Beckman Stichting, 95–146.
White, S. (1998) 'Interpreting the Third Way', *Renewal* 6, 17–30.
White, S. (ed.) (2001) *New Labour: the Progressive Future?*, Basingstoke: Palgrave.

2 Policy changes of European Social Democrats, 1945–98

Andrea Volkens

Introduction[1]

Did European Social Democrats move to the right by incorporating policy positions of their centre-right competitors? Did they abandon traditional left positions to follow new Third Ways? And if so, how much and why did they change their policy positions? In this chapter these questions are addressed by estimating the policy positions on the basis of national election programmes from all major Social Democratic parties in the 15 European Union states between 1945 and 1998.

The empirical part of the chapter starts by outlining the measurement procedures for party policy positions based upon election programmes. Quantitative content analysis of election programmes using the classification scheme of the Manifesto Research Group (Budge, *et al.* 1987) offers unique opportunities to analyse policy changes of parties over long time periods as well as on different policy dimensions. Following this outline, the extent and the directions of policy changes of Social Democratic parties are described in traditional left–right terms. Although the left–right dimension may still be the major competitive dimension of party systems, literature on the Third Way suggests that nowadays Social Democratic parties may emphasise policy positions that cannot be reduced to left–right semantics. Therefore, the chapter compares left–right changes of Social Democratic parties to changes in Third Way positions. A measure for Third Way issues is derived by a content analysis of the Third Way Programme as given by Anthony Giddens (1998).

Even if one can easily portray policy changes of Social Democratic parties by such a content analysis of election programmes, the question of why Social Democratic parties may have changed policy positions is a difficult one to answer. In the following theoretical part of the chapter, existing studies on party policy change are utilised to derive hypotheses for the extent and the directions of policy changes by European Social Democrats. Based on the assumption that parties copy the successful policy strategies of their opponents, this chapter is a first attempt at investigating a competitive party hypothesis. It proposes a twofold hypothesis on the directions of policy changes: a 'contagion from the left' during the 1950s and 1960s followed by a 'contagion from the right' during the 1980s and 1990s.

Theories of party policy change

Policy positions of political parties are a central concern to representative liberal democratic theory. In the competitive struggle for votes, parties are seen as offering policy packages to choose between. The presumption is that the party or parties that win the elections will put the policy packages into effect when in government. Policy changes of governmental parties are thus assumed to result in changes in the status quo. Today, models of party policy change are usually based on spatial theories. In most spatial theories, parties are located on even graded scales between a left and a right pole:

> A party can then be described as standing far to the right, far to the left, and in the centre; to the right or to the left of another party; between two of the other parties, and so on. The scale can also be used to express changes: a party can move to the right, or to the left, or to the centre; it can change place in the sequence. The distance between two parties can be great or small; can increase or decrease. We can speak of party intervals of varying size.
>
> (Sjöblom 1968: 159)

Downs (1957) assumes vote-maximisation to be the basic motive of parties' behaviour. Therefore, the positions of parties are lined up according to the distributions of their voters. From this assumption follows that whenever voters change their positions, we see a '. . . shifting of the parties on the scale with the object of attaining vote maximisation' (Sjöblom 1968: 160). Studies on changes of parties indeed show parties to be concerned with vote-seeking. Panebianco (1988) describes sudden changes in party ideology for vote maximising reasons. In their comparative study on the possibility of party reform, Harmel and Janda (1982) reveal vote losses to be a major source of party policy change, and Thomas (1982) detects electoral decline to be the source of rightward shifts of Social Democratic parties. In addition, established parties react to the threat posed by new parties (Harmel and Svåsand 1997).

Although the literature on parties and party systems is abundant (Caramani and Hug 1998), comparative studies have mainly been devoted to changes in the strength or in the organisational structure of parties. Many organisational analyses start from the assumption that the type of major parties has changed to 'catchall parties' (Kirchheimer 1966) which are expected to abandon traditional ideologies for the sake of broader electoral support. Lately, parties have been diagnosed to be developing into cartel parties whose 'party programmes become more similar' (Katz and Mair 1995: 22). Both of these party organisation models predict that the main parties of a party system draw closer to one another. Changes in policy positions of parties have also been analysed implicitly in research on the polarisation of party systems, that is, 'the variation in the ideological distance between the political parties along the left–right scale' (Lane and Ersson 1987: 177). Results of empirical tests, though, are, at best, not comparable because of different countries and time periods covered or different methods employed, and, at worst, are contradictory (Volkens and Klingemann 2002). However, the major hypotheses of rational choice theories on party policy change – that parties will converge to the preferences of the median voter – has been rejected (Budge 1994; Macdonald and Rabinowitz 1998; Iversen 1994 a, b). Instead of converging to the median voter, parties kept their distance from one another.

Opposed to models that predict both Social Democrats as well as their main competitors to converge due to the same developmental processes, Duverger (1954) posits a counter-hypothesis that takes the competitive situation of parties into account. He supposes a 'contagion from the left' in that centre-right parties would be pressured to adopt the successful strategies of the socialist mass party model.

> *H1: 'Contagion from the left' during the 1950s and 1960s: in this time period, centre-right parties moved to the left.*

The 'contagion from the left', prevalent in the 1950s and 1960s, though, may have been replaced and superseded by a 'contagion from the right' for several reasons. Epstein (1980) and others have diagnosed the end of the socialist ideology. The disillusion with the leftist ideology has caused a neo-conservative movement, and the rise of neo-liberalism resulted in a rightward shift of conservative, Christian Democratic and liberal parties. Because this was a successful policy strategy of their opponents, Social Democratic parties may now be prone to a 'contagion from the right' just as their main competitors previously were prone to a 'contagion from the left'.[2]

There are more reasons to take over the positions of competitors. In addition to the successes of policy strategies, policy changes of competitors may also have a contagious impact on Social Democrats because the scope for programmatic changes of Social Democratic parties and their room for manoeuvring may depend upon programmatic changes of their competitors. Shifts to one side always give rise to the danger of losing votes on the other side. The stronger the competitors are and the bigger their shifts, the more it pays for parties to go for new floating voters. Thus, the amount of policy changes on the part of Social Democratic parties may depend upon the policy changes of their strongest competitors. When their strongest competitors move to the right, they leave an empty space and provide the opportunity for Social Democratic parties to gain votes.[3] Therefore, the hypothesis predicts:

> *H2: 'Contagion from the right' during the 1980s and 1990s: in the second time period, Social Democrats moved to the right as much as their main centre-right competitors moved to the right.*

The uni-dimensional left–right scale has been shown to be the major dimension of party competition and is, especially in advanced industrial societies, more important than any other dimension (Huber and Inglehart 1995). Sani and Sartori explain this superiority by distinguishing between domains of identification and the space of competition on which it is rewarding for parties to compete for floating voters. They conclude that 'the space of competition may well be a single space, regardless of how many cleavages and/or identification dimensions exist' (1983: 330). Despite this relative significance, the importance of left–right party semantics may have changed. Daniel Bell (1962) as well as Seymour Martin Lipset (1963) proposed the 'end of ideology' thesis which posits a decreasing relevance of these thought systems. Therefore, we hypothesise:

> *H3: The importance of the left–right dimension has decreased.*

Recent declines in the relevance of the traditional left–right dimension may also be due to new issues that may have become more prominent in the rhetoric of Social Democratic parties. Anthony Giddens (1998) argues that there has been a 'qualitative change' in the relevance of the left–right distinction. Although he agrees with Noberto Bobbio (1996) that the left–right distinction is still valid, he also advises Social Democratic parties to adopt new Third Way issues not implied in traditional left–right semantics. Insofar as Social Democratic parties are travelling on a new Third Way, they may have taken up new issues that are neither left nor right.[4] What these new issues might be will be shown later on through the results of a content analysis of Giddens' Third Way Programme. For now, we can hypothesise that:

> *H4: Social democratic parties changed to Third Way issues that are neither left nor right.*

Measurement of party policy change

Because of measurement difficulties, policy changes by parties have seldom been analysed comparatively, quantitatively, and over long time periods. Measures based on voters' judgements are reduced to available interview times and expert judgements raise problems of retrospective validity. Election programmes, on the other hand, are generally issued for each election by every party that contested national parliaments of the 15 EU member states since 1945. Opposed to other statements from party elites or factions of parties, election programmes are authoritatively endorsed by the party as whole and constitute the main policy premises for voters to choose between. Although election programmes are often criticised for being mere 'shopping lists' to attract voters and of being without relevance for the political behaviour of parties, a number of studies have shown programmatic positions to be translated into legislation (Pomper 1968; Ginsberg 1982; Rallings 1987; Thomson 2001) and into budgets (Klingemann *et al.* 1994).

Since 1979, the Manifesto Research Group and its continuation, the Comparative Manifestos Project, collected and content analysed election programmes according to a classification scheme with 56 broad categories grouped into seven policy domains (Budge *et al.* 1987). Each category is composed of a set of typical issues and political ideas. The classification scheme comprises 24 bipolar issues, such as 'Welfare State Expansion' as opposed to 'Welfare State Limitation', and 32 unipolar (or valence) issues such as 'Environmental Protection'. Each (quasi-) sentence of a programme is coded into one, and only one of the 56 categories. The Manifesto classification scheme is at the same time reasonably parsimonious, but permits three types of comparisons: (1) comparisons of changes in policy positions over time within specific parties, (2) comparisons of policy positions across parties, and (3) comparisons of policy positions of parties across countries. The basic data used to support such comparisons are the percentages of the total number of quasi-sentences devoted to each category. Thus, the Manifesto data generally combine a (one-) positional with a saliency approach in one measure (Volkens 2001). The saliency theory of party competition states that parties do not only compete by offering different positions of issues, but also by 'emphasizing the importance of different issues' (Budge and Farlie 1983: 269).

During the long life span of the project, the Manifesto Group has tried out a number of different operationalisations for left–right measures based on the 56 categories. Meanwhile, one of these operationalisations, the left–right measure employed by Laver and Budge (1993), has been shown to have the greatest face as well as correlational validity (McDonald and Mendes 2001 a, b). This measure will be used to analyse left–right movements of Social Democratic parties and movements of their competitors. The measure is derived by (1) adding up percentages of 13 categories that define the right pole, (2) adding up percentages of 13 categories that define the left pole, and (3) subtract the added left pole from the added right pole percentages.[5] The categories used to define the two poles cover socio-economic, societal, and foreign policy issues. Thus, the measure is an indicator for general left–right positions and encompasses all relevant policy domains. This measure can vary between −100 (100 per cent left position) and +100 (100 per cent right position).

Measuring Third Way issues

Although we can rely on an approved measure for traditional left–right positions of parties, measuring Third Way positions on the basis of the Manifesto classification scheme is complicated. What are the core concepts of the Third Way and are they captured by the Manifesto classification scheme? The Third Way Programme as given in Giddens (1998) book *The Third Way* on pages 69 to 153 was used to determine the core concepts of the Third Way. Every sentence on these pages is content analysed as coders are required to do when coding election programmes (Volkens 2002). Each (quasi-) sentence for which a category of the Manifesto classification scheme applies without doubt is marked with the respective code number of the category at the margin of the page. After this first round, a second round of coding is required to check all uncoded sentences.

My expectation was that I would find a large number of uncodable sentences due to a variety of factors: first, the classification scheme was developed to code the total content of election programmes which are written to be comprehensible to a mass audience. A book written for a political and scientific audience is necessarily more complex than our parsimonious classification scheme. Second, the classification scheme was largely developed at the beginning of the 1980s with only two categories added at the end of the 1980s. Therefore, Third Way concepts might not be included. Third, Giddens has been criticised of using many vague and 'as well as' (*sowohl als auch-Stil*) statements (Dahrendorf 1998: 20,25) which would be uncodable. This expectation proved to be true. Of the 1097 identified (quasi-) sentences, 455 (quasi-) sentences were left uncoded even after a second round as compared to an average of 8 per cent for election programmes (Volkens 2001). The reasons for this large number of uncoded sentences, though, was neither due to the non-applicability of the classification scheme to Third Way concepts nor to a particular vagueness of the text. Most of the uncoded sentences are devoted to descriptions of the general economic and societal situation at the end of the century, descriptions of historic developments, references to studies and particular countries as well as descriptions of the Old Left and New Right (328 quasi-sentences) that do not make up Third Way positions. In addition, many other sentences (127) could not be coded because they are due to a specific rhetoric of the text. A good example is the use of rhetorical questions which Giddens uses quite frequently.

During the second round of checking the zeros, I detected only one new concept that could not be subsumed under one of the 56 MRG categories. This was a new concept of 'public governance' in which state agencies assist economic and societal organisations in solving problems. Giddens (1998: 88) introduces this concept to fight crime, but it may also be used to tackle other economic and societal problems. There certainly are more new issues for which no Manifesto category is available at first sight, but in these cases, Third Way responses are straightforward. For example, there is no category called 'globalisation'. The Third Way response, however, namely increased international cooperation, is captured by category 'Internationalism: Positive'. For other categories such as 'No rights without responsibilities', the Third Way position is a combination of Manifesto categories: 'Social Justice', 'Welfare State: Limitation', and 'Governmental and Administrative Efficiency'. Most Manifesto categories, however, are broad enough to cover Third Way concepts. For instance, 'active civil society', 'social cohesion', and 'third sector' are all included in category 'Social Harmony'. That the Manifesto classification scheme is made up of broad categories that include many related issues – issues that may vary between parties and change over time – certainly conceals a lot of subtle differences between parties and time periods. This feature of the Manifesto classification scheme has to be kept in mind when interpreting empirical results, and will be discussed later on in detail.

The next step then was to identify core categories, defined as frequently appearing MRG categories, for each subchapter of the Third Way Programme. 24 categories appeared frequently. Of these 24 categories, 12 are used by the Laver/Budge left–right measure to define the traditional left (Military: negative; Internationalism: positive; Democracy; Market Regulation; Welfare State Expansion) and right pole (Freedom; Free Enterprise; Incentives; Productivity; Welfare State: Limitation; Law and Order; Social Harmony). That both the left and right pole categories appear in many subchapters indicates that the Third Way Programme as developed by Giddens is at least in part a mixture of the Old Left and Right (Faux 1999). The empirical analysis will show how far Social Democrats have changed to the right.

One frequently appearing category, 'Social Justice', has been a core concept of the Old Left, but was not used by Laver and Budge to define the left pole. The expectation for 'Social Justice' is that the percentages of election programs devoted to this category will not change over time because Giddens (1998: 40–2) pays particular attention to the lasting importance of social justice. This expectation will be investigated by looking at the percentages of single categories.

Eleven of the 24 core categories are not related to the traditional left–right dimension. Giddens' Third Way Programme is mainly concerned with 'Governmental and Administrative Efficiency', 'Decentralization', 'Traditional Morality: Negative', and 'Non-Economic Demographic Groups' (for children and elderly people). In addition, 'Against Corruption', 'National Way of Life: Negative', 'Multiculturalism: Positive', 'Underprivileged Minority Groups', 'Environmental Protection', 'Technology and Infrastructure' (in the sense of need for job training), and 'European Union: Positive' appear frequently in some subchapters. The added percentages of these 11 categories are utilised as a measure of Third Way issues which theoretically can range between 0 and 100 if Social Democrats are totally unconcerned with traditional left–right semantics. An increase in percentages over time indicates that parties are on a Third Way.

Empirical evidence from party programmes

In the following empirical part of the chapter, policy position of parties are presented as averages across all elections that were held in one of the six decades between the 1940s and the 1990s. The Social Democrats included in this analysis are the strongest Social Democratic parties from each of the 15 European Union member states that are represented in the group of the Party of European Socialists (PES) in the 1999 European Parliament. Because the Belgium party system is divided into a Flemish and a French part, 16 Social Democratic parties are taken into account.[6]

Left–right changes of Social Democrats and their main competitors

A brief glance at Table 2.1 already reveals that changes in left–right positions are quite usual for all European Social Democrats. This is true even though a lot of changes are hidden by the averages. For the sake of clarity, standard deviations within decades are not presented, but they are quite high, ranging up to 10 per cent on average. With two exceptions, changes are more pronounced during the 1980s and the 1990s than during the 1950s and the 1960s. Exceptions are the Finnish Social Democrats with a huge jump from +40 in the 1940s to −15 in the 1950s and the German Social Democratic party with a shift from −24 in the 1950s to −6 in the 1960s.

The average measures for all Social Democrats on left–right changes reveal a clear-cut pattern. Most Social Democrats moved to the left from the 1940s to the 1960s (−17 as compared to −25) as predicted by Hypothesis 1. While Social Democrats in Finland, France, Italy, the Netherlands, and Sweden shifted to the left, a freezing of policy positions is prevalent in Austria, Denmark, and Luxembourg. During this time period, there are three exceptions from the general trend. The Belgian and the German Social Democrats as well as the British Labour Party shifted to the right.

During the second half of this six-decade period, almost all European Social Democrats moved to the right from −24 in the 1970s to −17 in the 1980s and further moved to −11 in the 1990s as predicted by Hypothesis 2. Once more, there are only three exceptions from this general trend, namely the Francophone Belgian, the Portuguese, and the Spanish Social Democrats. Whether these exceptions are due to their competitors not moving to the right remains to be seen. In Greece, Portugal, and Spain, free competitive elections have been held uninterruptedly only since the 1970s. For these three countries, our data collection starts with the 1970s,

Table 2.1 Left–right positions of Social Democratic parties in six time periods

Country	*Party*	*1940s*	*1950s*	*1960s*	*1970s*	*1980s*	*1990s*	*45–98*
Austria	SPÖ	−14	−16	−15	−23	−14	+1	−14
Belgium	PSB/BSP	−32	−21	−17	−30	–	–	−25
Belgium-Franco-phone	PS	–	–	–	+1	−16	−16	−10
Belgium-Flemish	SP	–	–	–	−29	−24	−13	−22
Denmark	SD	−17	−13	−17	−14	−20	−17	−16
Finland	SSDP	+40	−15	−18	−41	−1	−6	−7
France	PS	−14	−25	−43	−40	−17	−18	−26
Greece	PASOK	–	–	–	−32	−21	−21	−25
Germany	SPD	−18	−24	−6	−18	−14	−16	−16
Ireland	LP	−19	30	−22	−18	−24	−10	−21
Italy	PDS (PCI)	−17	−15	−28	−14	−15	+12	−13
Luxembourg	POSL/LSAP	−34	−30	−35	−36	−23	−20	−30
Netherlands	PvdA	−17	−24	−28	−43	−23	−9	−24
Portugal	PSP	–	–	–	−7	−5	−14	−9
Spain	PSOE	–	–	–	−10	−15	−23	−16
Sweden	SdaP	−33	−32	−46	−19	−21	+5	−24
United Kingdom	Labour	−31	−32	−19	−28	−26	−11	−25
Average		−17	−23	−25	−24	−17	−11	−19
Sum of L+R in per cent of programme		50	48	45	49	48	47	48

Source: Comparative Manifestos Database (in Budge *et al.* 2001)

and some of the deviating patterns in theses countries may also be due to the fact that these three countries are the democratic latecomers of Western Europe.

Before examining the composite movements of Social Democrats and their centre-right competitors, we will take a closer look at the centre-right competitors and their policy changes (Tables 2.2a and 2.2b). The question of which party is considered to be the main competitor by the Social Democratic party in each of the 15 countries is a difficult one to answer. Therefore, a clear-cut if arbitrary definition was employed. The centre-right party which received the most valid votes, averaged for all elections between 1945 and 1998, is defined as the main competitor. However, in about a third of the countries, there are centre-right parties that on average are almost as strong as the main competitor, and these second strongest competitors received even more votes than the strongest competitors at least in some elections. Therefore, the strongest as well as the second strongest centre-right competitor will be taken into account.

A glance at Tables 2.2a and 2.2b is sufficient to show that the competitor parties vary considerably with respect to their party family membership. The competitors are of Christian democratic, conservative, liberal,

Table 2.2a Left–right positions of strongest centre-right competitor in six time periods

Country	*Party*	*1940s*	*1950s*	*1960s*	*1970s*	*1980s*	*1990s*	*45–98*
Austria	ÖVP	+32	+33	+9	+1	+15	+23	+19
Belgium	PSC/CVP	+16	+1	−7	–	–	–	+3
Belgium-Francophone	PSC	–	–	−13	−7	+5	−9	−6
Belgium-Flemish	CVP	–	–	−13	−8	+8	+2	−3
Denmark	Venstre	+10	+18	+13	+26	+26	+39	+22
Finland	SK	+0	+17	−10	−19	−24	+14	−4
France	Gaull./RPR	+25	+20	+17	+14	+26	−1	+17
Greece	ND	–	–	–	+14	+25	+18	+19
Germany	CDU/CSU	−12	+21	−1	+10	+20	+15	+9
Ireland	Fianna Fail	−12	+15	+22	+26	−10	+1	+7
Italy	PPI (DC)	+18	−11	−8	+0	+1	+25	+4
Luxembourg	PCS/CSV	+6	+6	−20	−15	−4	−18	−8
Netherlands	CDA	–	–	–	−12	−11	−2	−8
	KVP	+5	+6	−3	−20	–	–	−3
	ARP	+20	+14	−2	−16	–	–	+4
	CHU	+21	+22	+4	−18	–	–	+7
Portugal	PSD	–	–	–	+1	+13	−6	+3
Spain	AP (PP)	–	–	–	+12	+8	−8	+4
Sweden	MSP	+56	+50	+40	+14	+41	+40	+40
United Kingdom	Conservatives	+15	−14	+1	+11	+30	+27	+12
Average		+14	+14	+2	+1	+11	+10	+9

Source: as Table 2.1

agrarian or even Social Democratic origin. Most of the strongest and second strongest competitors are stable parties that competed in every election between 1945 and 1998 or, in Greece, Portugal and Spain, between the 1970s and 1998. Although the Dutch KVP, ARP, and CHU combined into the CDA and all Belgium parties including the Social Democrats have segregated into a Flemish and a Francophone party, one can easily compare the policy positions of the former parties to their followers. The French centre-right is not composed of stable parties but of spiritual families for which policy changes over time can be traced. The Spanish UCD ceased to exist in the 1990s. In this case, values of the 1970s are compared with values of the 1980s. The major exception is Greece, where the second strongest competitor in the 1970s, EDIK, has ceased to exist and was not replaced by another party worth mentioning. Thus, the only country in which we cannot trace changes during the 1980s and 1990s for two centre-right competitors is Greece.

Despite the huge variations in party families, there is a clear-cut pattern in policy changes. Almost all of these parties moved to left during the first time period and then to the right during the second time period with only

Table 2.2b Left–right positions of second strongest centre-right competitor in six time periods

Country	*Party*	*1940s*	*1950s*	*1960s*	*1970s*	*1980s*	*1990s*	*45–98*
Austria	FPÖ	+5	+4	−27	−14	+5	+39	+2
Belgium	PLP/PVV	+24	+22	+18	–	–	–	+21
Belgium-Francophone	*PRL*	–	–	–	*−0*	*+18*	*−2*	*+5*
Belgium-Flemish	PVV	–	–	–	+14	+20	−11	+8
Denmark	*KF*	*+10*	*+25*	*+32*	*+29*	*+32*	*+14*	*+24*
Finland	*KK*	*−2*	*−9*	*+15*	*+4*	*−24*	*+5*	*−2*
France	RRRS, CDS, *UDF*	+37	+6	−20	+11	+11	+7	+9
Greece	EDIK	–	–	–	−24	–	–	−24
Germany	FDP	+7	−1	−12	+11	+3	+2	+2
Ireland	Fine Gael	+52	+45	−2	−18	+3	+9	+15
Italy	PSI (FI)	−23	−18	−31	−21	−1	+8 (21)	−14
Luxembourg	PD/DP	−3	−8	−8	−19	+8	+15	−3
Netherlands	VVD	+20	+20	+10	+11	+10	+11	+14
Portugal	PP	–	–	–	+1	+21	−6	+5
Spain	*UCD*	–	–	–	−0	−7	–	−4
Sweden	*CP*	*−5*	*+5*	*−7*	*−16*	*−7*	*+13*	*−3*
United Kingdom	Liberals, LDP	−7	+1	−25	−8	−7	−14	−10
Average		*+10*	*+8*	*−5*	*−2*	*+6*	*+6*	*+4*

Source: as Table 2.1

Note
Italic: Second strongest competitor almost as strong as main competitor

very few exceptions. This said, we can now move on to look at the cross-tabulations between movements of Social Democrats and their competitor parties to investigate the contagion hypothesis.

A complete confirmation of Hypothesis 1 – contagion from the left during the 1950s and 1960s – is provided by the two upper left hand cells in Tables 2.3a and 2.3b, where the competitors moved to the left and the Social Democrats either stayed put or also moved to the left. When compared to movements of their strongest competitors, nine out of fourteen parties, when compared to the second strongest competitor, six out of twelve parties fall into these two upper left hand cells. Of the 26 competitor parties included, only five do not move to the left as predicted by 'contagion from the left'.

A complete confirmation of Hypothesis 2 – contagion from the right during the 1980s and 1990s – is provided by the lower right hand cell in Tables 2.4a and 2.4b, where both Social Democrats and their competitors moved to the right. When compared to movements of their strongest competitors, nine out of sixteen parties, when compared to the second

Table 2.3a Left–right movements of Social Democratic parties and of their main centre-right competitors, 1940s–1960s*

Strongest competitor	*Social Democratic parties*		
	Leftward trend	*No trend*	*Rightward trend*
Leftward Trend	Finland France Italy Netherlands: KVP Netherlands: ARP Netherlands: CHU Sweden	Austria Luxembourg	Belgium Germany United Kingdom
No Trend			
Rightward Trend	Ireland	Denmark	

Source: as Table 2.1

Note
Comparison of value for 1940s with value of 1960s; no trend = +/− 2 per cent

Table 2.3b Left–right movements of Social Democratic parties and of their second strongest centre-right competitors, 1940s–1960s*

Second strongest competitor	*Social Democratic parties*		
	Leftward trend	*No trend*	*Rightward trend*
Leftward Trend	France Ireland Italy Netherlands	Austria Luxembourg	*Belgium* Germany United Kingdom
No Trend	*Sweden*		
Rightward Trend	*Finland*	*Denmark*	

Source: as Table 2.1

Note
Comparison of value for 1940s with value of 1960s; no trend = +/− 2 per cent
Italic: Second strongest competitor almost as strong as main competitor

strongest competitor, five out of fifteen parties fall into the lower right hand cell. Of the 16 Social Democratic parties, only four, namely the Belgian PS, the Danish SD, the Portuguese PSP, and the Spanish PSOE did not move to the right.

Empirically, Hypotheses 1 and 2 have one thing in common. Both predict Social Democrats and their competitors to keep their distance. During the first time period from the 1940s to the 1960s, a complete contradiction to this non-convergence is given by the upper right hand, during the second time period, a complete contradiction is given by the lower left hand cell. There are three countries that really contradict the non-convergence thesis and conform to the catch-all party hypothesis by

Table 2.4a Left–right movements of Social Democratic parties and of their main centre-right competitors, 1970s–1990s*

Social Democratic parties	*Strongest competitor*		
	Leftward trend	*No trend*	*Rightward trend*
Leftward Trend	Belgium-Francophone Portugal Spain		Denmark
No Trend			
Rightward Trend	France Ireland Luxembourg		Austria Belgium-Flemish Part Finland Greece Germany Italy Netherlands Sweden United Kingdom

Source: as Table 2.1

Note
Comparison of value for 1970s with value of 1990s; no trend = +/− 2 per cent

Table 2.4b Left–right movements of Social Democratic parties and of their second strongest centre-right competitors, 1970s–1990s*

Social Democratic parties	*Second strongest competitor*		
	Leftward trend	*No trend*	*Rightward trend*
Leftward Trend	Belgium-Francophone Denmark Portugal Spain		
No Trend			
Rightward Trend	Belgium-Flemish Part *France* Germany United Kingdom	*Finland* Netherlands	Austria Ireland Italy Luxembourg *Sweden*

Source: as Table 2.1

Note
Comparison of value for 1970s with value of 1990s; no trend = +/− 2 per cent
Italic: Second strongest competitor almost as strong as main competitor

Kirchheimer during the first time period, namely Belgium, Germany and the United Kingdom. With respect to the second time period, there is a more differentiated picture with respect to the strongest and the second strongest competitors. Only in France did both the strongest and the second strongest competitors move to the left that results in an overall convergence of the main parties of the party system. In Ireland and Luxembourg, there is a pronounced but partial convergence because the strongest competitors, Fianna Fail and PCS/CSV, moved to the left. In the Flemish part of Belgium, in Germany, and in the United Kingdom, left movements of the smaller liberal parties result in a partial if slight convergence of Social Democrats and their second strongest competitors.

As with most other analyses of party and party system change, then, one can sum up this section by pointing out that there certainly are a number of different developments taking place in the European countries. This result was to be expected given all the variations in European party and party system features. However, it is also clear that the contagion hypothesis work much better than the convergence hypothesis. During both time periods, there are three cases of convergence but nine cases of contagion when comparing Social Democrats to their strongest competitors. Although there are deviating countries, there are clear overall trends: most major parties in Europe shifted to the left during the 1950s and 1960s and then to the right during the 1980s and 1990s. Even the former Communists in Italy, which today are part of the PES in the European Parliament, conform with this general pattern. Historical developments of the PCI during the 1950s and 1960s already contributed to this transformation (Panebianco 1988: 82–5).

Although one cannot prove casual relationships between movements of parties by just comparing changes over decades, there is indeed empirical evidence for contagion processes taking place. During both time periods, relationships between changes by Social Democrats and changes by their strongest competitors are stronger than relationships between changes by Social Democrats and changes by the second strongest competitor (1st time period: 9 out of 16 versus 6 out of 12; 2nd time period: 9 out of 16 versus 5 out of 15 cases). Thus, one can deduce that Social Democrats moved to where most of the new floating voters might have been gained.

But there is even more to it: during the second time period, four parties, the Francophone Belgium, the Danish, the Portuguese, and the Spanish Social Democrats did not move to the right – as predicted by 'contagion from the right' – but instead moved to left. And these are exactly the four countries, in which the second competitors moved to the left, competitors that are almost as strong as the main competitors. Except in Denmark, the strongest competitors as well moved to the left. These four cases, then, do no contradict the contagion hypothesis at all. In Ireland and Luxembourg, where the strongest competitors moved to the left, Social Democrats moved alongside with the rightward trend of their second strongest competitors. If one predicts a Social Democratic party to move along with the rightward trend of either the strongest or the second strongest competitor, there is only one exception left. In France, both competitors shifted to the left, but nonetheless the PS shifted to the right.

There are quite a number of possible explanations for this deviating party. In this chapter, attention is devoted to main centre-right competitors, only. Deviations may be due to the presence of other right- and left-wing competitors or even, in the French case, to differences between presidential and parliamentary regimes. Overall, however, there is a clear-cut picture: most of the major parties in Europe have firstly shifted to the left and then to the right during the last 20 years and, thus, conform to the contagion hypothesis.

Change to Third Way issues

Hypothesis 3 predicts that the left–right dimension is losing importance. With a content-analysis of election programmes, this hypothesis can be examined by looking at the sum of the 26 categories that together make up the left–right dimension. A decrease in the proportion of programmes devoted to the added sum of the 26 categories, shown at the bottom of Table 2.1, would denote a decrease in importance. Even if there is a slight decrease from an average 50 per cent of the programmes devoted to left–right semantics in the 1940s down to 45 per cent in the 1960s, the average percentage increases again in the 1970s and stays just under 50 per cent in the 1980s and 1990s. Thus, the left–right distinction today is as relevant to programmatic statements of Social Democrats as it was in the 1940s.

Although the importance of the left–right dimension has not decreased, the position stated in Hypothesis 4 – that Social Democrats changed to Third Way issues – finds empirical support. A brief glance at Table 2.5a, however, is sufficient to detect that this is not a recent development. When measured by the cumulative sum of the 11 categories derived from Giddens, it appears that Social Democrats all over Europe entered the Third Way as early as the 1950s. The average percentage of programmes devoted to the 11 categories rose from 10 per cent in the 1940s to 30 per cent in the 1990s. With each passing decade, European Social Democrats continually devoted more and more programmatic content to Third Way issues and so, too, did their competitors. There is an equally strong and almost continual rise of these issues for the strongest as well as the second strongest competitor parties. Since there is no decrease in the importance of left–right issues, increasing attention to Third Way issues is given at the expense of a variety of other issues with which parties had been concerned before.

Table 2.5b gives further evidence on changes to the Third Way by depicting averages for all European Social Democrats, but distinguishing between the single categories that are used to produce the combined Third Way measure. As predicted, Social Democrats were devoted to 'Social Justice' throughout the six decades. But most Third Way issues also received the same amount of (non-) attention in the 1990s as in the 1940s. This is true for 'Non-Economic Demographic Groups' although the

Table 2.5a Third Way positions of Social Democratic parties in six time periods

Country	*Party*	*1940s*	*1950s*	*1960s*	*1970s*	*1980s*	*1990s*	*45–98*
Austria	SPÖ	15	21	28	28	24	31	25
Belgium	PSB-BSP	11	27	33	33	–	–	26
Belgium-Francophone	PS	–	–	–	42	45	36	41
Belgium-Flemish	SP	–	–	–	23	28	34	28
Denmark	SD	6	6	14	6	17	24	12
Finland	SSDP	0	3	4	4	37	20	11
France	PS	16	11	22	24	24	22	20
Greece	PASOK	–	–	–	17	19	29	22
Germany	SPD	24	21	24	23	32	41	28
Ireland	LP	11	16	16	14	14	22	16
Italy	PDS (PCI)	7	6	10	24	25	27	17
Luxembourg	POSL-LSAP	3	10	20	26	37	38	22
Netherlands	PvdA	18	17	15	21	27	30	21
Portugal	PSP	–	–	–	8	20	33	20
Spain	PSOE	–	–	–	29	32	41	34
Sweden	SdaP	2	7	7	11	17	18	10
United Kingdom	Labour	10	6	11	19	20	30	16
Average		*10*	*13*	*17*	*21*	*26*	*30*	*20*
Average for 1. Competitors		*12*	*13*	*16*	*21*	*25*	*28*	*19*
Average for 2. Competitors		*14*	*12*	*19*	*21*	*27*	*31*	*21*

Source: as Table 2.1

Table 2.5b Average percentage of 11 Third Way issues and 'social justice' in election programmes of Social Democratic parties in six time periods

Category	*1940s*	*1950s*	*1960s*	*1970s*	*1980s*	*1990s*	*45–98*
301 Decentralization +	1	1	1	2	2	2	2
303 Gov./Admin. Efficiency +	1	1	2	2	3	6	3
304 Corruption –	1	1	0	0	0	1	1
602 Nationalism/Patriotism –	0	0	0	0	0	0	0
604 Traditional Morality –	0	0	0	0	0	0	0
607 Multiculturalism +	0	0	0	0	0	0	0
705 Minority Groups +	0	0	0	0	0	0	0
706 Non-Economic Groups +	3	4	6	4	5	4	4
501 Environmental Protection +	0	0	1	3	5	6	3
411 Infrastructure +	2	4	4	4	6	5	4
108 European Union +	0	1	2	1	2	3	2
503 Social Justice +	*8*	*6*	*6*	*8*	7	7	7

Source: as Table 2.1

percentages vary more over time than they do for 'Social Justice'. In addition, the four categories 'Against Nationalism/Patriotism', 'Against Traditional Morality', 'Multiculturalism', and Underprivileged Minority Groups' received next to no attention in the six decades. Social democrats, then, were and still are fairly traditional with respect to societal issues.

In the other hand, 'Anti-Corruption', which was a minor issue in the 1940s and 1950s, received attention again in the 1990s in accordance with Giddens' Third Way Programme. Slight increases are evident for 'Decentralisation', Infrastructure and Technology', and 'European Union: Positive'. There are only two issues with more pronounced increases, namely 'Environmental Protection' and 'Governmental and Administrative Efficiency'.

Is there any contagion process evident with respect to Third Way issues? In order to answer this question, one can look at the 11 single core categories for the strongest and second strongest competitors to determine which party took the lead. However, a look at the Tables 2.6a and 2.6b reveals that differences between Social Democrats and their competitors are, if at all present, tiny. Both the Social Democrats and their main competitors have been increasingly concerned with the same Third Way issues, namely environmental protection, technical training as included in category 'Infrastructure and Technology', governmental and administrative efficiency, European integration, and decentralisation. With respect to these issues, parties grew closer and converged. In contrast to the left–right dimension on which parties in most countries kept their distance, a parallel and, it seems, almost synchronised movement towards these Third Way issues has been taking place. There is only one issue for which a contagion process is evident: 'Governmental and Administrative Efficiency' was picked up by the competitor parties earlier and more pronounced whereas Social Democrats doubled their attention only from the 1980s to the 1990s from 3–6 per cent of the platform content.

As mentioned earlier, these same patterns also hide differences between the competing parties. For instance, governmental efficiency today is a valence issue to which all parties agree. This is what the

Table 2.6a Average percentage of 11 Third Way issues and 'social justice' in election programmes of strongest competitors in six time periods

Category	*1940s*	*1950s*	*1960s*	*1970s*	*1980s*	*1990s*	*45–98*
301 Decentralization +	1	1	1	3	2	3	2
303 Gov./Admin. Efficiency +	2	2	2	3	5	6	3
304 Corruption −	0	0	0	0	1	1	0
602 Nationalism/Patriotism −	0	0	0	0	0	0	0
604 Traditional Morality −	0	0	0	0	0	0	0
607 Multiculturalism +	3	2	1	1	1	0	1
705 Minority Groups +	1	1	0	1	1	1	1
706 Non-Economic Groups +	3	3	4	5	4	3	4
501 Environmental Protection +	0	0	1	3	4	5	2
411 Infrastructure +	2	3	4	4	5	5	4
108 European Union +	0	1	2	2	3	4	2

Source: as Table 2.1

Table 2.6b Average percentage of 11 Third Way issues and 'social justice' in election programmes of second strongest competitors in six time periods

Category	*1940s*	*1950s*	*1960s*	*1970s*	*1980s*	*1990s*	*45–98*
301 Decentralization +	1	1	3	3	2	3	2
303 Gov./Admin. Efficiency +	2	2	4	3	6	7	4
304 Corruption −	1	1	0	1	1	2	1
602 Nationalism/Patriotism −	0	0	0	0	0	0	0
604 Traditional Morality −	0	0	0	1	0	0	0
607 Multiculturalism +	1	1	0	0	0	0	0
705 Minority Groups +	1	0	1	2	1	1	1
706 Non-Economic Groups +	5	3	4	5	4	3	4
501 Environmental Protection +	0	0	1	3	6	7	3
411 Infrastructure +	2	2	4	2	4	5	3
108 European Union +	1	1	2	2	2	3	2

Source: as Table 2.1

Manifesto classification scheme can show, but it does not capture conflicts over the means to achieve this goal. The concept of centre-right parties for modernising the bureaucracy is new public management which includes curtailment of public spending, deregulation, and in general a withdrawal of the state from society (Pollitt and Bouckaert 2000). This concept for achieving efficiency deviates a lot from the Third Way concept of the 'active' and 'enabling' state that is based upon participation of all relevant groups. However, what one can conclude by using the Manifesto classification scheme is that most Third Way issues which are not included in the left–right dimension are neither new nor particular to Social Democrats, but have become valence issues to which all major parties agree.

Conclusions

Based upon content analysis of election programmes, this chapter attempted to test four hypotheses on the directions of policy changes of European Social Democrats. Changes on the left–right dimension have been put down to the fact that parties strategically choose to take over the successful policy positions of competitor parties for vote-maximising reasons. Hypothesis 1 – contagion from the left during the 1950s and 1960s – as well as Hypothesis 2 – contagion from the right during the 1980s and 1990s – received empirical support. There are strong indications of contagion processes having taken place. Between the 1940s and the 1960s, most of the main competitors of Social Democrats moved to the left as predicted by 'contagion from the left'. During this time period, most Social Democrats either stayed put or moved further to the left. On the other hand, between the 1970s and the end of the 1990s, most Social Democrats as well as their competitors moved to the right as predicted by 'contagion from the right'. Most major parties all over Europe, then, have kept their distance and did not converge. There are only few exceptions: In Belgium, Germany, and in the United Kingdom, movements of the parties during the first time period conformed to a 'catch-all party' pattern and their policy positions converged; during the second time period the major exception is France, because the French PS moved to the right although their main competitors shifted to the left.

Social democrats, as well as their main competitors, moved along the left–right dimension quite frequently but did not abandon left–right semantics as predicted by Hypothesis 3. In the 1990s, left–right semantics were as common in election programmes as they were in the 1940s. Nevertheless, Social Democrats increasingly adopted Third Way issues as predicted by Hypothesis 4. Third Way issues, then, were not adopted by abandoning left–right semantics, but at the expense of a variety of other issues with which the parties have been concerned before. The policy shift to new Third Way issues, however, is no recent development, but started as early as the 1950s. And it took place on the part of the Social Democrats and their competitors as well. Thus, decentralization, technical training, European integration and governmental and administrative efficiency have become valence issues on which all major parties of the 15 European member states agree. On most of these Third Way issues, Social Democrats and their main competitors moved in synchrony with each other. The only exception was with respect to governmental and administrative efficiency. On this issue, centre-right competitors took the lead, and Social Democrats picked up this issue later.

Half of the Third Way issues as identified by a content analysis of Giddens' Third Way programmme are included in the traditional left–right measure that today is frequently used for measuring policy positions of parties. About half of these issues define the left pole, while the other half defines the right pole. Thus, Giddens' Third Way programme, as far as it can be subsumed under left–right semantics, is a centrist programme. In accordance with Giddens' blueprint, most Social Democrats moved to the right during the last 20 years. At the end of the 1990s, they occupied a position in the centre of the party systems. These trends – a continuing importance of left–right semantics and rightward shifts on the part of the Social Democrats – confirm Kitschelt's diagnosis of the 'Transformation of European Social Democracy': 'Party programs are diluting the conventional tenets of the Keynesian welfare state with substantial doses of free market pragmatism, on the one hand, and ideas of participatory democracy and communitarian social life organized by citizens themselves, on the other' (Kitschelt 1994 preface).

Notes

1 Thanks to all participants of the ECPR workshop, especially to Ian MacAllister and Hans Keman and the two workshop directors, for valuable comments, and to Thomas Cusack for correcting my English.

2 The term 'contagion' has been used by a couple of authors in quite different ways. Epstein introduced this term 'to view business-oriented middle-class parties as pioneers of the new style of campaigning via the mass media' (1980: 257). Furthermore, it has been used to indicate 'that the elite autonomy and consequent strategic flexibility of modern centre-right parties has influenced modern centre-left parties, for example in Britain'. (Broughton and Donovan 1999: 276). In the approach of this chapter, 'contagion' is defined as the adoption of policy positions that were previously held by competitor parties.

3 Changes in policy positions, though, may not only be caused by successful strategies or policy changes of competitor parties, but may be due to third factors. Both Social Democrats and their centre-right competitors may have responded to changes in the electorates or to economic pressures. If we assume vote-seeking to be a major goal of parties, we expect parties to follow changes in policy positions of their voters. Correspondingly, in his major study on changes in the strength of Social Democratic parties, Kitschelt (1994) also shows strategic choices of parties to be of importance under the assumption of a rightward movement of electors. In the same vein, economic downturns may have forced Social Democratic parties to abstain from extending the welfare state further and instead adopt more market-oriented policies. In this chapter, no analysis of all these potential sources for policy changes is undertaken. Instead, we talk of contagion processes whenever parties take over positions formerly kept by competitors.

4 The left–right dimension seems to assimilate new meanings (Knutsen 1995). Thus, the New Politics dimension now is incorporated in left–right semantics (Knutsen 1998). However, even if Third Way issues may eventually be incorporated in left–right semantics, this absorption will take some time.

5 Laver and Budge (1993) use the following formula: ((per104 + per201 + per203 + per305 + per401 + per402 + per407 + per414 + per505 + per601 + per603 + per605 + per606) – (per103 + per105 + per106 + per107 + per202 + per403 + per404 + per406 + per412 + per413 + per504 + per506 + per701)); for definition of categories see Budge *et al.* 2001.

6 Data used in this chapter are published on a CD Rom attached to Budge *et al.* (2001). Descriptions of all parties included in the analysis as well as descriptions of the MRG/CMP categories are given in appendices I and II of the book.

References

Bell, D. (1962) *The End of Ideology*, New York: Free Press.

Bobbio, N. (1996) *Left & Right: The Significance of a Political Distinction*, Cambridge: Polity Press.

Broughton, D. and M. Donovan (eds) (1999) *Changing Party Systems in Western Europe*, London/New York: Pinter.

Budge, I. (1994) 'A New Spatial Theory of Party Competition: Uncertainty, Ideology and Policy Equilibria Viewed Comparatively and Temporally', *British Journal of Political Science* 24 (4): 443–67.

Budge, I. and D. Farlie (1983) 'Saliency Theory of Party Competition – Selective Emphasis or Direct Confrontation? An Alternative View with Data', in H. Daalder and P. Mair (eds), *Western European Party Systems*, London: Sage Publications, 267–306.

Budge, I., H.-D. Klingemann, A. Volkens, J. Bara, and E. Tanenbaum with R. C. Fording, D. J. Hearl, H. M. Kim, M. D. McDonald and S. Mendez (2001)

'Mapping Policy Preferences. Estimates for Parties; Electors, and Governments, 1945–1998', Oxford: Oxford University Press.
Budge, I. D. Robertson and D. Hearl (eds) (1987) *Ideology, Strategy and Party Change: Spatial Analysis of Post-War Election Programs in 19 Democracies*, Cambridge: Cambridge University Press.
Caramani, D. and S. Hug (1998) 'The Literature on European Parties and Party Systems Since 1945: a Quantitative Analysis', *European Journal of Political Research* 33 (4): 497–524.
Dahrendorf, R. (1998) *Ein neuer Dritter Weg? Reformpolitik am Ende des 20. Jahrhunderts*, Beiträge zur Ordnungstheorie und Ordnungspolitik 158 herausgegeben vom Walter Eucken Institut, Tübingen: Mohr Siebeck.
Downs, A. (1957) *An Economic Theory of Democracy*, New York: Harper and Row.
Duverger, M. (1954) *Political Parties: Their Organizations and Activities in the Modern State*, London: Methuen.
Epstein, L. D. (1980) *Political Parties in Western Democracies*, New York: Frederick A. Praeger 1967, 1980 by Transaction, Inc. New Jersey.
Faux, J. (1999) Lost on the Third Way, *Dissent* 46 (2): 67–76.
Giddens, A. (1998) *The Third Way. The Renewal of Social Democracy*, Cambridge: Polity Press.
Ginsberg, B. (1982) *The Consequences of Consent. Elections, Citizen Control and Popular Acquiescence*, New York: Random House.
Harmel, R. and K. Janda (1982) *Parties and their Environments. Limits to Reform?* New York & London: Longman.
Harmel, R. and L. Svåsand (1997) 'The Influence of New Parties on Old Parties' Platforms', *Party Politics* 3 (3): 315–40.
Huber, J. D. and R. Inglehart (1995) 'Expert Interpretations of Party Space and Party Location in 42 Societies', *Party Politics* 1 (1): 73–111.
Iversen, T. (1994a) 'Political Leadership and Representation in West European Democracies: A Test of Three Models of Voting', *American Journal of Political Science* 38 (1): 45–74.
Iversen, T. (1994b) 'The Logics of Electoral Politics. Spatial, Directional, and Mobilizational Effects', *Comparative Political Studies* 27 (2): 155–89.
Katz, R. S. and P. Mair (1995) 'Changing Models of Party Organization and Party Democracy', *Party Politics* 1 (1): 5–28.
Kirchheimer, O. (1966) 'The Transformation of the Western European Party Systems', in J. LaPalombara and M. Weiner (eds) *Political Parties and Political Development*, Princeton: Princeton University Press, 117–200.
Kitschelt, H. (1994) *The Transformation of European Social Democracy*, Cambridge: Cambridge University Press.
Klingemann, H.-D., R. I. Hofferbert and I. Budge (1994) *Parties, Policies, and Democracy*, Boulder: Westview.
Knutsen, O. (1998) 'Expert Judgements of the Left–Right Locations of Parties: A Comparative Longitudinal Study', *West European Politics* 21 (2): 63–94.
Knutsen, O. (1995) 'Value Orientations, Political Conflicts, and Left–Right Identification: A Comparative Study', *European Journal of Political Research* 23 (28): 63–93.
Lane, J. E. and S. O. Ersson (1987) *Politics and Society in Western Europe*, London/Beverly Hills/Newbury Park/New Delhi: Sage.
Laver, M. and I. Budge (eds) (1993) *Party Policy and Government Coalitions*, New York: St Martins Press.

Lipset, S. M. (1963) 'The End of Ideology', in S. M. Lipset (ed.), *Political Man*, Garden City, New York: Doubleday-Anchor, 439–56.

Macdonald, S. E. and G. Rabinowitz (1998) 'Solving the Paradox of Nonconvergence: Valence, Position, and Direction in Democratic Politics', *Electoral Studies* 17 (3): 281–300.

McDonald, M. D. and S. M. Mendes (2001a) 'The Policy Space of Party Manifestos', in M. Laver (ed.), *Estimating the Policy Positions of Collective Actors*, London: Routledge, 90–114.

McDonald, M. D. and S. M. Mendez (2001b) 'Checking the Party Policy Estimates: Convergent Validity', in I. Budge, H.-D. Klingemann, A. Volkens, J. Bara and E. Tanenbaum with R. C. Fording, D. J. Hearl, H. M. Kim, Hee Min, M. D. McDonald and S. Mendez, *Mapping Policy Preferences. Estimates for Parties, Electors, and Governments 1945–1998*. Oxford: Oxford University Press, 127–42.

Panebianco, A. (1988) *Political Parties: Organization and Power*, Cambridge: Cambridge University Press.

Politt, C. and G. Bouckaert (2000) *Public Management Reform. A Comparative Analysis*, Oxford, Oxford University Press.

Pomper, G. M. (1968) *Elections in America. Control and Influences in Democratic Politics*, New York: Dodd, Mead.

Rallings, C. (1987) 'The Influence of Election Programmes. Great Britain and Canada, 1945–1979', in I. Budge, D. Robertson, D. J. Hearl (eds), *Ideology, Strategy and Party Change: Spatial Analysis of Post-War Election Programs in 19 Democracies*, Cambridge: Cambridge University Press, 1–14.

Sani, G. and G. Sartori (1983) 'Polarization, Fragmentation and Competition in Western Democracies', in H. Daalder and P. Mair (eds), *Western European Party Systems. Continuity and Change*, London/Beverly Hills: Sage Publications, 307–40.

Sjöblom, G. (1968) *Party Strategies in a Multiparty System*, Studentliteratur Lund Sweden.

Thomas, J. C. (1982) 'Ideological Change in Competitive Labor Parties. A Test of Downsian Theory', *Comparative Political Studies* 15 (2): 223–40.

Thomson, R. (2001) 'The Programme to Policy Linkage: The Fulfilment of Election Pledges on Socio-Economic Policy in the Netherlands, 1986–1998', *European Journal of Political Research* 40 (2): 171–97.

Volkens, A. (2001) 'Manifesto Research since 1979: From Reliability to Validity', in M. Laver (ed.), *Estimating the Policy Positions of Collective Actors*, London/New York: Routledge, 33–49.

Volkens, A. (2002) *Manifesto Coding Instructions. Second Revised Edition*, Discussion Paper FS III 02–201, Berlin: Social Science Research Centre.

Volkens, A. and H.-D. Klingemann (2002) 'Parties, Ideologies, and Issues. Stability and Change in Fifteen European Party Systems 1945–1998', in K. R. Luther and F. Müller-Rommel (eds) *Political Parties in the New Europe: Political and Analytical Challenges*, Oxford University Press, 143–67.

3 Models of citizenship and Social Democratic policies

Dietmar Braun and Olivier Giraud

Introduction

The notion of citizenship is becoming more and more a hotly debated topic in partisan politics in general and for social–democratic parties in particular. Two developments seem to have influenced the resurgence of citizenship. First, economic competitiveness in a *globalised world* (economic efficiency) is increasingly considered as a constraint to maintaining a high level of social protection (social justice) being at the heart of the notion of 'social citizenship'. This discussion is pertinent because one of the major concepts of the 'old way' of Social Democracy, social citizenship, mainly introduced by T.H. Marshall (1950), seems to be contested in the discussions of the Third Way. Social citizenship is a concept narrowly related to the welfare state of Social Democratic origin and social policy in general. In Marshall's view, a full democratic participation of citizens not only depends on civic and political integration but also on social integration. Social citizenship must thus be understood as a basic condition of the modern inclusive democracy. In the words of one of the most insightful analysis of Marshall's work, 'social rights not only provide citizens with a sense of material security . . . social security encourages a sense of belonging and commitment to the kind of society, the welfare state, within which citizens live' (Hemerijck, 2001: 138). The right to real income is then not 'proportionate to the market value of claimant' and there should be a 'subordination of the market to social justice' (Hemerijck, ibid.). Second, another tendency, in part related to processes of globalisation and directly pertinent for the construction of citizenship, is the trend towards the *individualisation* of society (Beck and Sopp 1997). Individualisation can have disconcerting repercussions on social and political integration.

In order to understand how 'real life concepts' of citizenship of Social Democratic parties have changed facing the challenge of globalisation and individualisation, we believe that existing models of citizenship must be complemented, because their analytical treatment of the citizenship problem is insufficient.

Frameworks of citizenship[1]

The existing frameworks of citizenship combine two main dimensions: a model of political participation, and a model of social status (Crouch *et al.* 2001:262). They all focus on the universalistic character of citizenship and on the modes of the individual's inclusion into the citizenry. In our view, however, the discussion on citizenship is also about a double relationship between the individual and the groups and institutions relevant for the whole political community, i.e. the state. The analysis of the individual's inclusion into the citizenry only focuses on one way of the relationship, the bottom-up one from the individual into the collective, but does not really tackle the reverse relationship, the top down one, considering the modes of intervention of the state in the society and in the individual's existence and fate. The models focusing on the status provided or guaranteed by the state, offer a too limited view of the state's influence on society and on individuals. If we take the relational character of citizenship seriously, models of citizenship should also consider and analyse the development and nature of state intervention.

If this complementary notion is conceded, three analytical dimensions are pertinent to grasp at the notion of citizenship. First, *social integration* denotes the preferred way in the different national systems to encourage social cohesion. It partly depends on the states' intention and ability to guarantee or not the material conditions of life of citizens, on the one hand, and to integrate or not the citizen into a working life. This is, of course, the famous welfare and work distinction. The ways of social integration depend on how the role of the state and the individual is defined with regard to welfare and work. Behind the different solutions to welfare and work we often find, in addition, different belief systems concerning the relationship of the individual and the community/state.

Second, political integration is the mode different systems select to support political participation and commitment of the individuals or the social groups. We can distinguish four different ways to integrate the citizen into the political life. These ways are very much in correspondence with the modes of social order described by Streeck and Schmitter (1985): the market, hierarchy, association and community. We think that community – despite of all discussions by communitarians – is not a viable option in the current political discussion but there are elements of the communitarian philosophy integrated in the 'postmodern' type of 'active individualism' we regard as the fourth model of political integration.

Third, scope and style of state intervention refers to the conception, signification, and importance of the public apparatus influence and instruments on society and on the individuals' choices and destiny. The scope and style of state intervention demonstrates more in particular *how* the state defines the limits and extensions of its authority in relation to society. It shows us how much room is left for independent action of citizens in society.

Table 3.1 Four ideal-types of citizenship

	Social integration	*Political integration*	*Scope and style of state intervention*
Statism	Egalitarianism and redistribution; moral obligation of citizen	Subject	Centralisation
Paternalism	Protection and passivity; rights, no obligations	Member	Delegation
Market	Competition and consumer-orientation	Voter	Order function and privatisation
Active individualism	Enabling and facilitating; 'reflexive individual'	Participant	Deregulation; moderation; supervision

On the base of these three analytical dimensions we aim to develop 'ideal-types of citizenship', which will serve as our framework of interpretation for understanding the developments of Social Democratic policies with regard to citizenship. We contend that we find four such ideal-types today, three belonging to what one might – according to Beck, Giddens and Lash (Beck *et al.*, 1996) – call the first modernity[2] (market, statism, and paternalism) and one emerging model (active individualism) representing the second modernity or, according to other authors, postmodernity. The following typology summarises the main components of the four ideal-types.

The state model

The 'old' Social Democracy like we find it for example in Sweden, is very much based on a '*statist model of citizenship*' with an egalitarian conception concerning the allocation of resources and status differentials. The state has the task to 'decommodify' a substantial part of society relationships by an active welfare policy. This welfare policy is, however, based on the belief system that the citizen should keep his or her independence *vis-à-vis* the state and his or her fellow-citizen. Welfare should, therefore, not create an attitude of dependence but enable all citizens to actively participate in work. The state is, however, the central and collective institution for creating the favourable conditions fostering this goal by a redistribution of resources. Citizens have rights and obligations concerning the community. Old Social Democracy in Sweden searches a way between welfare and work with a strong emphasis on work. In this model, corresponding to the hierarchical type of social order, the state has a primordial role in defining the rules and contents of political life. The collective interest predominates and the citizen easily becomes a 'subject' in the sense of Almond and Verba (Almond and Verba, 1963).

Paternalism

In the '*paternalist model of citizenship*',[3] the state has the task to guarantee 'economic security' in the first place and strife for an 'equality of needs' instead of an egalitarian redistribution of resources. The role of the citizen becomes a different one in this context. Its role concerning social integration is a passive and dependent one but the citizen has the right to claim social protection without being supposed to fulfil too much obligations with regard to the community. In contrast to the former model, social integration is, in addition, based on the upholding of status differentials and on the family as the main addressee of state action. The '*paternalist model of citizenship*' builds much more on intermediary systems between the state and the individual. Associations and interest groups respectively are the predominant form of political organisation of citizens and citizens become first and foremost members of such groups and associations in order to participate in political life.

The market model

The '*market model of citizenship*' 'liberates individual self-interest' and fosters competition as the major principle of social order. The state has – as is described in Esping-Andersen's market welfare regime – a much more reduced function in protecting the material needs of its citizens. It acts as an institution of last resort in order to avoid the worst for people. The citizen is above all a producer and a consumer with no clear defined moral obligations versus the community. Freedom from state intervention (i.e. 'negative freedom') means a high degree of self-responsibility and active search behaviour on the labour market. Social integration takes place by anonymous market processes, or, in the words of Durkheim, by 'mechanic solidarity'. The '*market model of citizenship*' respects the liberal democratic state and guarantees the democratic voting rights of citizens. It is the 'Schumpeterian' view of democracy which rules in this model. The citizen is a voter in political life and not more.

Active individualism

These are the three types of social integration we find in the 'old world' during the first modernity. A fourth type is emerging which endeavours to take into account the new trends and developments and which represents according to us very much the philosophy of the 'new Social Democracy'. In this type – and we refer mainly to the concept developed by Anthony Giddens – citizenship is based on a mix of 'individualism and communitarianism' (Giddens 1997), i.e. an 'active individualism'. Individualism in so far as the self-responsibility for social integration and an 'entrepreneurial attitude' of citizens is stressed and communitarianism in so far as obligations *vis-à-vis* the community is stressed. The new and active individualism tries to overcome the 'egoistic attitudes' of an individualistic way of life by striving for a 'reflexive autonomy', meaning a behaviour that respects and even highly esteems the different opinions and interests of other citizens and that voluntarily searches for civil contract with others. In this way, an independent individual should take care of social integration. While this contains elements of the 'statist model' it becomes different concerning the role of the state with regard to social integration: the state should not protect or steer, but facilitate and enable the individual to take its responsibility. It is not the redistributing and egalitarian state which is demanded, neither the reactive and protective state but the pro-active 'social investment state' (idem), moderating and supervising the autonomous interactions of citizens. 'Empowerment' and 'positive welfare' become keywords in this model. The model reacts to the individualisation process in society nowadays: it reduces state authority and it envisages overcoming 'de-solidarisation' by empowerment and civic contracts.

The new model of '*active individualism*' aims to (re-)create – in the republican tradition of Aristoteles and Hannah Arendt and quite corresponding to the category of 'participants' in the work of Almond and Verba – active citizens participating in the civil society (or in 'sub-politics' in the sense of Ulrich Beck 1993). Giddens insists that in this model a normative and hierarchical political institution is no longer accepted (Giddens 1997: 79). Democracy becomes a 'dialog' between citizens while the established political elite is retreating.

'*Active individualism*' tries, as Giddens contends (Giddens, 1998), a balance between regulation and deregulation and a balance between economic and non-economic elements. But it is clear that, given the desire to decentralise political power to civil society and sub-politics, deregulation of state functions become one of the goals within this model. The state does not delegate, as in the paternalist model, but it deregulates and keeps the function of orientation and supervision. The state is not superfluous but an important device for 'de-commodification'. It should, however, serve the citizen and not become his or her 'superior'.

We think that this ideal-type, though one can find affinities with each of the other ideal-types, is sufficiently distinct to become an emerging new model of citizenship conducive to the political strategies of social-democratic parties nowadays, among other things because it allows to maintain a progressive orientation despite of the confines of globalisation and individualisation and because the ideal-type is sufficiently distinct from the other ideal-types – because it merges elements from each other type without becoming identical to neither type – to maintain a visible Social Democratic programmatic position in the party system. It is not excluded, however, that other parties may also embrace 'active individualism' as a suitable strategy in developing the notion of citizenship.

Countries with Social Democratic presence in government have, of course, followed different models of citizenship that do not correspond exactly to one of these ideal-types. One can, for example, state that the Netherlands demonstrate a combination of paternalism in social and political integration and of statism in the scope and style of state intervention, while Sweden has statist elements in social integration and state intervention but a paternalist element in political integration. France, to give another example, has a paternalist orientation in social integration but a statist tradition on the other two dimensions.

We contend, however, that most Social Democratic parties are today moving into the direction of this fourth and emerging citizenship model. In order to verify this statement we will compare two contrasted cases with Social Democratic participation in government, the Netherlands and Sweden. As both countries have different cultural and political backgrounds and have pursued different paths in the application of citizenship models, it will be interesting to see if our hypothesis of a converging trend in policies on citizenship is confirmed or if different historical paths and cultural traditions account for diverging strategies of adaptation to globalisation processes and individualising trends in society.

The case of the Netherlands

Citizenship in the Netherlands has been heavily influenced by Christian-democratic thinking and, therefore, the 'paternalist type' of social and political integration (see Becker 2000b). Until the end of the 1960s, the country was characterised by consociational procedures of decision-making built upon a segmentational structure of society and specific conceptions of social justice and of the state-society relationship:

- a strong leading and independent role of the different 'pillars' political elites (catholic, protestant, secular);
- a high degree of acquiescence of the citizens concerning political decision-making; and a very secretive and centralised style of bargaining where a preoccupation for consensus predominated;
- a high esteem of solidarity in the sense that the state had the responsibility to protect the poor and weak in society by a centralised redistribution of resources and built an advanced and well-protecting social security system with a strong emphasis on risk assurance (and not on risk prevention),[4]
- a strong and interventionist state with regard to income and price regulations, but also a high degree of tolerance concerning the self-organisation of the different pillars in society (subsidiarity);
- a strong emphasis on consensus and negotiation as the principle mode of interaction; and
- a tendency to delegate economic and social policies to the inter-

mediary level, i.e. to the social partners, integrated into a highly institutionalised system of intermediation ('corporatist structures of negotiation').

The kind of citizenship model emerging out of these basic features corresponds to the paternalist type we sketched above: a citizen whose claims for social protection are accepted but who lacks above all the possibility to use his or her formal political rights in a more active and participatory way. He or she is represented in the political arena by the political elite's and by interest groups.

Since the 1970s this original model has been contested on several occasions. The 'Partij van de Arbeid' (PvdA), the Social Democratic party of the Netherlands, for example, attempted to introduce a more 'statist' type of citizenship in the 1970s, where the main goals of social justice became equality of assets, income, power and knowledge and emancipation while discrimination was strongly opposed. The Christian-democratic and liberal coalition government in the 1980s by contrast initiated a certain '*liberalisation*' of the Dutch citizenship model.

The period we will discuss starts in 1989, when the social-democratic party joined a coalition with the Christian Democrats who remained the major party. After 1994, the first government without the Christian Democrats was installed, a coalition between the PvdA as the biggest party, and right-wing and left-wing liberal parties (the so-called 'purple coalition'). It is during this period, the 1990s and above all the period after 1994, that we should find an answer to the question what kind of citizenship model Social Democrats are defending today in the Netherlands. We will answer this question by passing along our three dimensions of citizenship.

Social integration preferences

The Social Democratic use of power in government during the 1990s has often been seen as a pragmatic approach and as a learning process rather than the application of a concise and refined ideological framework of action (Becker and Cuperus, 1998). The PvdA did not seek the way back to its 'old Social Democratic' attitudes concerning social and political rights in the 1970s. Quite on the contrary, few things changed once the PvdA participated in government instead of the liberals from 1989 onwards. The Social Democratic party subscribed the continuation of the deficit reduction of the former government though it put more emphasis on the maintenance of the social protection level and on a more sensible policy concerning the avoidance of poverty for the working poor (Delsen, 2000). This did not withhold the PvdA to launch, together with the Christian-democrats, one of the most radical reforms in the existing welfare state regime, i.e. the tightening of eligibility rules in the generous and costly disability scheme. This reform brought both parties almost at the brink of total defeat during the elections of 1994 where both parties lost a large number of votes.

The reform of the welfare state remained important for the Social Democrats in two senses: first, because the financial room for manoeuvre suffered seriously from the high rates of welfare transfers and made it impossible to reduce taxes and social charges for the enterprises which was regarded as the adequate economic policy in a period of globalisation, and second, because the understanding of the welfare state began to change. For the first time the unemployment crisis was largely seen as a crisis of inactivity, hence one finds a move away from the image of a protective and passive 'welfare taker' to a higher prioritisation of work (Green-Pedersen *et al.* 2000). In this context the policies concerning the unemployed also began to change.

There have been profound changes on the Dutch labour market, above all due to the growing willingness of women to enter into the labour market after the paternalist model and social cleavages ceased to hold their grip on the Dutch society. The developments on the labour market – often described under the title 'polder model' – are well known and will not be described here (Visser and Hemerijck, 1997; Becker, 2000a; Delsen, 2000; Hemerijck *et al.* 2000).

The Social Democrats intended to tackle the labour market segmentation in placing work before welfare. The high level of persons benefiting from the disability scheme and the high rates of long-term and youth unemployment were attacked through the reform of the Employment Service, the further tightening of unemployment and disability insurance eligibility rules and the reduction of labour costs. The purple government broke with a long tradition of a rather passive labour market policy and developed a large number of labour market schemes targeted to problem groups (Schmid, 1996; Hemerijk *et al.* 2000). The general orientation of most reforms resembled the ideas of 'workfare' implemented by the Blair government in the United Kingdom. Unemployed should have sufficient incentives to actively seek for jobs on the labour market: in a positive way through tax schemes supporting re-integration into the labour market and in a negative way by forcing the jobless to accept work below their educational level or to participate in training measures.

These policies were partly successful but strongly increased the rate of part-time activity and did not address the problem of precarious jobs. In 1996, the social partners developed – with the help of the government – some regulations on how to better protect the position of part-time workers.

The priorities of social justice became the integration into the labour market (the slogan of the 'purple coalition' was 'jobs, jobs, jobs') and, in words rather than deeds, a better education policy instead of high social protection standards and equality, as it was still the case in the 1970s. The lesser emphasis on the last two social justice goals did not mean, however, that they were radically abandoned. The protection of the 'weak' remains a highly valued and persisting element of all Dutch governments until today. If one stresses these shifts in social justice one should not forget that other policy values have or received an even stronger backing of governments, including the Social Democrats. Efficiency, for example, remained a top priority of all governments in the 1990s (Hoogerwerf, 1999) and liberal ideas of 'economic freedom' and 'competition' were increasingly accepted by the PvdA which, after 1994, was clearly dominated by the liberal wing of the party while the traditional radical wing lost power (U Becker 2000a).

The emphasis on labour market integration instead of welfare was the first element changing radically the view on citizenship and social rights. The second one was the change in the view on the foundation of the welfare state. Traditionally, in all 'risk assurance' welfare states, the transfer structure was directed to the male breadwinner representing the family as the most important economic and social unit. With the individualisation and emancipation process taking place in all countries, the male breadwinner model now is in discredit and replaced by the more neutral notion of the 'individual'. Several reforms have been undertaken in the Netherlands during the 1990s going into this direction (above all in the 'New Social Assistance Act' of 1996). Elements of this change were, however, already propagated by the Social Democracy in the 1970s (see above).

State intervention

The perception of the role of the state *vis-à-vis* society is also changing. Here, the new Social Democratic led 'purple coalition' has not followed a different course than its predecessor governments. The balance is clearly shifting in favour of a more liberal version of the role of the state, though some elements of the paternalist model and some new elements of the enabling model are integrated.

The retreat of the state for example, already among the priorities of the Christian-democratic and liberal government, belonged also to the priorities of the two 'purple governments' but it has received a somewhat different shade. First of all, the government wants to promote 'more market and less government' in economy. It is convinced that, in addition, the asset of having a corporate self-regulation of the social partners should be maintained. One even notices more delegation of economic and social decisions to the intermediary level than before while the state is supposed to limit itself to its main functions. While these priorities seem to continue in the direction of the previous governments in following a mix of liberal and paternalist elements in state intervention, there are other policy initiatives demonstrating that Social Democrats in the Netherlands have indeed included elements of the 'enabling state' model.

First of all, the government stresses not only delegation but also 'steering' as the main function of the state nowadays. The whole organisation of the public sector is under revision (Kickert 1998). Already in the 1980s, the juridical status of 'zelfstandige bestuursorganen' (ZBO) was introduced to give para-statal agencies more room to manoeuvre in executing public functions while the ministerial bureaucracy should develop a stronger guiding and orienting role and concentrate on the control of the functioning of these agencies. Later on, the status of so-called 'agencies' ('agentschappen') was introduced which followed clearly the model of the new public management (idem). Efficiency, a public service directed to clients and a stronger role for political guidance are the main elements ruling these reorganisation processes.

Second, despite of the emphasis of trusting the social partners to organise public tasks, there was a tendency to 'de-corporatise' the organisation of public tasks. A first indicator is the reform of the status of the traditional advisory body of the government in social and economic policies, the 'Social and Economic Council', a body comprised of trade union and employers´ representatives as well as of independent experts. The legally fixed obligation to ask for advice of this body before governmental decisions are taken was abolished in the beginning of the 1990s though the Social Democratic government still claims that it will not neglect this body if important decisions are to be taken. A second indicator is the reorganisation of welfare administration traditionally managed by trade unions and employers. Evidently, there were serious problems of 'segmentation' in the delivery of welfare services in the Netherlands, i.e. of 'rent-seeking' by those groups administering these welfare services. The government reduced the weight of the social partners in new bodies or even created 'independent' and 'neutral' bodies, like for example the 'Supervisory Board for Social Insurance' (Hemerijck *et al.* 2000). At the same time market incentives were introduced. All these reforms were clearly inspired by a will to raise the level of efficiency of governmental services. This also holds for the reorganisation of employment services, which was deregulated. Such a reorganisation did already take place in the beginning of the 1990s but, because this reform was not very successful, the purple government has once again reorganised the Employment Service according to the general philosophy of new public management. Nowadays, the Minister of Social Affairs and Employment is responsible for the budget and for developing the overall orientation in employment policies. The responsibility for the implementation is delegated to the semi-autonomous Central Board of the Employment Service that is financed according to its performance, i.e. by its ability to get people back to work. Efficiency by way of the new public management, deregulation and competition characterise the philosophy of the government in the making of public services nowadays.

Political integration

These shifts in the organisation of state and society demonstrate already that self-organisation of the society has become the predominant ideology of the Social Democratic party and the purple government. This shift is further demonstrated by claims and reforms concerning the political rights. In the new party programme of the PvdA ('De rode draden van de sociaal-democratie'; see van Kersbergen, 2000) it is demanded to further strengthen the 'cultural democracy', meaning a policy to reinforce the civil society and granting it more independence and autonomy from the still very prominent influence of the state in society. This claim is different from Social Democratic demands in the 1970s. It is based on the conviction that a new self-consciousness of the citizen has emerged that should be institutionalised and fostered by governmental policies. It indicates also that – quite according to the philosophy of the enabling model – the role of traditional 'politics' by the political elites is not anymore valued in high esteem. The political discussion in forums distinct from the state should be developed.

At least one reform has been introduced concerning the political rights of the citizen, being a new law on a 'corrective referendum' (1999). By way of a referendum (600,000 signatures are needed), people can now refuse a bill with a majority vote of at least 30 per cent of all eligible citizens having presented their vote.

Finally, the government is also stressing the principle of 'subsidiarity' because it wants to foster political structures that are situated as near as possible to the citizen. Politics should become an affair of the people and not the policy of a political elite ruling over an apathetic citizen, as it still was the case in the earlier paternalist model. As a direct consequence public tasks were as much as possible transferred to provinces and municipalities (Hoogerwerf 1999: 172). This is a large step away from the traditional centralisation mood in the Netherlands.

Conclusions

All this shows that it would be a stereotype saying that the Netherlands solved the challenges and problems of globalisation by re-activating their traditional consensus-model. The consensus model has helped to find pragmatic solutions to unemployment but at the same time there has been a major change in the citizen model of the Netherlands in the direction of both the market and the active individualism model. The integration into the labour market is put before social protection, though the maintenance of minimum social standards for the 'weak' is still strongly defended; labour market segmentation between part-time and full-time workers is accepted and even wanted for by a large number of people; a dualism on the labour market between those having work and those out of work still exists, but Social Democrats have begun to actively reduce those 'out of work' by a mix of different policy instruments. The role of the state in society is revised: there is more deregulation and delegation, but also more political guidance and more control; and there is also the willingness to free economic enterprises from state regulation and financial burden. There is an emphasis on more participation of the citizen and a more independent and active role, though concrete measures are still rare and the strengthening of political rights certainly has not belonged to the main priorities of the two purple governments; the integration by the corporatist self-organisation is increasingly replaced by more 'independent' bodies composed of experts; there is the demand to create stronger link between citizens and the state at the regional and local level instead of the central level. Compared to the traditional paternalist model and the 'old Social Democratic' model of the 1970s, one can contend that there is a shift going on in the Social Democratic view on citizenship during the 1990s. Clearly, the reforms address the 'individualisation' of society and are preoccupied with a stronger emphasis on individual responsibility and the creation of equal chances on the labour market and in society in general in order to also arrive at new forms of 'solidarity'. The promotion of the political active citizen, on the other hand, still remains vague and needs further elaboration.

The case of Sweden

Sweden stands for the archetypal model of the Scandinavian Social Democratic regime. Famous for its ability to conciliate social and economic goals, its developed welfare state, its centralised bargaining system of industrial relations and, its high level of public expenditure, Sweden has developed over time a regime of citizenship which appears to be a mix of both the statist and the paternalistic types. Resolutely egalitarian in the social integration dimension ('statist type'), relying on effective encompassing organisations in the political integration dimension ('paternalistic type'), the Swedish model of citizenship was carried out by a powerful and centralised state ('statist type'). Emerging from a society often characterised as homogeneous in both ethnic and religious terms, the power of the Swedish state used to be well accepted in the society (Olson 1993: 181) and the authority of its administrative elite was linked with the traditional culture of the protestant bourgeoisie (Rothstein, 1996). Egalitarianism, high level of associative discipline, loyalty and political participation, hierarchy, centralisation: most keywords characteristic of the Swedish type of citizenship appear to be particularly challenged by the ongoing trend toward the individualisation of modern societies. This mixed type of citizenship is often assimilated with the Social Democrats because the Social Democratic party (SAP) has been shaping the Swedish model since the late 1930s. Despite the proportional list voting system favouring the fragmentation of the partisan system, and despite of a high frequency of parliamentary elections,[5] the SAP stayed in power for long periods. Moreover, the party was able, if necessary, to build coalitions with the post-agrarian party (Centre) or with parties located on the Left (Arter 1994: 72).

How can the high integrative capacity of the Swedish Social Democratic party be explained? The analytical framework in terms of citizenship we developed in the second section of this paper might provide some help. We will firstly sketch the main characteristics of the Swedish post-war model according to our three analytical dimensions: social integration, political integration and role of the state. We will then investigate the first important alteration of the original Swedish model in the 1980s and 1990s; finally, we will examine the current agenda of reform of the Swedish SAP in power along the three dimensions defined above.

The post-war model

The construction phase of the Swedish Social Democratic regime is marked in each of our three dimensions by the predominant role of the industrial labour union. After the war and confronted with the electoral strength of the communist party, the Swedish business associations and the labour unions were inclined to commit themselves in forms of neo-corporatist partnership. In the political arena, the SAP preferred to form a coalition with the moderate Agrarian party than with the radical communists of the late 40s but had to find answers to the pressure emerging from the left spectrum. The 'Rehn-Meidner' strategy for the economy was based on two main features. Firstly, it was designed to introduce a remuneration of the labour force that would make up for the traditional wage discrepancies dividing the wage-earning category and the sector specific labour unions ('solidaristic wage policy'). Secondly, the strategy pursued the objective of raising the productivity of national firms, precondition for economic growth in an open economy but also for welfare state, real-wage expansion and an important growth of labour market participation (Pontusson 1994: 26). The state was the pro-active architect of the economic and social organisation of the model negotiated with the LO. It adapted its welfare and labour market policies but also its fiscal policies in order to favour productive investments.

Based on a strong intervention state and on encompassing interests associations, Sweden seems at first sight to constitute a very consistent model of citizenship. Though, it raises a puzzle concerning the degree of involvement, activity and empowerment of the individuals in this particular configuration favouring 'big organisations', i.e. the state and corporative actors. Many scholars argue that a strong welfare state discourages the citizens' participation and responsibility. In this perspective, developed corporatist patterns of social mediation and policy-making favour a medium or long-term divide between the political and organisational élite and the mass of voters and members. The passivity of citizens should be the outcome of this type of configuration (Goul Andersen and Hoff, 2001). Other scholars yet state that Sweden has continuously been demonstrating a high level of 'social capital' both in terms of political participation as well as of diversified and intense forms of civil society development or even of informal sociability and solidarity (Rothstein 2001). In our view, Sweden has been developing an original model combining both types of patterns:

- *Social integration* is based on two main pillars. On the one hand, the welfare state and economic policies, as well as the solidaristic wage strategy are oriented towards high standards of egalitarianism and protection. On the other, the individuals active involvement on the labour market (skill adaptation, mobility) and a fair use of social benefits are required. Social integration is provided through a contract like arrangement and not through the one-sided attribution of protection by the state. The Swedish model of social integration could be characterised as an 'active' form of statism.
- *Political integration* is based on a high standard of loyalty required by the 'big' industrial relations organisations for maintaining their involvement into corporatist arrangements; this type of arrangement both centralises and monopolises bargaining and regulative power in society (paternalism). In the Swedish case, high levels of citizens' political and associative participation moderate this pattern.
- *Scope and style of state intervention*: traditionally, the scope of the Swedish state's intervention is large and its style is rather centralised, rigid, and demonstrates a high level of authority.

In Sweden, as in many other industrial countries, the 70s shake this post-war model and heralded major changes. Confronted with the increasing incapacity of big firms to create employment, with high rates of inflation, with a growing demand for more consumption (Benner and Bundgaard Vad, 2000: 408), the SAP lost the 1976 election. This downfall pushed the party to develop an independent economic and social expertise and to take its distance from the trade union strategy.

First changes in the 1980s

Back in power from 1982 on, the SAP already used the banal image of a 'Third Way' – the 'third road' – in order to characterise its agenda of reform.

Social integration

In line with its traditional social justice values, the Social Democratic government cancelled the cuts in welfare benefits imposed by the previous government, introduced new taxes on capital income and heritages and even a soft version of the wage-earner funds first proposed in the 1970s. Later in the decade, a sixth week of annual vacation, a longer parental leave and the expansion of public-day care for young children were introduced. During the 1980s, the retrenchment from the original model in terms of social integration was not significant.

Political integration

The unstable economic and social context of the 1980s had more consequences in political integration matters. In 1983, the central bargaining system was abandoned and the tensions between labour and business and within the labour camp, between public sector and private industry unions, intensified. These tensions nourished the slide of the income policy, which caused high levels of inflation during the whole decade. The transformation of the corporatist framework strongly weakened the integration of the whole wage-earning category into the one and only pattern of the productive unionised industry worker. The state had to intervene in order to replace the corporatist regulation and built an expertise autonomous from the union in social and economic matters. These trends characterise an evolution from a paternalistic type of political integration toward a more state-centred version.

Scope and style of state intervention

Simultaneously, the new SAP administration conducted important reforms oriented toward an improvement of supply side factors: restore the profitability of private firms[6] and '*growth*' became higher priorities than '*redistribution*' (Pontusson 1994). State-owned companies were restructured and privatised; subsidies for declining sectors were cut. The money saved on these expenditures was dedicated to industrial policy programs favouring the development of the economy in basic industry or new technologies (Benner and Bundgaard Vad, 2000: 423). The growth of public spending was limited and important reforms of public administration were launched. Important segments of the administration were decentralised and open to new organisational forms such as 'corporatisation' – '*hiving off of auxiliary services to companies owned by local governments*' or other models of responsiveness and efficiency inspired by the private sector (Pontusson 1994: 36). Further on, the financial market was deregulated following the Anglo-Saxon path and the fiscal system was strongly amended in the line of American or British liberal fiscal reforms. Finally, the Swedish model of labour market intervention was transformed: the activation rate of spending was lowered and the centralisation of public administration for employment was attacked in favour of the municipalities. Decentralisation became a legitimate goal.

In terms of citizenship, the 'third road' of the 1980s should not be interpreted as a U-turn, leading away from the traditional direction of Social Democracy toward social justice, welfare, and social integration through full employment and economic efficiency. It does, though, represent a first alteration of the Swedish model. The withdraw of the corporatist arrangement, the end of the solidaristic wage, the introduction of an active limitation to public spending growth, and finally the state and tax reform are important factors corresponding to a first 'normalisation' of the Swedish system. The decision to join the European Union taken during the summer of 1991 was the logical next step in that direction. At this stage though, neither the decline of paternalism in the political integration dimension, nor the first reforms undertaken in the scope and style of state intervention dimension are clearly or explicitly targeted toward the active individualism model of citizenship.

Further development in the 1990s

Sweden had to face strong shocks in this last decade of the 20th century. The perspective of the integration into the EU, the choice of a hard currency strategy, the deregulation of the financial market and the transformation of the fiscal system had first a negative impact on the country's economic situation. The labour market went through a deep crisis, for the first time in the post-war period. The SAP lost the 1991 election but won the 1994 one and is still in power since that time. Because of the serious difficulties the country had to face, in public finances and on the labour market, both the conservative and the Social Democratic government introduced reforms and cuts in spending. Those cuts and reforms aimed in the first place to adapt the existing system to new conditions but in the end had an impact on the general patterns of the system (Benner and Bundgaard Vad 2000: 430–1).

Social integration

Firstly, the SAP government reformed the pension system in direction of a less universalistic and more Bismarckian type of benefit allowance. Secondly, the different governments of the 1990s reduced the level of generosity of the welfare state.[7] Thirdly, the Social Democratic government of the 1990s renewed its preferences for active labour market spending, in particular for training programmes. Despite these efforts and the bettering in the labour market situation in the second half of the 1990s, the level of labour market segmentation has grown in recent years. A high proportion of people are integrated in temporary programs and the creation of jobs in the home service sector has been encouraged (Björklund 2000: 154). More significant from a symbolic point of view, the SAP government decided to cut an important number of jobs in the public sector, especially low skill jobs occupied by women working part-time (Benner and Bundgaard Vad 2000: 433). In other words, the Social Democratic combat for radical egalitarianism on the labour market seems to be practically abandoned; the endowment of social policy has been seriously lowered. The political discourse appears to be the only stable element in that matter (Iversen 1999: 176).

Political integration

The SAP came back to power in the mid 1990s with ambitious priorities. The integration of Sweden in the EU occurred simultaneously with the arrival of thousands of refugees caused by different conflicts around the world and with the development of problems linked with the integration of immigrants. European integration outwards and multiculturalism inwards raise the problem of the relationship of the Swedes to other national and cultural communities. The acceptance of the end of the 'homogeneous Sweden' is the next step to go after the end of 'welfare state patriotism' and is still on the agenda of the present SAP government (Svensson 2001: 223). The failure of the corporatist arrangement and Sweden's integration into the EU also led to an irrevocable loss of power of the corporative actors. The key role played by the union in the paternalist Swedish model of political integration has been hollowed out. Most analysts state that the preservation of the very high membership rate in the union is principally due to the union's key role in the unemployment benefit system (Goul Andersen and Hoff 2001; Rothstein 2001). The crisis of the Swedish 'big institutions' – big state, political parties, encompassing corporative actors – has not led yet to a corresponding weakening of political participation or of associative participation. The citizens' values have rather been reoriented toward the conciliation of fulfilment of their own individual interests with the preservation of solidarity. The overall participation in Sweden to associative activities has recently increased but has been reoriented toward more individualistic activities and favours decentralised and less hierarchical forms of collective organisations (Rothstein 2001: 221).

Scope and style of state intervention

Finally, the continuing decentralisation process of public administration and welfare state implementation (school system, labour market policies), will have stimulating effects on local political communities. Moreover, the Swedish debate is currently centred on the ongoing process of state and Welfare state reform. 'Value for money' 'efficiency', and 'confidence in the public sector' are central keywords of this debate (ibid.). The improvement of public administration and its opening to new forms of direct democratic control – small scale democracy – is understood as the appropriate answer to political integration concerns and to necessary improvement of state action (Goul Andersen and Hoff 2001).

In each of our three dimensions, the very key words of Active Individualism appear to be engaged in the process of reform of the state/citizens relationship in Sweden (individualisation, differentiation, participation, decentralisation, efficiency). Only, the label 'Active Individualism' itself is absent in this national context.

Conclusions

The original model of Swedish citizenship has been altered in recent years. The egalitarian and paternalist patterns of both the social integration and political integration dimensions have been radically weakened by a number of factors: the plague of the corporatist arrangement, the end of the solidaristic wage, a significant shift in social policies strategy, the important transformations of the labour market, taxation and public employment policies as well as a reform of the state apparatus towards decentralisation and efficiency. These factors had a clear impact on both social and political integration. Sweden's adhesion to the EU and the intensification of immigration further on weakened the boundaries of the traditional framework centred on national encompassing organisations and on a unique model of citizen. In these both dimensions, the Social Democratic governments have been forced to transform or adapt the Social Democratic model to changing conditions.

The statist type of social integration based on a strong egalitarian model had to respond to the challenges of individualisation and differentiation. The traditional contract type of social integration (high level of protection for high level of individuals' commitment) has been transformed: less protection is provided, a higher level of social differentiation is accepted, and more commitment is required.

The paternalist type of political integration has been radically transformed. The encompassing and hierarchical organisations lost most of their power. The Social Democratic state seems, though, to have a hard time using the new forms of civil society engagements developed from below by citizens, who nowadays formulate needs for more individualistic and autonomous designed forms of collective action.

In the scope and style of state intervention dimension, the Social Democratic governments explicitly and deliberately organised both the reform and decentralisation of the public apparatus and of the Welfare state. The state style of intervention clearly moves toward decentralisation and efficiency, in other words toward a model valuing a market-oriented type of rationality tolerating inter-regional disparities and/or competition.

Especially along two of our three dimensions of citizenship – social and political integration – the Swedish Social Democrats have difficulties to design a cohesive model. The SAP is particularly reluctant to use the New Labour program in the United Kingdom as a model. The relation of the party toward the British 'Third Way' is regarded as a '*delicate affair*' (Svensson 2001).

'*Empowerment and employability*', keywords of the active social integration promoted by the Third Way, are regarded as '*Swedish exports*' (Svensson 2001: 223). The current challenges that the Swedish tradition of a developed welfare state, and high level of public employment and spending have to face are understood as opportunities to renew the contract founding the model between the state and the citizens.

Even if most key words of Active Individualism are in fact guiding recent reforms and transformation of the Swedish citizenship framework, both the government and the Social Democratic party are still very unwilling to erect it as a reference or a model. The Swedes might have abandoned their traditional welfare state patriotism, they still prefer to keep national references, values and traditions to build and delimitate the national political discourse and the national citizenship model. Officially, there should not then be any shift in that matter, but only an adaptation. The SAP chose to trigger a silent revolution – many changes in policies and in the distribution of power, high level of stability in discourse – rather than to take the risk to frighten and disorient its political clientele in order to mobilise it more actively around a new shape of citizenship such as Active Individualism. The richness and diversity of the Swedish Social Democratic repertoire of policy instruments and values allowed such a soft strategy that most European Social Democratics could envy.

Conclusions

The focus of this chapter was on the adaptation of the Social Democratic party strategies concerning citizenship in the Netherlands and Sweden in an environment of rapid change. We parted from the idea that traditional models of citizenship (market, statism and paternalism) are forced to come to terms with processes of globalisation and above all individualisation as the new cultural feature of modern societies. We suggested that a suitable alternative model for Social Democracy is 'active individualism'. Our intention was to analyse to what extent the Dutch model of citizenship (a combination of paternalism in social and political integration and statism in matters of state intervention) and the Swedish model (a combination of a statist pattern of social integration and state intervention with a paternalistic form of political integration) have changed their models into the direction of active individualism and if they followed different trajectories.

Our findings demonstrate that, indeed, the two countries integrate today a large number of elements characterising 'active individualism' but that they followed different trajectories, not only because their starting points were different, but also because the strategies and goals chosen by both countries are at least partially divergent. To make two long stories short, one could say that the Netherlands have followed a path which is radically deviating from the original model of citizenship and leading a long way towards the emerging model of active individualism. In the Swedish case, the reforms launched in the last two decades are more cautious and seem to adapt the Swedish model in order to keep it in function rather than to explicitly change it. The first striking difference between our two cases concerns, therefore, the intensity of change. The Netherlands are involved in a radical shift from their previous model, while Sweden is adapting its own system without having defined yet clear goals to reach.

The second notable difference between the two countries involves both the starting points and the trajectories chosen. The original Dutch paternalistic model of citizenship was characteristic for a divided society that had developed a consociational model of democracy. According to the famous analysis of Arend Lijphart (1984), these regimes were based on viable consensus-building procedures among the political élite who represented the different segments of society while citizens demonstrated a high degree of acquiescence and confidence in the ruling capacities of the élite. The protective type of social integration, the political integration by way of intermediary groups and the centralised state intervention created for a long time a stable form of citizenship. Already due to secularisation processes, but much more so by the actual tendency towards individualisation and demands for more autonomy on each dimension of the citizenship model, this model could no longer be maintained. It was in obvious conflict with the new needs, norms and interests accompanying the structural changes. This makes it more understandable that Dutch policy-makers in general and Social Democrats in particular were obliged to radically shift their model of citizenship.

The Swedish classical Social Democratic type of citizenship was under less pressure because it showed already features conducive to 'active individualism' but it lost some key elements, mostly, the performance that were achieved in the past by the national corporatist arrangement. First, the Swedish model of social integration was already based on strongly egalitarian and protective features where work and active involvement – typical features of 'active individualism' was already realised. Second, the associative type of political integration was also based on the ability of the Swedish wage earner citizens to self-regulation. Despite the inducing role of the Swedish state in corporatist affairs, wage restraint or the solidaristic wage implied the aware adhesion of the union members and of members of employers' associations to arrangements providing medium- or long-term compensations. These outcomes were more central to the Swedish type of citizenship focused on the egalitarian participation of all citizens to the labour market than in the Dutch case.

The only component of the Swedish model of citizenship that was clearly in conflict with active individualism was the centralised form of state intervention. And it was this dimension, which was subject to profound changes during the last decade. Hence, the higher congruence of the Swedish model of citizenship with active individualism made a radical shift less compelling than in the Dutch case. The other tremendous changes recently undergone by the Swedish case were linked with the failure of the traditional corporatist mediation and the integration into the EU.

However, the attempt of the Dutch Social Democratic party to create a new type of citizenship provides it with a convincing and offensive political agenda, which seems to be appealing to the electorate, exactly because it takes up the new belief systems and interests within the population. The Swedish SAP still tries to defend the old positions in a changing environment, which seems to be fundamentally in conflict with the universalistic and egalitarian belief system nourishing still most of the discussion of the SAP on citizenship. Here it becomes clear that, in order to survive politically, a simple formal congruence of the basic features of citizenship models (like the slogan work before welfare) does not suffice. It needs a reorientation in thinking about state, society, and citizenship, i.e. a change in the belief system backing up the citizenship model, to really cope with the structural shifts in society. In other words, as long as Swedish Social Democracy does not accept reflexive individualism, deliberative democracy and deregulation as basic features of its ideology, the gap between citizens and the Social Democratic party may widen.

Notes

1 We see four such models: the *republican* approach, which focuses on the active commitment of the individuals to collective tasks (see for example Habermas 1992; van Gunsteren 1994: 42; Barber, 2001); the *neo-liberal* approach focusing on autonomy, freedom of choice and equality of opportunity (Crouch *et al.*, 2001; Goul Andersen and Hoff, 2001: 2); the *communitarian* approach, which evokes the loyalty toward a clearly constituted group, a common identity and a set of values exercised in the context of family live, neighbourhood etc. (Barber 1984; Etzioni 1995; and the '*Social Democratic, Third Way*' approach, which seems to integrate elements from all three aforementioned models (Giddens 1998).

2 With constituting elements like 'industry, wage work and no recognition of female house work, national state, and class affiliation' (Giddens 1998).

3 The conservative and corporatist welfare regime of Esping-Andersen contains many of these features (1990).

4 Hence, the typical conservative and corporatist type of welfare regime in the terminology of Esping-Andersen (Esping-Andersen 1990: 27).

5 3 years term.

6 The government devaluated the national currency to improve the export performance of the Swedish firms.

7 The income replacement rate for unemployment, sickness or parental leave was progressively lowered from 90 per cent to 75 per cent.

References

Almond, G. A. and Verba, S. (1963) *The Civic Culture. Political Attitudes and Democracy in Five Nations*, Princeton, NJ: Princeton University Press.

Arter, D. (1994) 'The war of the roses: conflict and cohesion in the Swedish Social Democratic Party' in Shaw, E. and Bell, D. S. (eds), *Conflict and Cohesion in Western European Social Democratic Parties*, London: Pinter Publisher, 70–95.

Barber, B. (1984) *Strong Democracy*, Berkeley, Los Angeles, London: University of California Press.

Barber, B. (2001) 'How to make society civil and democracy strong ?', in Giddens, A. (ed.), *The Global Third Way Debate*, Cambridge: Polity Press, 269–9.

Beck, U. (1993) *Die Erfindung des Politischen.* Frankfurt: Suhrkamp.

Beck, U., Giddens, A. and Lash, S. (1996) *Reflexive Modernisierung. Eine Kontroverse*, Frankfurt a.M.: Suhrkamp.

Beck, U. and Sopp P. (1997) 'Individualisierung and Integration – eine Problemskizze' in Beck, U. and Sopp P. (eds) *Individualisierung und Integratio*, Opladen: Leske + Budrich. 9–19.

Becker, F. and Cuperus R. (1998) 'Dutch Social Democracy between Blair and Jospin' in R. Cuperus and J. Kandel (eds) *Social Democratic Think Tanks Explore the Magical Return of Social Democracy in a Liberal Era*, Amsterdam: De Bevrijding, 245–56.

Becker, U. (2000a) *Successful Adaptation by Consensus? Employment Development, Power Relations and Hegemony in the Dutch 'Delta Model*, IPSA World Congress, Workshop on 'Power in the New Millenium: Neo-Corporatism or Neo-Liberalism?', Quebec.

Becker, U. (2000b) 'Welfare state development and employment in the Netherlands in comparative perspective' *Journal of European Social Policy* 10, 3, 219–238.

Benner, M. and T. Bundgaard Vad (2000) 'Sweden and Denmark Defending the Welfare State' in F. Scharpf and V. Schmidt (eds) *Welfare and Work in the Open Economy – Diverse Responses to Common Challenges* (volume II), Oxford: Oxford University Press, pp. 399–466.

Björklund, A. (2000) 'Going different ways: labour market policy in Denmark and Sweden', in G. Esping-Andersen and M. Regini (eds), *Why Deregulate Labour Markets?*, Oxford: Oxford University Press, 148–180.

Crouch, C., Eder, K. and Tambini, D. (2001) 'The future of citizenship' in C. Crouch, K. Eder and D. Tambini (eds), *Citizenship, Markets and the State*, Oxford: Oxford University Press, 261–70.

Delsen, L. (2000) *Exit poldermodel? Sociaal–Ecoomische ontwikkelingen in Nederland*, Assen: Van Gorkum.

Esping-Andersen, G. (1990) *The Three Worlds of Welfare Capitalism*, Princeton: Princeton University Press.

Etzioni, A. (1995) *Rights and the Common Good: The Communitarian Perspective*, New York: St Martin's Press.

Giddens, A. (1997) *Jenseits von Links und Rechts*, Frankfurt a.M.: Suhrkamp.

Giddens, A. (1998) *The Third Way*, Cambridge: Polity Press.

Goul Andersen, J. and Hoff, J. (2001) *Democracy and Citizenship in Scandinavia*, Basingstoke: Palgrave.

Green-Pedersen, C., van Kersbergen, K. and Hemerijk, A. (2000) 'Neo-Liberalism, the "Third Way" or What?: Recent Social Democratic Welfare Policies in Denmark and the Netherlands', *Journal of European Public Policy* 8(2): 307–25.

Habermas, J. (1992) 'Citizenship and National Identity: Some Reflections on the Future of Europe', *Praxis International* 12(1): 1–19.

Hemereijck, A. (2001) 'Prospects for effective social citizenship in an age of structural inactivity' in C. Crouch, K. Eder and D. Tambini (eds), *Citizenship, Markets and the State,* Oxford: Oxford University Press, 134–70.

Hemerijck, A., Visser, J. and Unger, B. (2000) 'The Netherlands, Belgium, and Austria: can corporatism cope with reform?' in F. W. Scharpf and V. A. Schmidt (eds), *Welfare and Work in the Open Economy. Diverse Responses to Common Challenges* (Volume II) Oxford: Oxford University Press.

Hernes, H. (1988) 'Scandinavian citizenship', *Acta Sociologica* 31(3): 199–215.

Hoogerwerf, A. (1999) 'Policy successes and failures of the first purple cabinet' *Acta Politica* 34, 158–78.

Iversen, T. (1999) *Contested Economic Institutions – the Politics of Macroeconomics and Wage Bargaining in Advanced Democracies,* Cambridge: Cambridge University Press.

Kersbergen, Kees van (2000) 'De "derde weg", de PvdA en de rode draden, discussion paper, Nijmegen. Universiteit van Nijmegen.

Kickert, W. J. M. (1998) 'Aansturing van verzelfstandigde overheidsdiensten: Over *publiek* management van hybride organisaties', Alphen aan den Rijn: Samson.

Lijphart, Arend (1984) *Democracies – Patterns of Majoritarian Consensus Government in Twenty-One Countries.* New Haven: Yale University Press.

Marshall, T. H. (1950) 'Citizenship and social class', in T. H. Marshall (ed.), *Citizenship and Social Class and Other Essays,* Cambridge: Cambridge University Press.

Olson, J. (1993) 'Le tournant difficile de la social-démocratie suédoise' in M. Telò (ed.), *De la nation à l'Europe – Paradoxes et dilemmes de la social-démocratie,* Brussels: Bruylant, 180–200.

Pontusson, J. (1994) 'Sweden after the Golden Age', in P. Anderson and P. Camiller (eds), *Mapping the West European Left,* London: Verso, 23–54.

Rothstein, B. (1996) *The Social Democratic State – the Swedish Model and the Bureaucratic Problem of Social Reforms,* Pittsburgh: University of Pittsburgh Press.

Rothstein, B. (2001) 'Social capital in the Social Democratic welfare state,' *Politics and Society* 29(2): 207–41.

Schmid, G. (1996) *Beschäftigungswunder Niederlande?: Ein Vergleich der Beschäftigungssysteme in den Niederlanden und in Deutschland,* Berlin: Wissenschaftszentrum Berlin für Sozialforschung, FS I, 96–206.

Streeck, W. and Schmitter Ph. (1985) 'Community, market, state – and associations?: the prospective contribution of interest governance to social order' in W. Streeck and Ph. Schmitter (eds) *Private Interest Government: Beyond Market and State,* Beverly Hills and London: Sage, 1–29.

Svensson, C.(2001) 'Swedish Social Democracy & the Third Way – a delicate affair' in R. Cuperus, K. Duffek and J. Kandel (eds), *Multiple Third Ways: European Social Democracy facing the Twin Revolution of Globalisation and Knowledge Society.* Amsterdam: Colofon, 219–26.

van Gunsteren, H. (1994) 'Four conceptions of citizenship' in B. van Steenbergen (ed.), *The Condition of Citizenship,* London: Sage, 36–48.

Visser, J. and Hemerijck, A. (1997) *A Dutch Miracle,* Amsterdam: Amsterdam University Press.

4 Social policy in Belgium and the Netherlands

Third Way or not?

Renaat Hoop

Introduction

The Third Way seems to have filled the ideological gap left by the collapse of the communist system in Eastern Europe and in recent years has obtained increasing support. Still, defining the exact meaning of the Third Way remains problematic (Alterman 1998). At times, it is not even attempted to clarify the theoretical underpinning of the Third Way; it is seen as something essentially pragmatic, a policy (Le Grand 1998). With this chapter, I would like to make a contribution towards clarifying the normative tenor and bearing of Third Way thinking. After all, even if the Third Way is indeed only a pragmatic attitude, it will still, like every practice, have been inspired by some kind of theory or philosophy. And in order to be able to properly judge the Third Way on its merits, it seems essential to bring this philosophy out into the open.

I will try to bring about this clarification by evaluating the conformity of the social policies recently pursued in Belgium and the Netherlands with Third Way thinking as put forward in the work of Anthony Giddens. It is indeed my claim that the philosophical foundations of a political theory may not only be deduced from the theory itself, but also from policy measures based on that theory. This seems especially to be true for Third Way thinking since Giddens himself stated that: 'The need to reform welfare systems is a key part of Third Way political philosophy' (2000a: 103).

Studying Belgium and the Netherlands is equally motivated by Giddens' interpretation of the Third Way. According to him, Third Way politics is above all an endeavour to respond to the profound changes he described in his earlier book (Giddens 1994), which the traditional left is unable to do (Giddens 2000a: 27). The aim and the reasons for the inception of the Third Way are thus to be found in supplying a doctrinal and policy framework for a renewed Social Democracy. But this radical renewal he propagates not only concerns Social Democracy, but also needs to surpass its major current competitor, neo-liberalism. Third Way political philosophy is thus presented by Giddens as a midway position between socialism and liberalism, or as modernised Social Democracy (Giddens 2000b). Insofar as we accept that this attempt to overcome the opposition between socialism and liberalism, or in broader terms the left–right divide, constitutes the essence or the main feature of the Third Way, Belgium and the Netherlands seem to be the perfect testcases for studying and evaluating the existence of TW-politics since both countries are currently being led by so-called 'purple' governments.

These mixed governments of liberals and socialists constitute a recent and rather rare phenomenon in both countries. Since 1954 in the case of Belgium and since 1919 in the case of the Netherlands, Christian Democrats had always been in power and had been free to choose either liberals or socialists as their coalition partner. Consequentially, the formation of the first post-war purple coalitions was generally seen as a historical event. Especially, since these coalitions were not imposed on by the electoral results but seem to have been the result of a free and conscious choice. For the Netherlands this event took place after the elections of 1994 with the formation of the first (1994–8) and second (1998–2002) cabinet, under Wim Kok. These coalitions consisted of socialists (PvdA), left-wing liberals (D'66) and right-wing liberals (VVD). In Belgium the first purple government came into power in June 1999 under the leadership of prime minister Guy Verhofstadt, when liberals (VLD/MR),[1] socialists (SP.a/PS) and greens (Agalev/Ecolo) agreed to work together. If we interpret the Third Way as an attempt to reconcile socialism and liberalism, purple coalition governments like the ones in Belgium and the Netherlands seem to be ideally placed to develop Third Way policies.

The examination of the social policies that were conducted in those two countries by their purple government will therefore have a threefold purpose. First of all, I want to verify if those purple policies can indeed be seen as actual practices of Third Way politics. For this purpose I will compare the goals of the purple policies with the goals and ideals described by Giddens. Secondly, assuming that the answer on the first question will be positive, I want to use the analysis to clarify and evaluate Third Way politics. The policy mechanisms used by the purple governments can indeed be seen then as a more detailed elaboration of Third Way goals and ideals, and thus illuminate the precise content and implications of Third Way values. A critical evaluation of these values and of Third Way politics as a whole will then be possible. Thirdly and lastly, this analysis will allow to elaborate a little on the question whether purple coalition governments are or should be the natural and privileged partners of Third Way politics.

Taking this threefold purpose into account, it seems interesting to know to what extent these purple governments consider themselves as being part of the Third Way movement. That is why I will first briefly sketch the political discourse in the two countries. The subsequent policy analysis will be divided in two parts: first, I will discuss the policies towards non-working people, and afterwards, the policies to reconcile work and family life.

The government discourse

In the Belgian case, the historical unity of the coalition is stressed in the coalition agreement, which also contains an appeal or a wish 'to rise above the classical political concepts and recipes and break new ground'.[2] The latter is particularly the conviction of the liberal prime minister Verhofstadt who keeps stressing in his speeches that since the fall of communism, that perverted liberty and equality (the values of the French revolution) into their opposites, a new era has dawned in which these values can and have to be allies. An era in which a reconciliation between modern liberalism and Social Democracy, between economic growth and social protection becomes possible. New Labour in Britain, the New Democrats in the US, Die Neue Mitte in Germany, the Dutch Poldermodel and his own Belgian active welfare state are in his eyes all concrete manifestations of the search for guiding principles for this new era. Although he never states that the Belgian government is the Third Way as such, it is obvious that there is a certain identification with the Third Way or in any case with the policy measures which Blair stands for. In this context it is significant that Blair and Verhofstadt formulated a joint statement on preparation for the European summit in Lisbon on employment of March 2000 (Blair and Verhofstadt 2000). In that statement the two prime ministers plead for a significant increase in the employment rate as 'full employment is the foundation of greater social inclusion without which it is impossible to achieve greater social cohesion or a genuinely more equal society'. For this purpose societies will have to be transformed into active welfare states, 'which encourages work (making work pay) and where rights and opportunities are balanced by responsibilities'.

The other partners of the Belgian purple coalition are less enthusiastic about references to the Third Way. Frank Vandenbroucke, the socialist Minister of Social Affairs, acknowledges that there is a clear convergence amongst European Social Democratic parties on the socio-economic field towards an active welfare state, in which economic prosperity and dynamics and social protection are no longer enemies. But he equally stresses that there is an important difference, at least on a rhetoric level, between the (continental) active welfare state he stands for and Anthony Giddens' social investment state, in which in his opinion Keynsian macro-economic policy and redistributive social spending are too radically renounced (Vandenbroucke 2001b). However, he still regards the Presidency Conclusions of the Lisbon Summit, that incorporated most of the ideas of Verhofstadt and Blair, as the expression of the active welfare state view (Vandenbroucke 2001a). The greens, the smallest coalition partner are, on the contrary, very firm in their rejection of the British Third Way as their leader recently clearly stated: 'The Third Way is not my way' (*De Standaard*, 29–30/09/01).

In the Dutch case, the absence of Third Way terminology in political discourse is striking. For example, in speeches or publications of prime minister Kok, reference is never made to the Third Way in the same explicit way the Belgian prime minister does. Still, in the media and amongst political commentators, there is no doubting the Third Way-character of the two purple cabinets. On the contrary, it is often stressed that the socialist prime minister Kok can be seen and is seen by foreign colleagues, as the first real leader of the Third Way (NRC Handelsblad, 30/08/01). Kok has indeed gained high praise from colleagues such as Clinton and Blair for the Dutch Poldermodel and has always accepted this with gratification. It is also true that – in a publication of 1995 – that Kok noted the definite end of the vision that labour and capital were opposites and stated that the old ideologies were no longer capable of providing the answers for our time. Shaking off those ideological feathers could be relieving for a socialist party and is according to Kok a necessary condition for tackling the problems of the present time. This is indeed one important account of the Third Way.

One could conclude that, although they show a clear and open sympathy with Third Way discourse and its foreign representatives, the Belgian and Dutch government are on their guard against a too close identification with it. As to the Belgian case, it is striking and almost paradoxical that the sympathy of the liberals for the renewed Social Democracy of the Third Way seems greater than that of the Social Democrats. That there is some kind of similarity between the two purple governments and Third Way politics seems moreover not to be questioned by the public opinion. Illustrative in this perspective is the fact that Giddens' book *The Third Way: the Renewal of Social Democracy* was translated in Dutch under the title *Paars: De Derde Weg: over de vernieuwing van de sociaal-democratie* (*Purple*: The Third Way: the Renewal of Social Democracy).

Policies towards the non-working

Both purple governments have made an active labour market policy the core element of their reform of social security and the welfare state in general. Increasing the employment rate is the absolute top priority, since this will serve several goals. First, it will relieve the burden of the social security system, thereby safeguarding the broad public support it enjoys and giving a new dynamic to economy. Further, it will give people economic independence as well as opportunities to build up social networks. In this way, social participation through paid employment will also bring about social cohesion and inclusion in society. These are, in a nutshell, the general goals both governments want to realise.

Roughly speaking one can distinguish three different methods by which the Belgian and Dutch government are trying to achieve an increase of the employment level. The first method is the creation of new jobs, and this in a double way. First, labour is made cheaper. In the public and soft sector, employers can use a part of the benefits as a wage subsidy if they offer long term and/or low-skilled unemployed a contract in an additional job. In the private sector several instruments are used for the same purpose: a reduction of the employer's contribution to social security or a wage subsidy in case of hiring certain target groups (long term and low-skilled unemployed or welfarites, elderly people, returners), or an indemnification for part of the costs of on-the-job-training or of adjustments of the working place. Second, one tries to stimulate private initiative: by offering self-employed persons a better social security and by providing a safety net in case they fail,[3] by abolishing unnecessary administrative burdens, or, for the Netherlands, by granting special allowances directed at the start of a private business.

The second method consists in activating the work force, in expanding the actual supply of labour on the market. Two different paths are followed here. On the hand one tries to better equip those who are offering themselves or could offer themselves on the labour market. This is done by organising (re)training, further training courses and schooling facilities, offering work experience places, application training etc. Unemployed people who successfully complete such a course are often rewarded with a bonus on their benefit. In the Netherlands, parents who follow a reintegration trajectory can get their child care financed during that time. What is new in this field since the purple coalitions have been in power, is the cooperation with the private sector. In Belgium, private enterprises and temping agencies have been asked to cooperate in creating work experience places and social employment. If temping agencies succeed in offering difficult employable people a permanent contract, they receive a huge wage subsidy. In the Netherlands, legislation on temping agencies has been made more flexible and the realisation of reintegration trajectories has been put open for the private market.

On the other hand one tries to realise that those who can offer themselves on the labour market (if necessary after the offered training facilities), actually do offer themselves. One tries to achieve this goal by making work pay. Different groups are targeted here. The policy is oriented in the first place towards people who draw a benefit, since getting people out of social security has the most direct advantageous effect on the state's social budget. In Belgium, the Ministre of social affaires, Frank Vandenbroucke, has tried to eliminate the so-called 'unemployment traps', social security regulations who have the perverse effect of inhibiting people drawing a benefit from getting back to work. He has done this by reducing the social security contributions for employees with low incomes: as a result, they will end up with a higher net wage and the contrast with a possible former or future allowance will be bigger. Long-term unemployed people (one year or more) are also granted a once-only mobility premium if their new job brings about a long travelling time. And unemployed people who get back to work are guaranteed the higher family allowance they were entitled to while being unemployed, during a first period (six months) of re-employment or if they lose their job again within six months. Similar measures are taken for handicapped people and disabled employees: they can now cumulate more easily their allowance with a new labour wage or with that of their partner. In this way the Belgian government wants to stimulate all those people in taking 'the risk' of getting a job again. The same consideration has inspired the Dutch government to hold out the prospect of a tax-free premium of 1815 euro for welfare recipients and subsidised employees who succeed in finding a regular job.

More and more fiscal measures are used in order to make work pay. The Belgian income tax reform plans contain a whole bunch of measures which should lower the fiscal pressure on labour: a negative income tax of *c.*495 euro for the labour incomes between 3,718 and 12,395 euro; full exemption for the employer's indemnification for the cost of public transport; an increase of the fixed deduction for professional costs and a raise of the lowest tax brackets. This is also the way in which Dutch welfare recipients are stimulated. The new Dutch tax system provides for reductions to which only the employed are entitled, and it is announced that this reduction would become more important in the years to come.

But not only welfare recipients are encouraged in applying for jobs again. The favourable economic climate and the subsequent labour shortage[4] in both countries, has made it necessary to launch a similar activation policy towards other fractions of the potential workforce. One of these new targeted groups are elderly people. Where in former employment creation plans, older employees had to make room for young people, the general idea now is that older ones should be kept at work as long as possible. In Belgium, the idea has been launched to abolish or at least heighten the retirement age. Also early retirement schemes are from now on fundamentally wrong, although in practice still used. Still, the government seems to have taken into account the fact that employees wish to slow down their career a bit when they grow older. For this reason the possibilities for a reduction of working hours for employees aged 50 or more are expanded. Other measures want to stimulate employers in recruiting older unemployed: from April 2002 on they get an important reduction on their social security contribution when they take on people aged 58 or more. They can also be granted a subsidy for the improvement of the working conditions of their older employees. Older unemployed people themselves (aged 50 or more) should be stimulated by the fact that the acceptance of a job with a lower salary will not have negative effects on the calculation of their retirement pension. There is also broad consensus among the Belgian government concerning the possibility for (early) retired people to combine their pension with an additional labour income: former restrictions will be lifted.

Similar measures are taken in the Netherlands. The premium older employees can be granted by their employer in order to stay at work, is tax-free and the new tax system provides for a reduction to which only older employed people are entitled. The older one is, the bigger the reduction. The employers from their side have the advantage of a lower disablement insurance premium for each employee aged older than 58. Early retirement programmes are made less attractive and will be replaced by flexible forms of retirement, in which the level of the retirement pension will be closely linked to the age at which one retires.

A second group which is targeted are women. Both governments want to tackle the phenomenon that women tend to leave the labour market permanently once they have children. A solution is searched for in creating more, better quality and affordable day-care centres. The prices paid for this day-care are in both countries made more tax-deductible. In Belgium, single parents who re-enter the labour market are also granted a once-only premium, and women are stimulated to start their own day-care centre with starting premiums and subsidies. In the Netherlands, women who re-enter the labour market and their employers enjoy fiscal advantages, and the new tax system provides for reductions for people with young children who work. For single parents and for low incomes, the reduction is bigger. Agreements are also made between the Dutch government and industries with a high staff shortage in order to take on more women: (child)care, education, ICT, call-centres. Tele-work is also promoted as an instrument of reintegration suited for women. The policies to reconcile family life and work, which I will discuss later on, can also be seen as activation measures for women. In the Netherlands, the recent labour shortage has given rise to a third target group: the asylum-seekers, with an expansion since June 2001 of the eligible industries and the allowed periods of work.

A third method by which the Belgian and the Dutch government have tried to increase the employment rate is by stressing the own responsibility of enterprises and welfare recipients and taking measures which should stimulate them in assuming that responsibility. This policy is particularly followed by the Dutch government. Most importantly, they have privatised in 1996 the Health Law by obliging employers to keep paying their employees 70 per cent of their salary during the first 52 weeks of their sickness. Employers should also draw up a reintegration plan after 13 weeks of absence through illness; if not, they are fined almost 500 euro. In the Disablement Insurance Act, the government has introduced (since 1998) premium differentiation hoping that this will bring down the enormous number of people relying on a disablement allowance. The same will be done in the Unemployment Insurance Act in order to financially encourage employers to prevent short-term unemployment. Employers who dismiss employees aged 57.5 years or older will moreover have to pay part of the unemployment benefit as long as this unemployment lasts, except when it concerns an employee who had been engaged after the age of 50.

But also the welfare recipients are confronted with their own responsibility. As soon as they claim a benefit, welfare beneficiaries are offered a written contract in which their rights and duties as well as possible sanctions are laid down and are appointed a fixed case manager. This is part of the so-called 'preventive or sound approach' by which each unemployed person should be offered a job, a work experience or schooling place within the year. In general, it has been made more difficult to get entitled to an allowance since the conditions therefore have become more stringent. Welfare beneficiaries have also been put under greater pressure in making efforts to get back on the labour market. At the end of 1999, for example, Minister Verstand presented the idea to impose an obligation to apply for halftime jobs (24 hours a week) on single mothers on welfare, caring for one or more children under the age of five.[5] Present legislation actually exempts this category from this obligation. As a result of pressure from, among others, women's organisations, Parliament declined to side with its Minister on this proposal. And older employees (from the age of 57.5 upwards) have to register from now on with the employment agency and may no longer turn down fitting employment offered them, but they still need not actively look for a job themselves. However this exemption may be lifted in the future.

The Dutch Minister Vermeend has also announced that the fight against social security fraud will be monitored and dealt with more sharply. To local social services, responsible for the administration of the General Social Security Act, has been made clear that imposing the sanctions which the Act provides for, is not a competence but a duty. After the disconcerting results of an inquiry in Amsterdam, the Minister decided to subject all local social services to an inquiry concerning the administration of the Act. Each municipality also has the obligation to draw up an anti-fraud policy plan. And since 2002, a newly founded service, the *Sociale Inlichtingen- en Opsporingsdienst (SIOD)*, investigates complex and serious forms of social security fraud.

In Flanders, too, increased pressure on the unemployed is reported as far as their willingness to work is concerned; even employers allegedly no longer neglect their duty to report these days.[6] The Belgian government has, furthermore, promised to offer every youth a so called 'starter's job' within 6 months of leaving school or completing their studies. In order to keep this promise, employers are obliged to take on a certain number of the people belonging to this target group. From September 2001 on employers also have to organise outplacement when they dismiss employees older than 45 years. The contractualisation of social welfare was already introduced by the former (not purple) government: since

1993, each person younger than 25 who asked for a social benefit has to sign a contract in which obligations concerning training and applying for jobs are laid down. This contractualisation has been confirmed however by the new government: the reform plans for a new General Social Security Act mention the right to individual reintegration and participation in society rather than the right to an allowance at the subsistence level.

Policies to reconcile work and family life

Notwithstanding the fact that in both countries the pre-eminently family-oriented parties[7] were relegated to the opposition, the facilitation of the combination of work and family is more than ever given priority in the social policy of the Belgian and Dutch purple governments.

In the Netherlands, the aim of setting up a combination scenario is making it possible for each employee to realise a new balance between work and care. One explicitly hopes that, as a consequence of this policy, women will work and men will care more. For this purpose, an enabling Act Labour and Care was established and came into force on 1 December 2001. This Act expands and coordinates the leave arrangements and makes their conditions more flexible. New arrangements are added such as the legally formalization of the paid 16-weeks maternity leave and a paid two days paternal leave, a paid four weeks 'bonding' leaving in case of an adoption and the right to a paid ten days care leave to look after a sick child or partner. Since 1998 there has already been a system for career interruption, which gives the employee the right to break off his or her career during a certain period of time.[8] This break can be taken in order to take care of children, family or friends, in order to provide palliative care,[9] or for taking courses that will improve one's employability. If the employee is replaced during this period by a person drawing a benefit, he will be financially compensated[10] by the government. The system of parental leave,[11] which has existed since 1985, has also been stimulated: employers who continue paying 70 per cent of the minimum wage during that period, are awarded a fiscal compensation since January 2001. And as of the first of July 2000 there is also the *Wet Aanpassing Arbeidsduur (WAA)* (Working Hours Modification Act), which enables employees in businesses with a minimum of 10 employees to once every two years request of their employers that their working hours be either increased or decreased. Most of these arrangements are or will be incorporated in the Act Labour and Care.

One of the goals of this enabling act was to make flexibility possible in these leave arrangements. This goal is pursued in three ways: by making possible an interpretation made-to-measure with regard to certain modalities,[12] by providing a general proviso by which each demand for a leave has to be balanced against the interests of the company, and by making possible different kinds of exchanges within the arrangements.[13]

Creating possibilities to combine professional and private life is also a concern of the Belgian purple government, but unlike the Dutch proposals, the policy is less focused on the combination of work with caring activities, which contains an explicit emancipatory goal towards women.

The Act of 10 August 2001, concerning the reconciliation of employment and quality of life, firstly contains measures concerning the reduction of working hours. As from 2003 on, a working week will last at most 38 hours; employers who reduced the working hours in their firm to this new maximum before 2003, were awarded a once-only reduction of social security contributions. Similar reductions are announced for employers who reduce the working hours beneath this maximum or who adopt a four-day working week.

Secondly, the Act confirms the measures adopted by the interprofessional collective labour agreement nr. 77 that came into force on 1 January 2002. This agreement reforms the system of career interruption that had been in place since 1985.[14] From 2002 on employees are entitled to a so-called 'time-credit'. This global time-credit of one year[15] can be used to stop working (full-time or half-time) during a minimum period of three months at any time in the working career. In addition to this, each employee will also have the right to reduce his or her working hours with one-fifth throughout a maximum of five years during the whole career.[16] This maximum doesn't hold for employees older than fifty. The latter are moreover awarded an additional right to reduce their working hours to a half-time job, under the condition that they can prove a career of twenty years. These reductions are financially compensated[17] by the federal government. To promote the use of this time-credit, the Flemish government has announced the awarding of premiums (*c.*150 euro a month) if the career is interrupted for the following purposes: to take care of a sick child (up to the age of 18), parent (from the age of 70) or a seriously ill family member; or, for taking courses that will improve one's employability. Parents who reduce their working hours with a fifth to take care of their family will be granted *c.*50 euro a month, as well as employees older than fifty who switch to a half-time job. This new system of career interruption doesn't affect the arrangements for parental leave[18] and palliative care[19] that were already in place.

Finally, the Act announces the extension of the paternal leave from 3 days to 10 from 1 July 2002 on, as well as the extension of the possibility (till the end of 2002) to go on early retirement at the age of 55 (part-time) or 56 (full-time).[20]

Conclusions

What can we say about the conformity of these social policies with the ideas of the Third Way as presented by Anthony Giddens? In answering this question, I shall try to follow the distinction between discourse, values, goals and policy mechanisms suggested in Chapter 1. In analysing this conformity, I will try to mark some differences between the Netherlands and Belgium. Special attention will be given to the values, as clarifying the normative foundations of the Third Way was intended to be the main goal of my research. Finally, I will elaborate on the relationship between Third Way politics and purple governments.

Discourse, goals and policy mechanisms

As to the level of the *discourse*, both purple governments show a hesitant but undeniable tendency of identification to the ideas of the Third Way as embodied by Giddens and Blair. In the speeches of the prime ministers, one can clearly discern the rhetoric of reconciliation mentioned by Fairclough (2000) as well as the social, integrationist discourse (SID), centred around paid work (Levitas 1998). A new mixed economy, a co-operative effort of the public and the private sector by making use of market dynamics without losing sight of the public interest (Giddens 2000b: 112), in which the market is no longer approached as a possible enemy but as the driving force in the creation of wealth, constitutes beyond doubt the foundation for the purple social policies.

The central *goal* of these policies is the realisation of an active labour market, since the increase of the employment rate is considered the best way to consolidate the affluence and to create opportunities for inclusion and participation in society. Social security as a passive safeguard has indisputably been exchanged for a social security that actively stimulates people to do their utmost to stay or become self-supporting. This makes up the general idea of the Dutch sound approach and the Belgian starter's jobs[21] – work and training before income – and responds perfectly well to Giddens' concept of 'positive welfare' (Giddens 2000b, 137–8).

The *policy mechanisms* used to realise the central goal equally reflect the insights and suggestions put forward by Giddens. Both governments rely heavily on market forces to bring about the result wished for, and try to be accommodating at the supply side: by offering training, by making labour cheaper, by facilitating private initiative. This is precisely what Giddens is pleading for: a state that 'nurture(s) the human capital that markets themselves require' (Giddens 2000a: 36). Both policies also try to make work pay: by making child care more available and affordable, by eliminating poverty and unemployment traps, by granting in work benefits of tax credits, etc. Summarising, it may be said that the Third Way accepts that the game is played following the market rules and contributes to the state a new but limited role of bringing the players at the start in their best condition and making the prize money as high as possible.

The fiscal welfare is a real innovation in relation to previous policies. Also the partnerships made with the private sector seem to be a typical 'purple' feature. The Netherlands have been the most radical in this respect, by really privatising aspects of their social security system. The Dutch regulations also offer most room for supplementation and divergent implementation and elaboration at a company level. In both countries social security has become more contractarian or conditional in character: governments have tried to make clear that rights do not go without responsibilities. It seems that the Netherlands have most suited the action to the word: sanctions have been strengthened and the investigation to improper use of social benefits and the lack of sanctioning this has increased. In Belgium, on the contrary, the call for sanctions and more negative incentives[22] has only just started. The actual condition of the labour market may possibly explain this difference. The Dutch have had to contend with a labour shortage for some years. In Belgium this problem is of a more recent date and is mainly concentrated in one state, the northern state of Flanders; a federal approach is not always self-evident in such a situation.

The family friendly working environment Giddens is pleading for (2000b: 137–8) has been given shape to by the two purple governments by means of the combination scenario. In the Netherlands this new model is mainly promoted as a new step in the emancipation of women (a redefinition of the traditional role models towards work and care); in Belgium it is rather presented – through the influence of the green coalition partner – as a way to regain some quality of life.

To conclude, there are undeniable similarities between Giddens' criteria and the two investigated countries on all three levels (rhetoric, goals and policy mechanisms) which allow us to accord the purple social policies the Third Way label. Of course, these social policies should be seen as just one possible elaboration of Third Way thinking, and there are of course also differences between the two countries, especially with respect to the used policy means, but these should be seen as differences in nuance that can be explained by the particular situation in each country.[23]

Values

What is there to learn from the analysis of the purple social policies with regard to the *values* of the Third Way? The social policies that are currently being carried out in Belgium and the Netherlands not only show how the theoretical principles of the Third Way may be effected in practice, but can also help us in understanding the actual scope of the values that are being put forward by Giddens and the Belgian and Dutch government: social justice, responsibility, equality as inclusion, opportunity, involvement, participation, social cohesion, solidarity.

It appears that the responsibility required of the citizen is mainly directed at the market and that the social participation to be promoted is merely the participation in the formal labour market. The combination scenario does not spoil this effect. Firstly, the possibilities to interrupt temporarily the work exist by definition only for those who have a paid job; those who do not have a paid job aren't entitled to these new rights. On the contrary, as we have seen, the Dutch government has tried to move in the opposite direction by proposing to abolish current exemptions of the obligation to apply for jobs. Secondly, those new leave rights are conditional: in most of the cases, they can only be used with a certain purpose (care, training) and only if the company interest doesn't weigh heavier. The new Dutch paid 10-day care leave is a striking illustration of this conditionality: not only should the leave be balanced with the company interest, the employer also has to prove the necessity of the fact that precisely he, and not his spouse, needs to provide this care. If the combination scenario is effectively intended to ensure that parents, besides their jobs, take on an equal share in the responsibility of looking after their family, this is really quite a remarkable condition. This implies that it is preferable for the non-working spouse to assume care duties and that the primary responsibility of the working partner is to be found in work duties. This boils down to assuming responsibility for one's family is allowed, as long as this does not disrupt the labour market. Fostering '... conditions in which individuals are able to form stable ties with others, especially when children are involved ...' (Giddens 2000a: 47) is in other words a government function worthy of pursuing, but only for those who have already manifested themselves as being productive citizens in the formal labour market. The entire combination scenario seems to be based on this idea. The new facilities which have sprung up in this context therefore do not seem to be inspired so much by the recognition that the activities, which are made possible besides work, possess an intrinsic value both for those involved and for society as a whole (social cohesion and solidarity). These activities are only considered valuable when they are carried out in combination with paid employment. The productive citizen is the focal point, not the socially integrated citizen.

The combination scenario therefore fits much better within libertarian than within communitarian politics. The aim is apparently the maximisation of the labour supply. By granting employees the opportunity to interrupt their careers under certain conditions, it is hoped that their productivity will remain high and, at the same time, a flexible labour reserve is created. The conditions under which career interruptions are allowed will guarantee that employees are not absent for too long or altogether from the labour market, or that their availability is retained or even improved.

As a consequence, government policy is foraging ever further in the personal life sphere, into the area of reproduction: education, time off, relaxation, recovery. Government is increasingly interfering in the way in which family relations are organised. There is, however, considerable danger that this new social and family policy is being forced on the citizens (Dahrendorf 1999). Where neo-liberalism in the Giddens' sense consolidated the breadwinner model, the Third Way seems to impose a new model in the same authoritarian way and with the same disciplining effect: the combination scenario. This would mean a shared illness with the neo-liberalism Giddens so detested, with its combination of market fundamentalism and conservatism. The Third Way makes a similar combination, albeit that on the economic axis the state is no longer regarded as an enemy, but as an ally who can lend a hand in case of serious derailments and for the remainder mostly fulfils a market-supporting function.

The Third Way thus leads to a recommodification of the citizen. One may well wonder to what extent the Third Way distinguishes itself from neo-liberalism in this respect. The only remaining difference seems to be that the Third Way does not consider a free market as a goal in itself, but as a means to realise traditional socialist values such as solidarity, equality and social justice. The question is to what extent the means chosen can be adequate to attain the goal. Because modern Social Democrats are so intent on guarding against detracting from the viability of capitalism, they are time and again forced to give in to economic necessity and to deny his own initial intentions. This causes a need for the political and ideological position to be revised over and over again (Bieling 1998, 22). The redefining of 'social justice' as 'social inclusion' rather than 'equality' (Lister 2000) could serve as an illustration of this: holding on to the market mechanism – which inevitably produces inequalities – results in a vision where having a job on the labour market (inclusion) obscures the question of the outcome where such a position can lead to. In the end, Social Democrats will no longer ask themselves how social goals may be realised without upsetting the market too much, but how the market can be allowed to function optimally without giving up on too many social goals. But the question then becomes: to what extent can Social Democracy be transformed before it ceases to be Social Democracy?

Third Way theorists in my view all too easily believe that choosing a position that, at first sight, appears to be midway between two 'pure' positions will automatically lead to an ideal and workable synthesis. Third Way theorists are mistaken though: you do not turn citizens into winners by obliging them to take part in a game that needs losers, too. This is not social justice in the traditional Social Democratic sense, perhaps it is not Social Democratic at all.[24]

Third Way and purple governments

Earlier, I suggested that the purple coalition governments were ideally placed to develop Third Way policies, since their composition of parties that represent the first and second way presupposes some kind of reconciliation between these two ways. The question is whether it is a necessary feature to have a Third Way politics in a coalition system? This question has particularly become relevant since the 'purple formula' seems to be perishable and confined to two government terms. While the Belgian coalition partners seem to be ready and enthusiastic for a second 'purple' term[25] – just as the first Dutch purple government did in 1998, a third purple coalition in the Netherlands appears to be out of the question as liberals and socialists do not consider each other anymore as possible coalition partners.[26]

It seems that the Third Way need not necessarily be linked with Social Democracy. For in Belgium, it is the liberal prime minister who identifies himself most openly and convincingly with the Third Way, and it is the liberal family that weighs most heavily on government policy. In the Netherlands, the socialists are the major party, but there as well, the liberals try to usurp the Third Way label. Prominent Dutch liberals, such as Frits Bolkestein (2000) and Hans Dijkstal, have repeatedly declared that the Third Way is in essence a confession of faith to liberal ideas, 'an ideological shortcut that leads to liberal ground' (Dijkstal 2000). If this is true, Third Way policies can equally be pursued by other coalitions, as long as they are prepared to confess themselves to the liberal market ideology.

To a certain extent this idea finds support in reality, since a lot of the purple policy mechanisms can somehow be seen as the logical continuation of what was already initiated by previous non-purple governments: active labour market policy, the combination scenario, contractarian welfare. Is it a mere (electoral) coincidence then, that Third Way ideas knew their break through under purple coalition governments? Not completely, I think. Firstly, the Third Way as a concept was developed by left of centre parties (New Democrats and New Labour), so other Social Democratic parties were in the best position to adopt this concept in a credible way. Secondly, as I have argued above, Third Way politics is all about the participation of productive citizens in the formal labour market, and this focus responds best to the traditional key values of both liberalism, fixated on economic values and socialism, founded on an ideology of work (cf. Anthony 1977). Nevertheless, I believe that Third Way policy will last longer than the purple coalitions, and that it has the potential to return, with minor difference of course, in other political constellations as well. After all, Giddens' accent on social inclusion and participation and the importance of a strong civil society, could easily be recuperated by communitarian inspired political parties such as the confessional parties on the continent. However, it does not look as if the Dutch case will soon be able to deliver proof for this position. At the discourse level, 'purple' has become a political term of abuse in the Netherlands since the Fortuyn-era, and a next government surely will not want to identify itself with purple or Third Way politics. But also at a more substantial level, it remains questionable whether a next government will pursue real Third Way-politics. The election campaign and programmes are based on the assumption that the Netherlands is near to a budgetary and economic crisis. This together with the enormous electoral defeat of the purple coalition partners in the Fortuyn-election of May 2002, provokes a certain ideological retrenchment and a resurgence of traditional left-right positions. Will Third Way-politics be able to survive? Time will tell.

Notes

1 Each political tendency is represented by a Dutch- and a French-speaking party.
2 My translation.
3 Belgium has created a bankruptcy insurance, which entitles small businessmen to a benefit during six months and which guarantees them family allowances and a medical insurance during one year after their bankruptcy.
4 In Belgium the labour shortage is most keenly felt in the northern state of Flanders.
5 The situation is illustrated by the fact that the discussion about the proposal of Minister Vermeend still related to the extension of the exemption to include single mothers with children under the age of 12.
6 *De Standaard*, 24 and 25 February 2001.
7 For Belgium these are the CVP (recently renamed as CD&V) and PSC; in the Netherlands the CDA is the largest family party.
8 A minimum period of two months and at least part-time; a maximum period of six months.
9 As of 1 January 2001 the Netherlands no longer maintain a minimum period for palliative care and compensation is paid to the amount of the minimum wage (1,123 euro). Also, there is no replacement obligation.
10 A maximum of 444 euro a month.
11 A maximum period of six months for each child under the age of 8.
12 In the parental leave arrangement for example, employers are free to continue paying (part of) the salary and can negotiate with the employee the number of hours per week the leave will be taken.
13 Since 2001, it is possible for example to save up salary and have this paid during a future unpaid leave.
14 Initially, this system of career interruption was set up as an employment measure. Therefore, the employee interrupting his career had to be replaced by an unemployed entitled to an allowance. From January 2002 on, the replacement is no longer an obligation. This has something to do with the actual labour shortage of course but also illustrates the change in policy towards the creation of a combination-model.
15 This maximum period of one year on a whole career can be extended to five years by a collective labour agreement.
16 The right should be taken for a minimum period of 6 months each time.
17 To a maximum of *c*.500 euro in case of a full leave.
18 For each child up to the age of 4, to be taken 3 months full-time or 6 months part-time. Compensation: *c*.525 euro.
19 Interruption for 1 or 2 months to be taken part-time (1/2, 1/3, 1/4, 1/5) of full-time. Compensation: *c*.525 euro.
20 The latter is clearly in contradiction with the earlier mentioned rhetoric concerning the need to get rid of these schemes.
21 The same reasoning was put forward by the Belgian socialist minister of social integration, Vande Lanotte, when arguing that making the social benefits inflation-proof again had to be postponed until 2002 and 2005 in favour of programs aimed at getting people back to work and eliminating unemployment traps (*De Standaard*, 31/12/99).

22 This was one of the advices of the High Council of Employment (Hoge Raad voor de Werkgelegenheid), *De Standaard*, 22/02/01.
23 This applies for example to target groups. The Dutch have a huge number of disabled persons; in Belgium the low education of many unemployed is the main problem.
24 This question has become very relevant in the Netherlands after the result of the parliamentary election of 15 May 2002. The Dutch social-democrats (PvdA) lost half of their seats in favour of the newly founded right-populist party by Pim Fortuyn (LPF). Fortuyn, who was shot 9 days before the election, had made the exposure of the 'purple mess' the central element of his campaign.
25 The Belgian prime minister, Guy Verhofstadt, declared himself in favour of a continuation of the current coalition and launched the 'responsible welfare state' as the coming purple project (De Standaard, 09/01/03). The next parliamentary election in Belgium is set on 18 May 2003.
26 In the Netherlands parliamentary elections were held in January 2003 since the right-wing government with christian democrats (CDA), right-wing liberals (VVD) and the right-populist party of the late Pim Fortuyn (LPF) put together after the elections in May 2002, lasted only 82 days. In the January election, the CDA received the largest number of seats. The LPF lost heavily, while the PvdA gained seats. At the time of writing a coalition between the CDA and PvdA looked most likely.

References

Alterman, E. (1998) 'Third way? No way', *Nation*, 10 December.

Anthony, P. D. (1977) *The Ideology of Work*, London: Tavistock Publications.

Bieling, H.-J. (1998) 'Neo-liberalism and Communitarianism: Towards a New Type of Employment Policy in Western Europe?', Amsterdam International Studies, working paper 54, Amsterdam: UVA.

Blair, T. and Verhofstadt, G. (2000) 'UK–Belgium Joint Statement on Preparation for the Lisbon Special European Council', Brussels.

Bolkestein, F. (2000) 'Speech to the 50th Congress of Liberal International', Ottawa/Hull.

Dahrendorf, R. (1999) 'Whatever Happened to Liberty?', *New Statesman*, 9 June.

Dijkstal, H. (2000) 'Olympic Performances', Speech to the 50th Congress of Liberal International, Ottawa/Hull.

Fairclough, N. (2000) *New Labour, New Language?* London: Routledge.

Giddens, A. (1994) *Beyond Left and Right: the Future of Radical Politics*, California: Stanford University Press.

Giddens, A. (2000a) *The Third Way and Its Critics*, Cambridge: Polity Press.

Giddens, A. (2000b) *Paar. De Derde Weg*. Antwerpen/Baarn: Houtekiet (Dutch translation of *The Third Way: the Renewal of Social Democracy*)

Le Grand, J. (1998) 'The Third Way begins with CORA', *New Statesman*, 6 March.

Levitas, R. (1998) *The Inclusive Society?: Social Exclusion and New Labour*, Basingstoke, Macmillan.

Lister, R. (2000) 'To RIO via the Third Way', *Renewal* 8(4): 9–20.

Vandenbroucke, F. (2001a) 'The active welfare State: a social-democratic ambition for Europe', *The Policy Network Journal*, Issue 1, March 2001.

Vandenbroucke, F. (2001b) 'European Social Democracy and the Third Way: Convergence, Divisions and Shared Questions' in S. White (ed.), *New Labour and the Future of Progressive Politics*, London: Macmillan.

5 The Portuguese socialists and the Third Way

Marina Costa Lobo and Pedro C. Magalhães

Introduction

In October 1995, after having spent an entire decade in the opposition, the Socialist Party (*Partido Socialista* – PS) obtained its best electoral result in twenty years of free elections in Portugal, returning to power with only four seats short of an absolute majority in parliament. In retrospect, this victory can be viewed as the founding event of the 'rose revolution' that, by the end of the 1990s, would put Social Democratic parties in control of the majority of governments in the European Union. The PS's leading role in this European-wide electoral shift could be interpreted as a mere chronological accident or the result of an electoral cycle. However, and although the PS has explicitly refused to classify its agenda as part of any 'new way', the political platform advanced back in 1995 had already shed most remnants of traditional Social Democracy and sought a new compromise between social concerns, economic liberalism, and budgetary orthodoxy. Thus, the Portuguese Socialists were arguably first in taking to power a political agenda that fell inside what has been called 'new Social Democracy' or the 'Third Way'. Additionally, in the first half of 2000, the Portuguese Presidency of the European Council transposed for the first time to EU level many of the ideas 'Third Way' leaders have been trying to implement in their respective countries. This was a remarkable transformation for a party that, in the early 1980s, still espoused Marxism in its statutes, and spent a good part of the 1980s and 1990s in internal crisis and under the hegemony of its centre-right adversaries in the party system.

This chapter attempts to explain the ideological and programmatic transformation of Portuguese Social Democratic politics in the last three decades, its similarities to that experienced by other European Social Democratic parties that have espoused some sort of 'Third Way', and the extent to which that transformation was translated into policy practice. In the early 1990s important changes at the domestic and international levels allowed the PS to openly dispute the centrist vote without fear of major losses to its left. Under the leadership of António Guterres, the PS swiftly and effortlessly abandoned what had been the (mostly rhetorical) traditional Social Democratic components of its programme, turning the pragmatism, centrism, and Europeanism they had always displayed in their political practice into an asset rather than a liability. Particular attention will be paid to the period since 1995, tracing the policies which have been implemented by Prime Minister Guterres, in an attempt to determine the extent that changes amount to a 'Third Way', in line with the discourse and practices of Northern Social Democratic parties. The *causes* of change of the Socialist Party will be discussed, arguing that the European integration process, as well as changes in the domestic political environment were at the root of the policy and programmatic change which occurred in the Socialist party. Finally, the last section analyses the demise of Third Way policies in Portugal, during the second Guterres mandate, which ended due to the Prime Minister's resignation in December 2001.

The PS before Guterres: between the rock and a hard place

By the mid-1980s, two aspects about the Portuguese Socialist Party's identity, support base, and role in the party system distinguished it from comparable cases. First, the PS had become 'one of the most conservative Social Democratic parties of Western Europe' (Merkel 1991: 199). Among the members of the Party of European Socialists (PES), only the *Partito Socialista Democratico Italiano* (arguably not a Social Democratic party and thus expelled from the PES in 1994) and the *Partito Socialista Italiano* were seen as more conservative (Huber and Inglehart 1995). Public opinion studies consistently showed that the PS's electorate was even further to the right in comparison with other Social Democratic electorates in Southern Europe, a puzzling phenomenon for a party that, at least until 1983, explicitly espoused Marxism and a peculiar brand of 'democratic Socialism' in its statutes (Gunther and Montero 2001: 105). The second noticeable peculiarity about the PS in that period was the fact that it was in the opposition. While PSOE and PASOK took less than a decade to achieve supremacy in their respective Spanish and Greek party systems, the PS had followed almost the opposite path: from a leading role among the pro-democratic forces to a subordinate position in the Portuguese party system. The explanation of the profound crisis in which the PS was plunged by the mid-eighties has to be sought in the confluence of two interrelated factors: the nature of Portugal's democratic transition and the political and economic legacies it produced; and the unfortunate timing of the Socialists' brief accessions to power both in 1976 and 1983.

Before the 1974 coup that brought down the Portuguese authoritarian regime, the major opposition force was not the PS, but rather the Portuguese Communist Party (PCP). The PCP's pre-eminence in the political process was reinforced in the months following the coup, when the struggle for power in a highly unstructured political environment moved from the electoral arena to the military barracks, the unions, the fields, and the streets. The position of the PS in the Portuguese party system was to be defined in reaction to this process. Although the Socialists persisted in a markedly leftist anti-bourgeois discourse in what concerned distributive policies, they sought nonetheless to occupy the centre of a highly left-skewed political spectrum in which the conservative right had been totally delegitimised, drawing the dividing line between themselves and the extreme-left on what had become the lowest common denominator among its own increasingly diverse rank and file and the forces to the right of the PCP: the option for an 'European-style' pluralist democracy, in opposition to the 'popular democracy' and 'third-worldist' orientation shared by the radical parties and military.

This strategy ultimately paid out. In the 1975 elections, the PS obtained the largest share of the vote (37.9 per cent), revealing the distance between the extreme-left's control of the transition process and the actual preferences of the electorate. At the polls, they had obtained substantial support from sectors of the large agricultural and industrial working-class, but also extended their influence across classes, regions, and the urban/rural divide, capturing even an important share of the Catholic vote and other factions of the electorate that were clearly to the ideological right of their proposed policies and discourse (Opello 1985: 127; Bacalhau 1994: 110). In the 1976 elections they triumphed again at the polls, forming a minority cabinet and successfully completing the strategy 'whereby the PS acted as a pivot in a political system where no party had an outright majority' (Gallagher 1990:29).

However, what seemed to be a recipe for unqualified success also turned out to lay the ground for long-term crisis, by placing the PS between a rock and a hard place. The 'rock' remained on its left: the Communist Party. The PCP was incomparably better organised than any other party in Portugal, and enjoyed strong electoral support both in Lisbon's industrial belt and among rural wage labourers in the South. Their electoral clout (around 14 per cent of the vote) was compounded by the *de facto* power that resulted from the extensive nationalisation of land, the heavy industry, and the banking sector that took place in 1975, allowing the PCP and its strictly controlled trade union to politically penetrate the management of these productive sectors. The PS's strategy during the transition – assuming the leadership of pro-democratic struggle in a tacit alliance with the moderate members of the military and the remaining anti-Communist parties – made competing for the leftist vote even more difficult.[1]

On the other hand, the 'hard place' was the tragic economic legacy of authoritarianism and consequences of revolution. Structurally, Portugal was characterised by a huge and backward agricultural sector and an equally antiquated and uncompetitive industry. The economic consequences of 'revolution' were also troubling, including depressed investment and exports that had caused negative economic growth and a massive and largely inefficient nationalised public sector, that included the entire banking system and heavy industry. Under what was already a difficult competitive electoral context to its left, the newly formed PS government was forced to adopt unpopular economic restructuring and stabilisation policies. In sum, the Portuguese Socialists could not follow the successful strategy adopted by their Spanish and Greek counterparts, which used their opposition years to absorb the Communist vote by adopting radical ideological appeals, immediately replaced by more centrist positions once the Communist parties had been squeezed out of the party system (Kitschelt 1994: 289).

Throughout the following decade, the consequences of this double constraint would be repeatedly felt. In 1978, the PS government had managed to stabilise the economy, but only at the expense of rising unemployment, two consecutive years of drops in real wages, and the growing hostility of the left. In the 1979 elections, the PCP bled the PS out of much of its previous share of working and lower-middle class constituency (Opello 1985). The Socialists ended up with only 27 per cent of the vote and in opposition. In the 1980s, they were again forced to coalesce with the right by forming a coalition cabinet with the centre-right PSD in 1983 (the Central Bloc), in a difficult economic context and in the final stage of negotiations for EEC membership.[2] This PS-led government embarked on the 'most drastic austerity programme to be implemented by any western socialist leader' (Gallagher 1990), and was able to bring down inflation and stabilise public finances, with negative electoral consequences for the PS. In the 1985 elections, the PS almost lost its status as second major party, obtaining only 20.8 per cent of the vote forced to share electoral space to the left not only with the Communist 'rock' but also with a newly formed party, the PRD.

The Socialists' attempts to escape this narrow electoral niche were often frustrated in the following decade. The Communists' ideological orthodoxy and relentless opposition to European integration throughout the 1980s contributed little to approximate the two parties. Besides, the governments led by their centre-right adversary, the PSD, were able to accompany liberal reforms with the neutralisation of the social costs associated to these measures. With economic growth at home and abroad, political stability, privatisation receipts, and EC structural funds, the PSD government promoted real growth in social expenditures in rates that had been unseen since the 1970s, while, at the same time, the weight of those expenditures in the total budget remained stable. In sum, in the late eighties and early nineties, the Socialists' adversaries in the centre-right followed what was the 'natural' but always unfulfilled destiny of the PS: to strike a balance between stabilisation, expansion, and egalitarianism, the same kind of balance that Social Democratic governments in Spain and Greece had obtained throughout the 1980s with remarkable electoral results (Maravall 1997: 177). In 1991, the PSD obtained a second consecutive absolute majority and its dominant position in the party system seemed virtually unshakeable.

The 'new' PS: programmatic reconfiguration

In the 1992 Congress, in the aftermath of PS's third consecutive electoral defeat in parliamentary elections, António Guterres became the party's leader. Guterres represented a clean break with the past. He was not a close follower of historic leader Mário Soares, nor was he from the leftist wing of the party, like Jorge Sampaio (leader from 1987 to 1991). Besides, and unlike all previous PS leaders, Guterres was a devout Catholic, which distinguished him from the Socialists' traditional secularism. After 1992, Guterres managed to combine the advancement of a new social policy agenda with the full embracing of the pragmatic liberalism that, in fact, the PS had long given to its political and policy practice. To what extent has this programmatic reconfiguration approximated the transformation of Social Democracy in other countries? And to what extent has it been reflected in the policy practice of the Socialist government?

There is some degree of consensus on the 'Third Way' core set of principles that have been adopted by left-wing parties in the 1990s. The first element of that core set is a redefinition of social policy goals. Without completely abandoning the 'equality' goal in favour of a purely meritocratic distribution of resources in society, the 'Third Way' redefines equality as 'inclusion', i.e., as equality in terms of 'real' social citizenship rights and opportunities (Giddens 1998; White 1998). In consequence, state-provided benefits that aim at pure equality of outcomes are deemed excessively blunt social policy instruments due to their emphasis of remedial over preventive action and their disincentive to individual responsibility (Esping-Andersen 1999).

The alternative advanced by the 'Third Way' is an 'employment-centred social policy', that views integration in the labour market as the most effective protection against exclusion (White 1998). This integration is to be achieved through regulatory, selective benefits and/or social investment strategies, such as work-sharing, basic income rights, or the redistribution of skills and opportunities by investment in education and professional training (Weber 1999; Lister 2000). Finally, the very role of the state in social policy is redefined. While financing and regulating social policy are preserved as state tasks, production of welfare goods is to be increasingly discarded and delegated on other providers (Le Grand 1989; Wright and Wright 1996; Giddens 2000), an option that neatly ties into a specifically political and institutional dimension of the 'Third Way': reinventing governance and devolving power to civil society and the community (Halpern and Mikosz n.d.; Le Grand 1998; Marquand 1999).

The Portuguese Socialists have remained adamant in rejecting the notion that their programmatic principles belong to any kind of 'new way', third or otherwise.[3] However, their electoral platform for the 1995 elections clearly followed – and, in some cases, surprisingly prefigured – many of these core elements of the 'Third Way'. The similarities start with the process that led to the drafting of the PS's 1995 electoral manifesto. In the summer of 1994, the PS initiated a series of discussion meetings that increasingly counted with the participation of independent intellectuals, scientists, cadres, and entrepreneurs identified not only with the moderate left but also with PCP splinter groups and the PSD faction more associated with the old Central Bloc government. A final and highly publicised general session was held in March 1995, in which Guterres signed a *Contrato de Legislatura*, which, similarly to the British Labour Party 1997 election manifesto, was symbolically depicted as a 'contract' between the Socialist Party and Portuguese civil society.

Despite listing a remarkably high number of 'absolute priorities' (employment, education, health care reform, fighting poverty, European Monetary Union (EMU), fiscal fairness, 'the information society', fighting drug addiction, and so on), the *Contrato* presented a clear hard core of policies. First, the party's political practice of the past was wholeheartedly embraced through the adoption of an overarching commitment: 'Europe', or more specifically, meeting the convergence criteria for EMU. Another major Socialist goal was 'Employment', to be achieved under the constraints of EMU. In other words, this meant the creation of jobs would have to be achieved through reducing working time and lowering non-wage labour costs, rather than increasing public expenditure.[4] However, and more importantly, 'Employment' was defined as a 'transversal goal, and actually included in the manifesto's section dedicated to 'solidarity policies'. The major objective of a PS government's economic and social policy was defined as 'providing all Portuguese the opportunity to work', giving citizens 'not only a source of income but also a powerful means of personal fulfilment'.[5] The positive integrative effects of job creation were particularly stressed in the case of female employment, a domain in which the Socialists vowed to increase what was already a relatively high rate of female activity (42 per cent in 1994).[6]

The role of the state also received great attention in the manifesto. First, as an overarching principle, the PS now placed the state as a market regulator and rule-enforcer, rather than a producer of goods and services.[7] Second, the manifesto redefined the doctrinal goals of social and fiscal policies, favouring the principles of 'Solidarity' and 'Equity' over 'Equality'. The significance of this terminological subtlety was clear: the PS would abandon any broad redistributive goals. Instead, in the fiscal domain, the PS proposed to promote 'Equity' by attacking the inefficiency of taxation and the rampant tax evasion that structurally favoured the self-employed.[8] In what concerned social policy, the PS's major objective besides promoting employment would be a targeted war on poverty and social exclusion, using instruments as a means-tested guaranteed basic income (*Rendimento Mínimo Garantido* – RMG). In fact, social inclusion, the role of welfare providers other than the state, and the 'Employment' goal were seen as intrinsically tied. Recipients of RMG would have to be available to work and to attend vocational training, and non-profits and the mutualist sector would co-operate in the programme's administration.[9]

The last major goal of the new PS platform was education, the only exception to the overall containment of public expenditures. However, investment in human capital was portrayed not only as a means to increase productivity, but also as social policy instrument, that would create employment in emerging technologically advanced sectors and enhance skills and capabilities necessary for labour market integration.[10]

Therefore, it is easy to see that, by 1995, the Portuguese Socialists had already adopted several of the basic 'Third Way' themes: equality as inclusion, inclusion through employment, employment through increased skills, and an overall shift towards a less interventionist and more regulatory state. In fact, by the mid-nineties, the time was already ripe for this platform's electoral success. Since 1992, the crisis triggered by the Gulf War and rising oil prices prevented the PSD government from simultaneously keeping up with EMU convergence criteria, prolonging the 'economic bonanza' of the eighties, and consolidating the expansion of the incipient Portuguese welfare state. In the October 1995 elections, in a context of negative economic indicators, the PSD lost approximately 15 per cent of their previous vote to the Socialists, which in turn obtained 43.5 per cent of the vote and came four seats short of an absolute majority, their best electoral score ever.

Guterres' policies: implementing the Third Way

The first Guterres administration, (1995–9), benefited both from positive external economic factors, namely a fall in interest rates and commodity prices, a rise in EU transfers after 1995, and from the previous effort at curbing inflation and consolidating the public sector through privatisation, effected by the PSD government (OECD 1999:1). Between 1995 and 1999, real GDP growth was on average 3.3 per cent, a higher rate than the rest of the EU, where it averaged 2.2 per cent (EC 1999: 269). Not only were economic circumstances highly positive, but also, on 22 May 1998, the European Council of the EU announced the list of countries that would participate in EMU from 1999 onwards, and included Portugal on that list. The EMU objective had thus been fulfilled, and was an important success for the government in that its main commitment to European integration for the period was accomplished. It had been achieved whilst simultaneously increasing public expenditure on social services, even if to a limited degree,[11] decreasing the budget deficit, and decreasing unemployment from 7.3 per cent to 4.7 per cent (Barreto and Preto 2000).

We can now turn to the analysis of the Portuguese Socialists policies in particular areas, namely privatisation, employment and social policy. These areas were chosen because they were emblematic of Socialist rule and they epitomise the understanding of the 'Third Way' policies in Portugal.

Privatisation

The Socialists privatised the economy with much more vigour than their right-wing predecessors (Corkill 1999: 64). This drive to privatise was in part due to imperative need to decrease the budget deficit and the public debt, in order to be able to join EMU in 1999. Indeed, proceeds from privatisations in 1996–7 *exceeded* the total obtained in the previous six years (1989–95) (Corkill 1999: 63). During the first Socialist administration, between 1996 and 1999, twenty-nine companies were privatised, involving a total of eighteen firms. The sectors targeted included the petrochemical, telecommunications, banking, cement, chemical industry, tobacco, agribusiness, naval construction, steel and paper sectors (Alves 1999: 63). This was not only in accordance with EMU convergence criteria but also with Guterres' views on the optimum balance between state and market forces, whereby state intervention was to be circumscribed to essential functions such as the provision of social services, and should be mostly restricted to regulatory powers over the market. During the late 1980s, privatisation had concentrated on revenue-generation (Corkill 1999: 59), but Cavaco Silva's last Finance Minister reformulated the privatisation strategy, shifting the emphasis towards wider share ownership, and the consolidation of large national economic groups. This strategy was continued and reinforced by the Guterres government. In part, its success was due to the lower interest rates for most of the 1990s, which encouraged Portuguese savers to shift from low-interest-bearing savings accounts to shares. The sale of Portugal Telecom, in 1996, attracted 800,000 new investors. Perhaps the most emblematic sale during the first Guterres' government was the sale of EDP, the state electricity company, with three quarters of a million people applying for shares (Corkill 1999: 63). Whereas in 1994, the state economic sector accounted for 11 per cent of GDP and 3.2 per cent of employment, in 1999, these figures had decreased substantially to 5.5 per cent and 2.6 per cent respectively (Alves 1999: 73). Thus, privatisation has served the twin PS's goals of transforming an interventionist state into a regulatory one, and of extending share ownership, whilst preventing the foreign control of Portuguese firms.

Employment policies

Since 1995, a few active employment schemes were created, which sought to decrease the 'social exclusion' of certain vulnerable groups, such as the unemployed and the poorest sections of the population. Some measures taken by the Socialist Party sought to facilitate the entry into the labour market of both long-term unemployed and young first-time entrants. To this end, the government created two types of incentives: a 36-month exemption of social security payments for these employees, to the firms hiring them; financial support to the firm, corresponding to 12 minimum incomes for each worker employed; and 'independent workers' who started their own business were exempt from paying social security contributions for the first twelve months (Comissão do Livro Branco Segurança Social 1998: 65).

The decrease in unemployment to 4.7 per cent was partially the result of the Strategic Social Pact, signed between the government and the two main trade unions, the InterSindical and the UGT, in December 1996. This pact envisaged an annual rise of employment by 1 per cent until 1999 (OECD 1998: 90). To achieve such an increase, the unions agreed on wage moderation and on furthering the flexibility of the labour market, in exchange for the government's commitment to draft laws regarding several aspects of the labour market, including changes in the legislation concerning the protection of pregnant workers. Perhaps one of the most important measures agreed in the Pact was the levelling of social security contributions made by those who are self-employed, to equal the contributions of those under dependent employment. In Portugal, firms have been encouraged in the past to hire labour as self-employed, even if they are effectively dependent employees, to lower their costs in terms of social security contributions. This was clearly unfavourable for workers who lost out on the benefits of being dependent employees of a company, although it may have been one of the factors that enabled unemployment to stay at relatively low levels in the past compared to other European countries (Brassloff 1992: 508–34) At the same time however, redundancies were made easier for firms, with compensation costs for labour being decreased, and 'atypical' forms of labour regulated, which favours their very existence (OECD 1999: 4).

Social policies

Social policy in Portugal has suffered from historic underdevelopment. During the authoritarian regime (1933–74), a few welfare schemes were created, which followed the continental European corporatist-conservative tradition of social security. However, these consisted of a weak system of mutual aid societies, with only 20 per cent of the population actually insured (Esping-Andersen 1994: 119). Unemployment insurance (1975,

1977) and the national health service (1979), for instance, were only introduced after democratisation. Even so, despite the huge effort by democratic governments to create a European welfare regime, the social safety net in Portugal continues to be rather weak and coverage and benefit levels are low (Esping-Andersen 1994: 120). When the socialists came to power in 1995, the Portuguese welfare regime still distributed modest benefits. This has not prevented it from being in permanent deficit. Thus, the Socialists faced the goal of reforming the welfare regime, to make it more efficient in fighting exclusion and poverty, whilst simultaneously finding ways of improving its finances.

On the first of these two complementary fronts, the Socialist government focused on making benefits somewhat more selective and on addressing situations of extreme poverty. On the one hand, unemployment benefits were reformulated (lengthened differentially according to age groups), and diverse types of family allowances (maternity, early childhood) were merged into one and made means-tested (Guillén *et al.*: forthcoming). On the other hand, lower social pensions were systematically increased and, following an experimental phase in 1996, a minimum income guarantee (*Rendimento Minimo Garantido*) scheme was implemented in 1997, similar to schemes in thirteen other EC countries. The objective was to combat social exclusion, by providing a security net to those below the poverty line in Portugal. However, in line with the previous 'Third Way' active social policies, it created not only rights but also duties for the beneficiaries. In exchange for receiving a monthly income, granted for twelve months, and renewable, the person must be available to participate in work and training programmes, age and health permitting. This subsidy was supposed to have various positive side-effects. Firstly, by identifying the families which are eligible to receive the subsidy, it would be possible to better target them for social inclusion, thus for instance, encouraging the children of the beneficiaries to attend school. Secondly, the training schemes would ensure that it is indeed the most vulnerable elements of society who receive the training. According to the government, by singling out those who face social exclusion, it would provide added incentives for those institutions working locally to co-ordinate efforts to promote their well-being. In fact, the scheme was largely successful: by December 1999 there had been four hundred and thirty thousand beneficiaries, amounting to 4.4 per cent of the Portuguese population (Barreto and Preto 2000).

On the second front – reforming the financing of social security – the most important steps were taken already during the Socialists' second administration (1999–2001). A new Social Security law, passed in 2000, opened the possibility of mixing public-funded and private-capitalisation in the social security system, and changed the formula for calculating the amount of pensions (lowering them on the average) (Guillén *et al.*: forthcoming). Besides, the new legislation also concretised the principles followed during the Socialists' previous term in government: ensuring that social security became more flexible, and thus better able to respond to differentiated needs; and targeting the most vulnerable groups in society, and not all citizens indiscriminately. While this would contribute to the inclusion of those living below the poverty line, it would also (and most crucially) lighten the financial burden of the welfare system. However, within the Socialist party, and the Left more generally, traditional Social Democratic values such as the universality of benefits have clashed with notions of solidarity towards the most needy, given that the welfare system is already facing serious financial difficulties. Parties to the left of the PS have been unwilling to approve any reform which questions the principle of the universality of benefits. Given that the PS ruled without an absolute majority since 1995 and understandings to its left remain undermined by the exclusion of the Communist Party's from the governing arch in Portugal, it had considerably more difficulty than other Third Way governments, particularly that of Tony Blair, to implement its policies.

Both concerning the redefinition of the state and the social sector, it seems therefore that the Socialist government was guided by the core principles of the 'Third Way'. It emphasised equity, not equality for the social sector, and responsibility for recipients of state benefits. Benefits for the most vulnerable sectors of society were tied to 'active employment' policies in an effort to combat exclusion. Regarding the state, it continued to extricate it from various economic sectors, transforming itself from an interventionist into a regulatory actor. However, not all Socialist policies contributed to the shrinking of the state: as the government extricated itself from the economy, it has still continued to expand in terms of GDP and the increase in state expenditure which occurred after EMU entry crowded-out private investment. As we shall see, this ended up playing an important role in the demise of Third Way policies in Portugal.

Explaining the new PS

How can the repositioning of the Portuguese socialists, in terms of political rhetoric and adopted policies, be explained? Two factors, one internal and other external, can be advanced as the most likely candidates. The first is the decline of the Communist Party, more strongly felt since 1989. This decline has made it considerably easier for the Socialists to position themselves more to the centre of the political spectrum, without fear of losses to their left. The second is the role that European integration has played in determining Portuguese national policy. Since entry to the EU in 1986, Portugal has faced a series of European challenges (the Single Market, the Exchange Rate Mechanism, and more recently EMU), which have shaped national policy to a large extent.[12] Conditioned by external EU objectives and goals, European states have tended for some degree of policy convergence to achieve them. Portugal, and the PS government since 1995, did not escape that trend.

The unfreezing of the Communist electorate

In the past, the pragmatic liberalism adopted by the PS-as-government had always resulted less from choice than from external pressures and/or unavoidable necessity, namely, the catastrophic economic situations faced by every Socialist incumbency and the need to deal with the political and economic legacies of democratisation. As a result of these joint pressures, the Socialists had remained unable to actively erode their competitors to the left, while they had also failed to give the centrist electorate a plausible reason to support them after costly austerity policies.

What allowed the Socialists to escape these contradictions was a change in the competitive environment faced by the PS to its left. In other words, the Communist 'rock' began to erode on its own. In 1987, disappointing electoral results for the PCP were followed by acute internal strife between the ruling orthodoxy of the PCP and emerging critical factions. While the latter were forced to abandon the party, with many of them joining the PS, the Communist leadership moved to a *fait accompli* view of democracy and EC membership. In the eyes of the Socialists' leftist faction, this doctrinal shift was perceived as reducing the need for the PCP's exclusion in the party system. In 1989, that faction's foremost representative and then party leader, Jorge Sampaio, rehearsed an approximation to the Communists in the 1989 local elections, successfully running for Lisbon Mayor under a PS/PCP joint ticket.

However, the 1991 general elections would dictate the end of this particular strategy. On the one hand, the PS still failed to capture most of the centrist electorate, which went on to renew its confidence on a PSD government riding high in popularity and economic performance. On the other hand, the 1991 elections also revealed a new interesting fact for the Socialists: the increased legitimisation of the PCP was accompanied by the 'unfreezing' of its electorate. For the first time, the PCP dropped below 10 per cent of the vote, and electoral behaviour studies showed that about one of out five of its previous voters moved to the PS (Lima 1991). Guterres thus decided to reject any further approximations with the Communists, and jumped to a clear centripetal strategy of competition for a PSD vote now threatened by economic decline (Bosco 2001). From this point of view, the Socialists 1995 'Third Way', in what it comprised of an unashamed embrace of budgetary orthodoxy and reduced state interventionism, resulted from Communist decline, for the first time allowing the PS to compete for the large and volatile centrist vote without being threatened by major losses to its left.

The process of European Integration as a motor for policy change

The constraints of European integration have shaped the PS's policies since its foundation in 1973. In the transition and consolidation phase of Portuguese democratisation, the Portuguese Socialists distinguished themselves from other left-wing parties by their commitment to the European project, and most crucially to a European-style pluralist democracy (Álvarez-Miranda 1996: 181–7). Later on, in the mid-80s, the Socialists returned to power with the goal of successfully completing the lingering negotiations with the EC in order for Portugal to be admitted as a member. This commitment shaped the Socialist government policies between 1983 and 1985, which meant the imposition of draconian economic measures, in order for the economic criteria of accession to be met. Thus, the process of European integration has traditionally been key to Portuguese Socialist policy (Lobo and Magalhães 2001).

Once again, on returning to power in 1995, the Socialist programme had an overarching European objective, that of joining the Euro in 1999. However, this time, compliance with EMU convergence criteria (the need to reduce inflation, debt, and expenditure) appeared as an opportunity to subjugate most elements of traditional Social Democratic discourse to the requirements of economic pragmatism. Thus, the Euro objective forced budgetary restraint, which represented a broad constraint on all other policies implemented by the Socialists. At the same time, however, the PS perceived that it also needed to widen the boundaries of the Euro objective, in order to include something more than monetary convergence and the strict financial measures it required. First, because these measures were precisely what the increasingly unpopular PSD administration were equated with. Second, because they had contributed to fuel the growing disenchantment with the EU among Portuguese voters, a disenchantment that might benefit the smaller 'eurosceptical' parties and, particularly, reverse the electoral decline of the PCP.[13] The end result of the PS government's simultaneous pursuit of EMU and the introduction of a 'social' component in the integration agenda was a 'Third Way' programme and practice.

The demise of 'Third Way' policies in Portugal

In the PS' second administration, which started in 1999, changing political circumstances contributed to alter its programmatic outlook, distancing the government from the Third Way principles implemented during the first mandate. In fact, the repeated failure to obtain an absolute majority of the votes, coupled with the absence of a clear EU objective, led to programmatic inaction and to a decrease in budget orthodoxy, thus contributing to its premature ending in December 2001.

Given the positive governmental record since 1995, it was largely expected that the Socialists would obtain an absolute majority in Parliament in the 1999 legislative elections. However, this objective was not accomplished, with the Socialists obtaining half of all parliamentary seats.[14] Indeed, in those elections, the only notable changes in the evolution of the Portuguese party system were the containment of the PCP's electoral decline and the emergence of a new political party to the left – the Left Block (BE), composed by an assortment of Maoist and Trotskyist parties, former Communists, and 'new politics'-type citizens' groups. Naturally, it can be argued that the failure to obtain an absolute majority is no reason to abandon the fundamental policy mix which characterised the first mandate, as described above, since the PS had been a minority government between 1995 and 1999. However, it is necessary to take into account that, precisely in anticipation of an absolute majority, various fundamental reforms had been postponed by the Socialists to the second mandate, especially concerning the fiscal, judicial, social security and health systems.[15]

These difficult reforms would still have been possible by resorting to *ad hoc* coalitions with other parliamentary parties, and indeed the 2000 social security reform discussed above, is a clear example of this. However, the disappearance of an overarching EU objective made all parliamentary negotiations much more difficult. Until 1999, the convergence of the major parties around the EMU objective provided the government with an objective of almost uncontested political legitimacy, contributing to make majority-opposition relations less adversarial. Yet, from 1999 onwards, with the accomplishment of the EMU objective, the lack of a decisive majority in parliament seemed a much more ominous obstacle to governability in the near future. Implicitly also, for the government, it was no longer necessary to adhere to strict 'Third Way' criteria, which had been the essential axis of their approach to monetary union, distinguishing them from the PSD's emphasis on exclusively financial objectives within EMU. For the Socialists, once the objective was met, there was an incentive to increase fiscal spending, free-riding on the Euro's credibility, and anticipating that the consequences of that behaviour could be politically contained.

Thus, the first 'post-Euro membership' 2000 State Budget indicated a substantial loosening of the government's previous commitment to fiscal orthodoxy, resulting in an increase in inflationary pressures and a rise in the fiscal deficit. The 2001 Budget was then forced to apply the brakes on the economy to reduce the fiscal deficit from 1.9 per cent (2000 Budget) to 1.1 per cent in 2001 and lower the growth rate of public expenditure to 5.9 per cent (10.9 per cent in 2000). At the same time, the economic circumstances began to deteriorate, with inflation and unemployment beginning to rise, culminating in a EU Commission warning concerning the excess budget deficit in 2001 (OECD 2001). The Socialists had difficulty in responding to these developments, with successive ministerial reshuffles confirming the image of a government devoid of a clear programme. In the second mandate, therefore, due to the political circumstances and the change in external environment, the Socialists lost the programmatic drive that had characterised the previous period. Had the 'Third Way' been a consistent ideology, rather than an expedient to achieve the EMU objective, it might have been possible to continue the implementation of such policies after 1999.

It was in these circumstances, fuelled by growing government unpopularity, that the Socialist party fought the 2001 local elections. In it, the PS did not lose a substantial share of its vote in relation to the previous 1997 local elections, even managing to win a few traditional Communist councils such as Évora, Loures, and Barreiro. Yet, it lost some of the most important cities in Portugal, namely Lisbon, Porto, Coimbra, and Sintra to the PSD (Lobo and Magalhães, forthcoming). In the event, Prime Minister António Guterres took the opportunity to resign from his post, as well as from the post of Secretary-General of the Socialist Party. Following this surprise resignation, the PS had to find a new leader to contest legislative elections. After a few candidates failed to concretise their bid for leadership, Eduardo Ferro Rodrigues put himself forward and won the support of the party. He had been one of the most popular ministers of the previous governments. In charge of the Employment and Social Solidarity portfolio, he was responsible for the most emblematic measure of the Guterres era, namely the RMG-Guaranteed Basic Income, described above. Given the constraints, Ferro Rodrigues ran a good campaign, with opinion polls showing the voting intention for the PS steadily increasing until election day. Still, it was difficult for him to disassociate from the failings of the previous government, since he did not criticise it when in office. In the ensuing legislative elections, the PSD won by a small margin of votes, albeit falling short of an absolute majority. Following the campaign pledge made by all parties to ensure government stability, the PSD then formed a coalition with the right-wing CDS–PP (*Centro Democrático Social–Partido Popular*). Ferro Rodrigues has nonetheless been maintained as party leader. Despite defeat, the Socialist party had the highest score ever obtained by the main opposition party, and the general feeling in the party on election night was that he had done a good job in difficult conditions.

Conclusions

After a decade in opposition (1985–95), the Socialists, led by moderate António Guterres formed government. The first Guterres government had what could be characterised as a Third Way electoral programme, although the party rejected such terminology. Various elements of civil society contributed to an electoral programme that shed all remnants of left-wing socialist rhetoric and presented new key ideas for the PS and

Portugal, combining both a market economy and an emphasis on social cohesion. In the first administration, the government was considered very successful: entry into EMU was achieved, within a context of positive economic performance, and moderate increases in social spending. This programmatic reconfiguration of the PS was achieved in part due to the unfreezing of the Communist electorate, which eased the cost for the PS of positioning itself unambiguously at the centre of the party spectrum. It was also a result of the EMU objective that functioned effectively as a positive constraint on the government's actions.

In retrospect, the abandonment of a coherent Third Way programme during the second mandate helps to shed light on the nature of the PS' government policy between 1995 and 1999. Seen from 2002, the programmatic coherence that Guterres brought to the government appears more as a tactical adaptation to the economic and political circumstances, as explained above, than a robust ideological commitment to that particular reformulation of Social Democracy. That is indeed very much in line with the nature of the Portuguese Socialist party since its foundation in 1973: a pragmatic party which tries to implement the 'necessary policies', given the external environment.

Notes

1 One of the manifestations of this alliance was the PS's jump to an unqualified defence of EEC membership, associating democratisation and economic recovery to the political and economic support that integration in the Common Market would bring (Sablosky 1996: 1013). In this way, the Socialists turned European membership into a political weapon, but that also meant plunging into a politics of exclusion of the PCP rather than competition for the Communist vote (Álvarez-Miranda 1996: 181).
2 The economic policies pursued by a previous centre-right cabinet, combined with the effects of a second international recession, had resulted in new gains in real wages (1.9 per cent per year on average from 1978 to 1983) but again, a new jump in public expenditures (from 38 per cent to 49 per cent of the GDP), huge public and balance of payments deficits (financed by escalating foreign debt), and an inflation rate of 26 per cent.
3 The motion for reelection of António Guterres as party leader in the 1999 Congress stated that 'the Portuguese Socialist Party has no need to search for 'new ways' – the third, fourth or fifth – nor to promote any act of refoundation, but only to persist in its goal of facing the challenges of the future.' The sentence was later withdrawn after the protests by some members of the party's parliamentary group.
4 As stated in the PS's 1995 electoral manifesto, 'the active employment policies – a central commitment of the PS government and the New Majority – (will be) more complex and diversified that the simple (and increasingly ineffective) manipulation of macroeconomic policy instruments or the concession of fiscal benefits to corporations' (Part II, Chapter 4).
5 Ibid., Part 3 ('Solidarity Policies'), Chapter 1 ('For a Society of Solidarity').
6 Ibid.
7 Ibid.

8 Ibid., Part 2, Chapter 4 (Macroeconomic Policies).
9 Ibid., Part 3 ('Solidarity Policies'), Chapter 4 ('Work and Employment').
10 Ibid., Part 4 ('Education, Scientific and Cultural Policies').
11 According to Barreto and Preto (2000), social expenditure in 1994 with education was 5.14 per cent of GDP and in 1997 was only 5.46 per cent. Given that Guterres had announced it as the PS' passion at the beginning of the legislature, it does not seem like a very large increase in expenditure. Health and Social Security follow the same pattern. Health expenditure also increased from 4.41 per cent to 4.52 per cent of GDP in the same time period, and Social Security only from 3.89 per cent to 4 per cent.
12 The EU co-finances some 'Third Way' national policies, such as active labour employment policies, which have some importance in determining the economic policy of the cohesion countries (Ireland, Portugal, Spain, Greece).
13 In 1992, and for the first time since 1985, more than 10 per cent of the Portuguese express negative feelings towards membership. This decline in support for membership was shared throughout Europe, reaching its lowest levels since the 1970s (see *Eurobarometer: Public Opinion in the European Union. 25th Anniversary*, 50 [Autumn 1998]). The electoral dangers of 'euroscepticism' for the PS, a party which traditionally supported European integration, were acknowledged in the 1995 pre-election manifesto: 'Situations emerge everyday which feed the fears of (Portugal's) further integration in Europe. That leads to nationalisms on the left and right (...) which are liable to receive support from certain sectors of society. In this context, a clear European project is necessarily one of the main instruments to fight this grave crisis' (*Contrato de Legislatura*, p. 106).
14 Although pre-electoral surveys pointed to an absolute majority of parliamentary seats, the PS did not increase its voting share substantially, winning only two extra MP's.
15 See 'Governo obrigado a negociar reformas com PCP e PP,' *Expresso*, 16 October 1999.

References

Álvarez-Miranda, B. (1996) *El sur de Europa y la adhesión a la Comunidad. Los debates políticos*, Madrid: CIS and Siglo XXI de España Editores.

Alves, C. (1999) 'Preparação e execução dos Programas de Privatizações 1996–1999', in DGEP- Ministério das Finanças, *Privatizações e Regulação – a experiência Portuguesa*, Lisboa: DGEP.

Bacalhau, M. (1994) *Atitudes, Opiniões e Comportamentos Políticos dos Portugueses: 1973–1993*, Lisbon: author's edition.

Barreto, A. and Preto, C.V. (2000) *A Situação Social em Portugal*, Lisbon: ICS.

Bosco, A. (2001) 'Four Actors in Search of a Role: the South European Communist Parties', in Diamandouros, P. N. and Gunther, R. (eds), *Parties, Politics, and Democracy in the New Southern Europe*, Baltimore: Johns Hopkins University Press.

Brassloff, W. (1992) 'Emprego e desemprego em Portugal no contexto europeu', in *Brotéria*, 135: 508–34.

Comissão do Livro Branco da Segurança Social (1998) *Livro Branco da Segurança Social*, Lisboa: INA.

Corkill, D. (1999) *The Development of the Portuguese Economy: a Case of Europeanisation*, London: Routledge.

EC (1999) *European Economy*, no.69, Brussels: EC.

Esping-Andersen, G. (1994) 'Budgets and Democracy: Towards a Welfare State in Spain and Portugal, 1960–1986', in Budge, Ian and McKay, David (eds), *Developing Democracy: Comparative Research in Honour of J.F.P. Blondel*, London: Sage, pp. 112–28.
Esping-Andersen, G. (1999) *Social Foundations of Postindustrial Economies*, Oxford: Oxford University Press.
Gallagher, T. (1990) 'The Portuguese Socialist Party: The Pitfalls of Being First', in Gallagher, T. and Williams, A. M. (eds), *Southern European Socialism*, Manchester: Manchester University Press.
Giddens, A. (1998) *The Third Way. The Renewal of Social Democracy*, Cambridge: Polity Press.
Giddens, A. (2000) *The Third Way and Its Critics* Cambridge: Polity Press.
Guillén, A., Álvarez, S. and Adão e Silva, P. (forthcoming) 'Redesigning the Spanish and Portuguese Welfare States: The Impact of Accession into the European Union', *South European Politics and Society*.
Gunther, R. and Montero, J. R. (2001) 'The Anchors of Partisanship: A Comparative Analysis of Voting Behavior in Four Southern European Democracies', in Diamandouros, P. N. and Gunther, R. (eds), *Parties, Politics, and Democracy in the New Southern Europe*, Baltimore: Johns Hopkins University Press.
Halpern, D. and Mikosz, D. (n.d.) 'The Third Way: summary of the NEXUS online discussion', http://freespace.virgin.net/www3.org/3way/summary.htm
Huber, J. and Inglehart, R. (1995) 'Expert Interpretation of Party Space and Party Locations in 42 Societies', *Party Politics* 1(1): 73–111.
Kitschelt, H. (1994) *The Transformation of European Social Democracy*, Cambridge: Cambridge University Press.
Le Grand, J. (1989) 'Markets, Welfare and Equality', in Le Grand, J. and Estrin, Saul (eds), *Market Socialism*, Oxford: Oxford University Press.
Le Grand, J. (1998) 'The Third Way Begins with CORA (Community, Opportunity, Responsibility, and Accountability)', *New Statesman*, March.
Lima, J. A. (1991) Aníbal de estimação, *Expresso-Revista*, 12 October.
Lister, R. (2000) 'To RIO Via the Third Way', *Renewal* 8(4): 9–20.
Lobo, M. C. and Magalhães, P. (2001) 'From Third Wave to Third Way: The Socialist Party and European Integration', in *Journal of Southern Europe and the Balkans*, 3(1): 25–35.
Lobo, M. C. and Magalhães, P. (forthcoming) 'Election Report – the local Elections 2001 and the Legislative Elections 2002', in *South European Politics and Society*.
Maravall, J. M. (1997) *Regimes, Politics, and Markets: Democratisation and Economic Change in Southern and Eastern Europe*, Oxford University Press, Oxford.
Marquand, D. (1999) 'Populism v Pluralism', *Prospect*, June 1999.
Merkel, W. (1991) 'After the Golden Age: Is Social Democracy doomed to decline?', in Maravall, J. M. *et al.*, *Socialist Parties in Europe*, Barcelona: Institut de Ciénces Politiques i Socials.
OECD (1998) *Report on Portugal*, Paris: OECD.
OECD (1999) *Report on Portugal*, Paris: OECD.
Opello, W. C. (1985) *Portugal's Political Development: A Comparative Approach*, Boulder and London: Westview Press.
Przeworski, A. (1985) *Capitalism and Social Democracy*, Cambridge: Cambridge University Press.

Sablosky, J. A. (1996) 'A actividade partidária transnacional e as relações de Portugal com a Comunidade Europeia', *Análise Social* 31(138).

Scharpf, F. W. (1991) *Crisis and Choice in European Social Democracy*, Ithaca: Cornell University Press.

Weber, H. (1999) 'Parti socialiste français et New Labour britannique: convergences et divergences', *Revue Socialiste*, 1.

White, S. (1998) 'Interpreting the Third Way; Not One Route, But Many', *Renewal* 6(1): 17–30.

Wright, A. and Wright, T. (1996) *Socialisms: Old and New*, London: Routledge.

6 Turning ideas into policies

Implementing modern Social Democratic thinking in Germany's pension policy

Martin Hering

Introduction

For the Social Democratic Party of Germany (SPD), the 1998–2002 legislative period was a period of transformation. Before the SPD's landslide victory in the 1998 federal election,[1] the party built a reputation as the defenders of the welfare state. During its 16 years in opposition, the Social Democrats heavily attacked the Kohl government on social issues. Continuing this tradition, the SPD fought the 1998 election as 'the party of social justice'. But after less than a year in office, the SPD became a very different party. Gerhard Schröder, the head of the government and the new leader of the party, reoriented Social Democratic policies and programmes. Schröder strengthened the party's competence in economic policy and focused on turning the SPD into 'the party of fiscal discipline'. To this end, the Social Democratic government implemented major welfare state cutbacks. The chancellor made the strengthening of individual responsibility into an important objective of SPD social policy.

The 2002 federal election was the first test of the SPD's ability to win office by giving priority to the consolidation of public finances instead of social justice (SPD 2002). The Schröder government was re-elected in an extremely close contest. The SPD lost 2.4 percent of the vote, but its losses were largely compensated by gains of its coalition partner, the Greens.[2] The Social Democrats lost a lot of support among workers in the West. In the East, however, the SPD gained significantly, mostly because of Schröder's clear stance against an attack on Iraq and the chancellor's high popularity in the wake of Eastern Germany's flood of the century. In sum, the 2002 federal election showed that the SPD has a very hard time winning office as 'the party of fiscal discipline', especially if budgetary consolidation does not coincide with economic growth and the creation of jobs. Without a strong emphasis on social justice, the Social Democrats have enormous difficulties in mobilizing their core constituencies. Modern Social Democratic issues – most importantly Schröder's plan for labor market reform – did not generate much enthusiasm among SPD voters during the 2002 federal election campaign.

In this chapter, I analyze Schröder's politics of modernizing the German Social Democratic Party by examining the redefinition of SPD pension policy.[3] The party's transformation is most visible, yet at the same time most puzzling in this area. In brief, the argument that I will develop in this chapter is the following: Schröder pursued a strategy of polarization to redefine Social Democratic pension policy. By polarizing the SPD, the chancellor marginalized the left wing and abruptly replaced the party's existing pension policy approach with his own conception of it. Schröder's redefinition of policy alternatives produced a change in the SPD's ideas concerning pension policy. These ideational changes, I argue, were the key to Schröder's success in modernizing the SPD.

The modernization of the SPD

The SPD nominated Gerhard Schröder as candidate for chancellor in April 1998, a few months before the fall election. The nominee stood for modernist positions that paralleled many of the ideas popularized by Tony Blair under the label 'Third Way'. But the SPD delegates did not rally behind Schröder because his positions appealed to them. Schröder's appeal came from his favorable public image that promised to lead the party to victory after 16 years of defeat at the polls. The party congress, by contrast, passed an election manifesto that emphasized traditional Social Democratic objectives: preserving the welfare state, lowering taxes for people with low and medium incomes, and protecting workers and the unemployed (SPD 1998; Lafontaine: 1999, 98–110). After the triumph in September 1998, the SPD showed no signs of change in ideas or policies. The position of the modernizers within the SPD, including that of the chancellor himself, remained weak. Proving the strength of the Social Democratic policy inheritance, the Schröder government's social and economic policies closely followed the path outlined in the party's election manifesto. During this time the SPD first rescinded many of the Kohl government's social cutbacks, most importantly in the area of pensions, and then implemented the alternative social and economic policy program that it had developed during its oppositional years.

The month of June 1999, however, was the beginning of a radical change of both the ideas and the policies of the SPD. The renewal of German Social Democracy was completely unexpected, even more so since the SPD had won against the Christian Democrats by capitalizing on its traditionally strong competence in social policy. In June 1999, Gerhard Schröder initiated his modernization of the party program from above. Without prior debate within the SPD, the chancellor went public with a paper that he had jointly authored with Tony Blair. The Neue Mitte *(The New Centre)* paper outlined a new direction for Social Democracy (Blair and Schröder 1999). In the same month, the Schröder government launched its ambitious Future Programme 2000 *(Zukunftsprogramm 2000)*

(Bundesregierung 1999). It marked the beginning of a fundamental reorientation of the SPD's social and economic policies. The SPD was deeply divided about the ideas expressed in the Neue Mitte paper and the policies contained in the Future Programme. Schröder's paper proposed a new supply-side agenda for the left that entailed the lowering of company taxes and of employers' non-wage labor costs. Moreover, it demanded substantial cutbacks of public spending, especially of large social programs on pensions and health care. Sound public finances and economic policy competence were declared to be the new trademarks of Social Democracy. The Future Programme 2000 included huge expenditure cutbacks of over 80 billion Euros within the next four years, announced major tax cuts for businesses and people with higher incomes, and made the commitment to achieve a balanced budget by the year 2004.

The most controversial feature of the Neue Mitte paper and the Future Programme was a particular combination of policy measures: tax relief for businesses, but social cutbacks for employees, pensioners and the unemployed. These policies conflicted strongly with the traditional Social Democratic objective of reducing social inequality. Rudolf Dreßler, the party's long-time social policy expert, warned Schröder against destroying the Social Democratic identity, one that is rooted in the pursuit of social justice (Dreßler *et al.* 1999). In a similar vein, the premier of the Saar state, Reinhard Klimmt, accused the chancellor of selling the party's soul. Schröder's attempt to modernize German Social Democracy caused deep intra-party conflicts, and led to major electoral losses in the fall of 1999 both in state and in local elections.[4] Less than three years later, however, the renewal of the SPD's policies and programs was almost complete. The 2000 tax reform and the 2001 pension reform, Schröder's two most important reform projects in the 1998–2002 legislative period, best evidence the dramatic change in policies. A major step in redefining the SPD's program followed at the 2001 party congress. The party leadership motion, entitled Security in Times of Change *(Sicherheit im Wandel)*, was almost unanimously approved by the delegates. It was a synopsis of the social, economic and fiscal policies implemented by the Schröder government (SPD 2001a). To conclude, between June 1999 and November 2001, the ideas contained in Schröder's Neue Mitte paper have been turned into governmental policy and have become the party's official programmatic stance. The inclusion of Schröder's ideas into the SPD's revised party manifesto would complete the process of modernization. The thrust of the interim report from the Party Manifesto Commission *(Grundsatzprogrammkommission)* indicates that the completion of the SPD's programmatic modernization is very likely (SPD 2001b).

In the remaining part of this chapter, I will study the political process of Social Democratic renewal in Germany. The overarching question is how Social Democratic modernizers are able to turn their ideas into policies. The chapter seeks to answer this question by focusing on the key actor in the modernization of German Social Democracy: chancellor Gerhard Schröder. It traces the process of change in one of the most important fields, that of pension policy. First, pension policy best reflects the SPD's changing approach to social policy since pensions are by far the largest social program in Germany's welfare state. Second, because the reform of Germany's pension system is an important instrument in stabilizing public finances and in reducing non-wage labor costs, it also mirrors the SPD's new approach to fiscal and economic policies. Third, the fact that the SPD's policy inheritance is especially strong in old-age security makes pension policy a good test case for Social Democratic modernization. Finally, Schröder's pension reform has long-lasting consequences: the partial privatization of public pensions is a major institutional change in Germany's welfare state that creates the possibility for further shifts of responsibility from the state to the market.

Explaining the paradox of Social Democratic renewal in Germany

It is a paradox that Schröder's attempt to modernize Social Democratic pension policy was a success. First, the SPD is known as a programmatic party whose basic social policy positions evolve over time, but do not change abruptly.[5] But the Old-Age Provision Act of 2001 *(Altersvermögensgesetz)* turns the SPD's long-established approach to pensions on its head. It is a radical break with inherited Social Democratic pension policy, was not part of the 1998 coalition agreement between SPD and Greens, and contradicts the policies pursued by the Schröder government at the outset of the 1998–2002 legislative period. Second, attempts to modernize the party initially had little chance to succeed when the SPD government was formed in 1998 because the modernizers were in a weak position.

The 2001 pension reform ended the near-monopoly of public pensions by partially substituting them with private pensions. It put a mechanism in place that lowers public pension benefits substantially between 2002 and 2008. At the same time, it encouraged the growth of private pensions. Schröder's private pension tier is a novelty for the German welfare state. By contrast, throughout most of the post-war period – between the establishment of Germany's modern pension system in 1957 and the implementation of the Future Programme in 1999 – the central goal of SPD pension policy was the preservation of the public pension system. Social Democrats defended the core function of Germany's generous pension system: the public provision of income-replacing pension benefits *(Lebensstandardsicherung)*. Before June 1999, partial privatization of pensions was unthinkable for the SPD. For Rudolf Dreßler, the key architect of SPD social policy during the 1980s and 1990s, the Old-Age Provision Act constituted a 'paradigm shift in pension policy'.[6] Schröder's modernization of pension policy entailed a departure from several long-held, "iron" principles in German Social Democracy, most importantly from the guarantee of income-replacing pensions, from parity financing by employers and employees, and from solidaristic old-age insurance. The focus of the SPD pension policy shifted from guaranteeing generous pension benefits to guaranteeing stable contribution rates. Old-age security ceased to be the exclusive domain of the state. Strengthening individual responsibility became an integral part of Social Democratic pension policy.

In the German Social Democratic Party, the modernizers were weak and the policy inheritance was strong. Why, then, did Schröder succeed? I will show in this chapter that ideational changes within the SPD were the key to Schröder's success in transforming Social Democratic pension policy. The German case of Social Democratic modernization thus suggests that the success of modernizers in turning their own ideas into policies critically depends on their ability to change the ideas of Social Democratic parties. At first, Schröder attempted to reach a bipartisan agreement on partial privatization by negotiating with the CDU/CSU over the course of six months. After these negotiations had failed in June 2000, however, the chancellor depended on the unity of the SPD parliamentary party to pass the Old-Age Provision Act in the Bundestag. During the first year of the reform process, from June 1999 to June 2000, Schröder's pension reform plans were heavily contested within the SPD. But Social Democratic ideas about pension policy changed between July 2000 and January 2001. As the ideas changed, intra-party opposition vanished. When the Old-Age Provision Act was passed in the Bundestag, the SPD parliamentary party was highly united. The best evidence for the ideational reorientation of the SPD is the behavior of the party's left wing, formerly the strongest defender of long-established Social Democratic principles and the most hostile opponent of Schröder's ideas. Although the SPD left wing had enough votes in the Bundestag to block the Old-Age Provision Act, it actively backed the reform legislation. Social Democratic left-wingers even claimed credit for the modernization of the German welfare state.

But how did Schröder bring about these ideational changes in the SPD? How did the chancellor overcome 'the vast deadweight of accumulated practices and ways of thinking' (Heclo 1974: 17–18)? How were the new principles in pension policy – individual responsibility and contribution stabilization – established? I will demonstrate that the redefinition of ideas depended on the purposeful removal of the old alternative from the menu of options. Given the existence of strong policy inheritance, removing the SPD's traditional pension reform plans was critical for Schröder. These plans were well developed, had strong support in the party and were implemented after the 1998 election had been won. Therefore, proposing a new alternative was impossible without first removing the old one. I further show that the removal was a political process that was initiated and sustained by purposeful actors. Social and economic circumstances did not make the SPD's traditional approach to pension policy obsolete. Exogenous economic shocks or social crises do have the potential to invalidate existing alternatives and to make way for other approaches. During the 1990s, however, the German pension system was not confronted with either a shock or a crisis. After unification, the full institutional transfer of West Germany's pension scheme to the East did not change the fiscal development of the system.

What was the driving force behind the political process that caused the redefinition of alternatives? As I will show in this chapter, Schröder accomplished the removal of the old alternative, and the SPD's change in ideas about pension policy, by pursuing a strategy of polarization. Modernizers have the choice between two basic strategies to redefine a party's policy alternative: a strategy of persuasion and one of polarization. Either they can attempt to demonstrate the weaknesses of the existing alternative and persuade the party of the merits of their new approach – the change in ideas will follow the redefinition of alternatives; or they can attempt to reduce the political influence of the leading supporters of the old alternative, polarize the party, and push the new alternative to the forefront by force. Here, the redefinition of alternatives precedes the change in ideas.

This is precisely what happened in the SPD under Schröder. Changes in ideas about pension policy were not produced by a reciprocal process of persuasion. On the contrary, Schröder used the powers available to him as chancellor and party leader to move forward with an authoritative redefinition of the SPD's approach to pension policy. There was no prior debate within the party. The chancellor's pension reform plan of June 1999 caught the SPD completely by surprise. In subsequent months, there was massive intra-party resistance. But Schröder declared the new principles of Social Democratic pension policy – individual responsibility and stable contribution rates – to be fixed and non-negotiable. The SPD leader defended them relentlessly against opposition from the parliamentary party and from regional party leaders. By using his leadership powers and by polarizing the SPD, Schröder managed, first, to marginalize the defenders of the party's policy inheritance, and second, to convert a majority of Social Democrats to the ideas that were contained in the 1999 pension reform plan. I further show that a change in power relations within the SPD was the precondition for employing a strategy of polarization. As mentioned before, the modernizers in the SPD were in a weak position at the beginning of the 1998–2002 legislative period. But Schröder was able to reduce the political influence of the traditionalists while strengthening and consolidating his own power, both in the party and in the cabinet. Without a series of advantageous personnel decisions and changes, the pursuit of Schröder's strategy of polarization would have been doomed to fail.

The polarization theory advanced in this chapter contrasts with theories of ideational change that stress the causal role of persuasion and downplay the significance of power, pressure and polarization (Heclo 1974; Kingdon 1984; Majone 1989). According to Kingdon, the removal of an old alternative is the result of a very long process of persuasion. Modernizers attempt to get policymakers slowly used to new ideas. For a long period of time, there is a gradual diffusion of new ideas. But then a point is reached at which an explosive diffusion of these new ideas sets in. The change of ideas is followed by a redefinition of alternatives. In Kingdon's persuasion theory, ideational change is 'the culmination of years of agitation'.

In the following sections, I will first describe the obstacles against modernization that Schröder faced. I will outline the party's inheritance in pension policy as well as Schröder's contrasting positions. The next section describes the preconditions that permitted Schröder to pursue a strategy of polarization. It examines the personnel decisions and changes that shifted the balance of power between modernizers and traditionalists within the SPD. The third section continues with a detailed analysis of Schröder's strategy of polarization that redefined the Social Democratic approach to pension policy. The fourth section examines the outcome of Schröder's strategy: the change of Social Democratic ideas about pension policy. The chapter concludes with a discussion of the causal significance of power and polarization in explanations of ideational changes.

The Social Democratic policy inheritance

The SPD's most influential programmatic statement, the report of the Old-Age Security Commission, dates back to its oppositional years in the mid-1990s, when a profound change took place in German pension politics. From the 1950s to the early 1990s, there had been a broad consensus between Social Democrats and Christian Democrats on the core features of the German pension system. Although there had frequently been intense party competition concerning pension policy, the two major parties had almost unanimously supported the four big pension bills of the post-war period: the establishment of the modern German pension system in 1957, its expansion in 1972, its consolidation in 1989 and the institutional transfer to the Eastern Länder in 1991. In 1996, the CDU ended Germany's celebrated 'pension consensus'. The Christian Democrats planned to depart from the shared commitment to provide income-replacing pensions by implementing massive benefit cutbacks.[7] The most contentious piece of legislation was the Pension Reform Act 1999. It was passed by the Kohl government against Social Democratic opposition in 1997, only one year before the federal election.

In reaction to the reforms planned by the Kohl government, the SPD established an expert commission, the Old-Age Security Commission *(Alterssicherungskommission)*, which developed an alternative plan. The commission was chaired by Rudolf Dreßler, the party's veteran social policy expert. The plan aimed at preserving the public pension system and thus reinforced the SPD's post-war inheritance in pension policy. The 1997 commission report stated that a fundamental change in Germany's public pension system was neither desirable nor necessary (SPD 1997b). First, the existing benefit level of 70 percent of an employee's income was inviolable. Any substantial reduction was a break with the guarantee of income-replacing pension benefits. This principle of *Lebensstandardsicherung*, the commission report emphasized, belonged to 'the core of our social security system' (SPD 1997b: 1). Second, there was absolutely no reason for altering Germany's Bismarckian pension system. To maintain generous benefits, to ensure the financial sustainability of the system in the long-term and to slow the growth of pension contribution rates, reforms within the existing system were sufficient. The Dreßler commission proposed two measures to reinforce the characteristics of the long-established pension programme. The first was to relieve the system from funding non-contributory benefits, especially childcare credits. Federal transfers to the pension system were to be increased. The second was to broaden the base of contributors. The steadily growing group of part-time employees, the commission proposed, should no longer be exempt from paying social insurance contributions.

The 1997 report of the Old-Age Security Commission was highly influential. Until the Nuremburg congress in November 2001, it defined the content of the SPD's political program. And between October 1998 and June 1999, it became law by shaping the content of pension legislation under the Schröder government. When the Social Democrats were in opposition, the SPD parliamentary party introduced a resolution in the Bundestag that contained the proposals of the commission report (Deutscher Bundestag 1997). Next, the federal party endorsed the report at the SPD congress in Hanover in December 1997. The delegates passed a resolution that committed the SPD, first, to repeal the pension reform of the Kohl government after an election victory in 1998, and second, to implement its own reform alternative (SPD 1997a). These commitments were reaffirmed in the SPD's election manifesto that was adopted at the Leipzig congress in April 1998 (SPD 1998). In the 1998 federal election campaign, the preservation of Germany's pension system was one of the party's key electoral promises.

When the SPD came to power, the Schröder government implemented the party's political program at an impressive pace and thus closely followed the democratic model of 'responsible party government' (Katz 1997: 32–5). The coalition agreement between the SPD and the Greens of October 1998 took over the SPD's positions on pension reform from its 1998 election manifesto (SPD and Bündnis 90/Die Grünen 1998). The SPD was determined to fulfill its election promises within the first 100 days in office. In December 1998, the red–green coalition rescinded the cutbacks of the Kohl government, which would have reduced pension benefits from 70 to 64 percent. In January 1999, the government implemented the two most important measures proposed in the report of the Old-Age Security Commission: first, it increased the federal transfers to compensate for non-contributory benefits, and second, it widened the base of contributors by making part-time employees liable to pay pension insurance contributions. These measures enabled the Schröder government to maintain the existing pension benefit level of 70 percent and to lower the pension contribution rate significantly.

The SPD's pension reform alternative and governmental policies were the exact opposite of Schröder's understanding of modern social policy. Schröder planned to transform Germany's generous, income-replacing pensions into basic, poverty-preventing pensions. The chancellor's plan was, first, massively to cut public pension benefits in order to lower contribution rates, and second, to strengthen individual responsibility by encouraging private retirement provision.[8] For Schröder, the significance of reforming pensions went beyond the creation of a modern pension system. Pension benefit cutbacks were essential for the chancellor to balance Germany's budget: reducing pension expenditure automatically lowers the size of federal transfers to the public pension system, which represents about 30 percent of total federal expenditure. Schröder wanted to make fiscal discipline into the trademark of modern Social Democracy. The chancellor's pension reform plan was developed by Bodo Hombach, his key policy advisor, who was also the author of the *Neue Mitte* paper (Hombach 1998: 205–18).

At first, the SPD's policy inheritance was amazingly strong. In May 1998, shortly after the SPD had nominated Schröder as candidate for chancellor, the nominee called for a fundamental reform of Germany's pension system. Rudolf Dreßler responded by declaring that the SPD's pension policy was defined by the party's election manifesto, not by its candidate for chancellor. Dreßler was proven right. Anti-cutback legislation and a massive increase of federal transfers to the public pension system were implemented by the SPD government soon after it took office. The modernizers in the SPD were still too weak to reorient the party's policies. Moreover, the political stakes for a pension reform in line with Schröder's ideas were high: it implied a break with the SPD's party program and a reversal of precisely those governmental policies that were supposed to prove that the Social Democrats keep their electoral promises and are accountable to voters.

Schröder's consolidation of power

The strength of the SPD's policy inheritance and the weakness of the modernizers within the party were major obstacles against turning the new ideas into policies. A number of personnel decisions and changes in the SPD were the precondition for Schröder's strategy of polarization. First, the chancellor appointed a modernizer as labor minister and made sure that Dreßler did not receive any responsibility for social policy in the cabinet. Second, Oskar Lafontaine's resignation as finance minister and party leader gave Schröder more control over the SPD and over cabinet decision-making. Third, Schröder gained more influence by replacing the SPD secretary, by incorporating the leader of the SPD parliamentary party into the inner circle of governmental decision-making, and by restructuring the office of the chancellor. These changes weakened the influence of traditional Social Democrats and consolidated Schröder's power in the SPD.

Schröder's first decision after being nominated as candidate for chancellor caught the SPD by surprise: Schröder nominated Walter Riester, the vice-chairman of the metal workers' union, as the very first member of the SPD's shadow cabinet. The SPD parliamentary party did not like Riester's nomination as shadow labor minister: Riester was not a member of the Bundestag and was known as an independently minded modernizer within the IG Metall, Germany's largest trade union. But most importantly, Schröder completely ignored Rudolf Dreßler, the parliamentary party's candidate of choice. Dreßler had served as the leading critic of the Kohl government's social policies for 16 years. He was also the chairman of AfA, the group that represents workers' interests within the party. Schröder never conferred with Dreßler about his decision, neither before nor after Riester's nomination. He also did not consult the SPD parliamentary party before making this decision.

Schröder did not want Dreßler, or other proponents of traditional SPD policies, to have any influence over social affairs, neither in the cabinet nor in the parliamentary party. Dreßler, a noted expert in health policy, was interested in becoming health minister. But Schröder passed over him, for a second time, by giving the health ministry to the Greens. To reduce Dreßler's power in the parliamentary party, Schröder, shortly after the election victory in 1998, offered him two attractive jobs, that of minister of construction or that of German ambassador to Israel. But Dreßler declined and remained member of parliament. His influence over pension policy was nonetheless diminished due to personnel changes within the leadership of the parliamentary party. Dreßler gave up his long-term responsibility for labor market and pension policy, and was replaced by Ulla Schmidt, a newcomer in the party leadership. Schmidt's election proved to be favorable for Schröder. First, she belonged to the SPD right-wing and therefore did not have a strong attachment to traditional Social Democratic principles in social policy. Second, Schmidt developed good relations with labor minister Riester and skilfully managed the government's pension reform in the Bundestag. In January 2001, the month the Bundestag passed the pension reform bill, Schröder rewarded Schmidt by appointing her minister of health even though Schmidt had no prior experience in health policy. Dreßler was frustrated by the SPD's 'paradigm shift' in pension policy. In July 2000, he decided to leave the Bundestag and take up Schröder's offer to become German ambassador to Israel.

The most important, and also most spectacular, personnel change in the SPD occurred in March 1999, when Oskar Lafontaine resigned all of a sudden as finance minister and as chairman of the SPD. Lafontaine was known as a left-winger. He had Keynesian economic ideas, reinforced the SPD's image as 'the party of social justice', and regarded workers, pensioners and the unemployed as the party's core constituencies (Lafontaine 1999). As the most influential cabinet member after Schröder, Lafontaine had the ability to block a shift in pension policy. Before his double resignation in March 1999, the party chairman ensured the survival of the old reform alternative. Lafontaine persistently defended the SPD's reform plans against Schröder's challenges. An incidence in May 1998 best illustrates Lafontaine's veto power: when Schröder went public with his ideas about transforming Germany's pension system, Lafontaine thwarted the candidate for chancellor. The SPD chairman called an end to the debate on pensions and warned Schröder against destroying the SPD's 'lead in expertise' in pension policy. Lafontaine's position as leader of the SPD and as high-ranking cabinet member put tight restrictions on Schröder's ability to propose a new alternative in pension policy.

Lafontaine's departure changed the power relations within the SPD substantially. The loss of its powerful leader left the SPD left wing in disarray. At the same time, Schröder consolidated his power step-by-step. First and most importantly, Schröder assumed the chairmanship of the SPD. This ended the separation between the offices of chancellor and party leader and gave Schröder the power to shape the party program, which he soon thereafter did by publishing the *Neue Mitte* paper. Second, the chancellor appointed Hans Eichel as finance minister who, unlike Lafontaine, shared Schröder's ideas about fiscal discipline. Third, Schröder laid the groundwork for a smooth coordination between the government, the party and the SPD parliamentary party. The SPD chairman installed a new party secretary, co-opted the SPD's parliamentary leader and restructured the chancellor's office. This period of power consolidation lasted from March to September 1999 (Bannas 2000).

Three personnel and organizational changes improved Schröder's difficult relationship with the party base and with the parliamentary party. First, Schröder altered the party's organizational structure. The chairman created the new office of the general secretary, in effect the SPD's executive leader, above the existing office of the federal party secretary. He filled this powerful position with Franz Müntefering, a Schröder loyalist who at the same time was respected by the SPD left wing. Ottmar Schreiner, a left-winger and social policy expert, resigned as SPD federal party secretary, clearing the way for Müntefering. Second, Schröder created the conditions for a close relationship with the SPD parliamentary party. Peter Struck, the chairman of the SPD parliamentary party, replaced Lafontaine in the Schröder government's inner circle of decision-making. This circle consisted of only four people, two members of the SPD and two members of the Greens (Bannas 1999). A better coordination with the parliamentary party became essential for Schröder after Lafontaine's resignation. In party-line votes, the SPD left wing had enough votes to veto legislation initiated by the government. Given that Lafontaine's power in cabinet was lost, the threat to block legislation in the Bundestag became more important in order for the left wing to represent its interests. Therefore, Lafontaine's resignation strengthened the role of the SPD parliamentary party, and consequently the role of its chairman. It was advantageous for Schröder that Struck filled the void left by Lafontaine. Unlike Lafontaine, he did not belong to the SPD left wing. Struck was one of the few people in the SPD who immediately supported Schröder's *Neue Mitte* paper.

Nonetheless, one major obstacle for a smooth relationship between Schröder and the SPD parliamentary party remained: Bodo Hombach, Schröder's Minister for Special Tasks *(Minister für besondere Aufgaben)* and head of the chancellor's office. Hombach, the co-author of the *Neue Mitte* paper and the architect of Schröder's pension reform plans, was not popular among the SPD Bundestag members because he seemed unwilling to coordinate the government's policies with the parliamentary party. In June 1999, Schröder replaced Hombach with Frank-Walter Steinmeier, formerly Hombach's deputy in the chancellor's office, who was a long-time Schröder confidant and an experienced background negotiator. To strengthen the link between the chancellor's office and the SPD Bundestag members, Schröder filled Steinmeier's previous position with Hans Martin Bury, a young member of parliament. In the SPD parliamentary party, Bury had distinguished himself by making proposals for the modernization of Germany's pension system. Bury's ideas had many similarities with Schröder's.

Schröder's consolidation of power contrasts sharply with the disintegration and marginalization of the SPD left wing. First, as a consequence of Lafontaine's resignation, the left wing was no longer represented in the SPD's decision-making center and, as mentioned above, in the government's inner circle (Bannas 2000).[9] Second, the loss of a leader led to a loss of orientation for the left wing. This state of confusion lasted for over a year, until June 2000. In that month, the SPD left wing changed both its leadership and organizational structure. It also started to revise its policy positions. The three-decade old Frankfurt Circle *(Frankfurter Kreis)* was replaced by a more professional organization, the Democratic Left Forum 21 *(Forum Demokratische Linke 21)*. As their new leader, the small group of 70 left-wingers elected Andrea Nahles, a young member of the Bundestag and former chairwoman of the SPD youth organization. Nahles announced that the SPD left wing would take on a completely different role. It would no longer concentrate its work on criticizing the party leadership, on outlining broad political visions and on acting as the SPD's 'social conscience'. The reconstituted left wing would end its isolation from governmental decision-making, build an alliance with the party's center, and 'develop pragmatic policy solutions' (Nahles 2000). The support of Schröder's pension reform is evidence of the left-wing's pragmatic turn. But the greater willingness to cooperate with the chancellor did not bring an end to the left's marginalization within the Schröder government.

Redefining the pension reform alternative

The political strategy pursued by Schröder to redefine the SPD's pension policy was based on polarization, not on persuasion. During the year and a half long reform process, Schröder did not engage in a discussion over the best alternative. It was never part of Schröder's strategy to promote the gradual diffusion of new ideas. The government did not appoint an expert commission to evaluate different reform options, as the Kohl government had done in the late 1980s and late 1990s. Instead, Schröder paved the way for the SPD's new pension reform alternative through a coup. Immediately after assuming the party leadership, Schröder took action: in June 1999, the government presented the first outline for a transformation of Germany's pension system. When Lafontaine was still the leader of the party, the chancellor did not make any attempts to bring about a change in pension policy. Nor did Schröder resist the implementation of the SPD's existing reform alternative after the 1998 election victory. In the following months, it was Schröder's strategy of polarization and relentless defense of his plan against intra-party resistance that secured the survival of the new reform alternative. The chancellor's intransigence became plainly evident when he silenced union protests in November 2000. At the congress of the ÖTV, Germany's large public sector union, Schröder ended the debate about the government's pension reform plans by declaring: 'The introduction of a private pension pillar is a necessity, and we will do it! Basta!'.[10]

In effect, Schröder's coup and polarization strategy amounted to an abrupt and complete replacement of the SPD's pension reform alternative. The objective of providing income-replacing pension benefits was replaced by that of stabilizing contribution rates in the long-term. The preservation of the public pension system gave way to the introduction of a private pension tier. For the Social Democrats, accepting Schröder's new objectives meant abandoning the SPD's old principles because they were diametrically opposed to each other. In the face of population ageing, stable contribution rates imply declining pension benefits. Therefore, it was impossible to maintain the principle of guaranteeing an employee's standard of living during retirement. Moreover, a sizable private pension tier is by design a partial substitute for, not a supplement to, Germany's public pension program. If it were a mere supplement, people would neither have an incentive nor the ability to save. Accepting private pensions therefore meant abandoning the commitment to preserve the public pension system as it had existed between the 1950s and the 1990s.

Two government proposals were important for the redefinition of the SPD's pension reform alternative: first, the labor ministry's original reform outlines of June 1999, and second, the joint reform plan of the SPD and the Greens of May 2000 (Bundesministerium für Arbeit und Sozialordnung 1999, 2000b). These proposals established the principles of contribution rate stabilization and individual retirement provision and prepared the ground for the 2001 Old-Age Provision Act. In June 1999, in conjunction with the government's Future Program 2000, the labor minister presented the first outlines for the reform of Germany's pension system. Riester's paper provoked a wave of criticism and protests from the SPD, the Greens, the opposition parties and the trade unions. Two proposed measures were especially provocative. First, Riester broke with the principle of *Lebensstandardsicherung* by planning to reduce the benefit level from 70 to 67 percent. In the Bundestag, Riester told his fellow party members that they were living a lie after they stuck to the promise to guarantee a person's living standard during retirement. Second, Riester departed from the principle of parity financing which governs social insurance in Germany. His plan called for a private pension tier financed entirely by contributions from employees. Employees were obliged to pay 2.5 percent of their wages into private pension plans, while employers were not required to make any contributions. This fuelled especially strong opposition from the trade unions. Klaus Zwickel, the chairman of the IG Metall, called Riester's pension reform plans 'a shame for a Social Democratic government'.

The presentation of Riester's outlines was a coup since it had been prepared in secret. The parliamentary parties of SPD and Greens did not know about the government's pension reform plans before Riester made them public (Meng 1999). Schröder pushed the plan in record speed through the cabinet and the SPD parliamentary party against strong intraparty opposition. It was advantageous for Schröder that Ulla Schmidt, not Rudolf Dreßler, was in charge of pension policy in the parliamentary party's leadership. Schmidt publicly backed the government's plan, justified the substantial benefit cutbacks as unavoidable and promoted the introduction of private pensions. As had been expected, Dreßler heavily criticized Riester's reform plan.

In June 1999, the SPD parliamentary party reluctantly endorsed Schröder's Future Programme 2000 that contained the measures to reduce pension benefits to 67 percent and to introduce a private pension tier. The controversy over the party's course in pension policy continued throughout the summer.[11] Notwithstanding the opposition from the SPD left wing, the Future Programme became law: the government's Budget Consolidation Act *(Haushaltssanierungsgesetz)* was passed in the Bundestag in November 1999. Schröder's strategy of polarization had paid off. An initial round of benefit cutbacks had been legislated. But the legislation of the new private pension tier had to wait for another year because there were too many unresolved issues.

In May 2000, the labor minister presented a second proposal that had been developed in cooperation with a special working group of the SPD and the Greens (Koalitionsarbeitsgruppe SPD und Bündnis 90/Die Grünen 2000). This reform concept generated another wave of criticism from the SPD parliamentary party and the trade unions. It was much more radical than the original proposal of June 1999. First, the plan was to reduce the level of pension benefits well below 61 percent. It meant that the Schröder government's benefit cutbacks were much more severe than the cutbacks of the Kohl government which were rescinded by the SPD in 1998. Second, the size of the private pension tier was made larger. Instead of 2.5 percent, employees were supposed to contribute 4 percent of their income to private pension plans. Third, the plan specified an even lower level for contribution rates than the original proposal had done. The ceiling for the pension contribution rate was set at 20 percent until 2020 and at only 22 percent until 2030.

Schröder once again employed a strategy of polarization. He first presented the reform plan with little prior input from the party. He then pushed it through the SPD parliamentary party and the SPD Executive Committee against massive opposition from his critics. The protracted decision-making processes in the parliamentary party and the Executive Committee reveal the power struggles within the SPD. Riester's pension reform plan was first vetoed in both bodies, but then endorsed at the next meeting. In both cases, there was a simple reason for the initial veto: the absence of the key modernizers. Peter Struck, the Schröder loyalist, was unable to attend the June meeting of the SPD parliamentary party due to illness. Rudolf Dreßler, the staunchest defender of the SPD's social policy inheritance, chaired the meeting in place of Struck and was able to block the passage of Riester's proposal in the parliamentary party, if only for a short while. The June meeting of the SPD Executive Committee followed a similar decision-making pattern. Schröder was absent because he was attending the meeting of the European Council. Therefore, the supporters of the old alternative had the power to veto Schröder's pension reform proposal. But Schröder and Struck were able to overcome the resistance within the SPD. On July 3, 2000, the SPD Executive Committee approved Riester's reform plan in a narrow and restricted vote (SPD 2000). Out of 45 committee members, only 19 voted yes. The combined number of abstentions and no-votes was therefore larger than the number of yes-votes. As the chair of the meeting, Schröder did not permit any votes concerning amendments. The following day, the almost 300 members of the SPD parliamentary party voted under Struck's chairmanship with a majority of only 70 percent for the government's pension reform plan.

Schröder's strategy had again been a success, even if the party remained divided. Because of the decisions taken in July 2000, Schröder's new pension reform alternative became official party policy. Despite strong resistance from traditionalists within the SPD, Schröder had removed the old alternative from the menu of options. Between July 2000 and January 2001, when the Old-Age Provision Act was passed, there was no debate about the direction of SPD pension policy anymore. The objectives to stabilize contribution rates at 20 percent and to introduce a private pension tier became non-contestable. For the SPD left wing, the two options left were either to veto the reform bill in the Bundestag or to bargain with Schröder about some of the details of the legislation while accepting the wholesale redefinition of the Social Democratic pension reform alternative.

Ideational change in German Social Democracy

The majoritarian endorsement of Riester's reform concept by the SPD Executive Committee and the SPD parliamentary party was the tipping point for the change in ideas. After the decisions about the fundamentals had been made, it did not take long to build a new pension policy consensus in the SPD. In September 2000, Riester presented the draft law of the Old-Age Provision Act (Bundesministerium für Arbeit und Sozialordnung 2000a). By that time, Schröder had generated a critical amount of support within the SPD. The supporters of the old alternative had become a minority and now found themselves politically isolated. In summer 2000, the SPD left wing reorganized itself and made a strategy shift from obstruction to negotiation, marking the beginning of the left-wing's change in ideas.

In November 2000, the approval of Riester's draft law by the SPD parliamentary party went smoothly. Out of almost 300 members, there were only about 10 votes against Riester's plan and about 10 abstentions. By comparison, a few months earlier, almost a third of the SPD Bundestag members had voted against it or had abstained. The positive reaction to Riester's draft law contrasts sharply with the hostile reaction to the government's original proposal in June 1999. The broad agreement in the parliamentary party evidences that a consensus had been created in the SPD regarding the long-term stabilization of contribution rates at the 20 percent level. The trade unions also converged on this position. At a summit with the bosses of the large trade unions, Schröder and Riester reached an agreement with the union movement. The agreement of December 17, 2000, stated that the trade unions support the goal to stabilize contribution rates at the level specified by the government. The unions' backing of the Schröder plans further strengthened the supporting stance of the SPD left wing.

The Chancellor's openness regarding some of the details of the legislation helped Schröder win the active support of both the left wing and the unions for the key features of his pension reform, stable contributions and private pensions. These concessions were negotiated by Struck, the chairman of the parliamentary party. First, Schröder had to give up his plan to avoid blame by targeting the benefit cutbacks on the younger generations while sparing the current generation of pensioners.[12] By applying the cuts to all generations, it became possible to make the long-term reduction of pension benefits less radical, while achieving a similar amount of expenditure cutbacks. The level of benefits was reduced from 70 to 64 percent, not to 61 percent. Second, the unions received more generous tax-incentives for occupational pension plans. Shortly before Christmas 2000, in a vote on the revised version of Riester's draft law, the SPD parliamentary party was even more highly united than in November 2000. There were only 5 no-votes and 8 abstentions. The stage for the passage of the Old-Age Provision Act in January 2001 was set.

The SPD parliamentary party, the SPD left wing and the trade unions were enthusiastic about the concessions they had negotiated with Schröder, although these were small when compared with the large-scale change in pension policy brought about by the Old-Age Provision Act. In the end, there seemed to be only winners. Struck claimed credit for getting Schröder to make concessions and was proud to say that the SPD parliamentary party plays 'a special role'. Nahles, the left-wing's leader, praised the Old-Age Provision Act as a 'success for the SPD left wing' and as 'a truly Social Democratic pension reform' (Nahles 2001: 4). The real winner, however, was Gerhard Schröder. Over the course of a year and a half, the chancellor had redefined the very meaning of 'truly Social Democratic'. The chancellor's strategy to polarize the SPD turned out to be a complete success.

Power, ideas and policy change

The fact that the left wing claimed credit for the partial privatization of the German pension system leaves no doubt as to the SPD's profound change of ideas. Moreover, at the 2001 party congress in Nuremburg, the 500 delegates voted almost unanimously for the motion of the party leadership that contained the new guiding principles of Social Democratic pension policy. It seems to be a paradox that Schröder's initiative to modernize the SPD was successful. The strong Social Democratic inheritance in pension policy put a premium on the guarantee of income-replacing pensions. But under Schröder's leadership, stable contribution rates became the overriding concern in SPD pension policy. This commitment requires that the pension benefit level varies according to available revenue. It made the guarantee of a given level of benefits sufficient to replace an employee's income unfeasible. Up until the late 1990s, a variable pension benefit level would have been simply unimaginable for the Social Democrats. How do we explain this paradox? How did Schröder turn his ideas into policies? In this chapter, I showed that it was Schröder's strategy of polarization that produced a change of ideas about pension policy in the SPD. By polarizing the party, the chancellor managed to remove the SPD's long-established alternative in pension policy from the menu of options. The change of ideas made the passage of the Old-Age Provision Act possible and was the key to Schröder's modernization of the SPD.

The 2001 pension reform of the Schröder government is an excellent case for the study of the relationship between power and changes in ideas. In the literature on ideas, the role of power in policy change is often downplayed.[13] Instead, ideational scholars usually emphasize the appeal of new ideas and the slow process of persuasion (Heclo 1974; Kingdon 1984; Majone 1989). Heclo argues that changes in the relationships of power are an insufficient explanation for changes in policy. The findings of Heclo's study on *Modern Social Politics* are that:

> a great deal of policy development – its creation, alteration, or redirection – has been settled prior to or outside of substantial exercises of power. In the end, when analysis, deliberation, and persuasion failed to reach agreement . . . political power has been resorted to and sometimes proven decisive.
>
> (Heclo 1974: 306)

Heclo is correct in pointing out that policy change is not the direct outcome of exercises of power. Strong policy inheritance and institutional path-dependence prevent governments from imposing major policy change. But the literature on ideas tends to overlook the causal significance of power in redefining policy alternatives and changing the ideas of political actors. I argue that persuasion is only one force that drives ideational change. In some cases, it plays an even negligible role. The analysis provided in this chapter shows that polarization is the second force that produces changes in ideas. In Schröder's case, polarization was the dominant mode of action.

There are three fundamental differences between these two strategies of ideational change. First, persuasion is a two-way interchange, while polarization is not: the new guiding policy principles are set from the beginning, and remain fixed throughout the process of modernization. Second, persuasion leads to the gradual substitution of the old policy alternative with a new one. By contrast, polarization means the abrupt removal of the old alternative. Third, the force of persuasion comes from the appeal of new ideas, while the force of polarization depends on the political power that modernizers have. Therefore, polarization is a risky strategy. If modernizers are not powerful enough, the attempt to change ideas by means of a strategy of polarization backfires. Weak challenges tend to reinforce existing policy alternatives instead of redefining them. Strong challenges, however, can overcome the deadweight of ideas, as Schröder's modernization of SPD pension policy shows.

The author would like to thank Karen Anderson, Giuliano Bonoli, Traute Meyer, Bruno Palier, Martin Powell and Martin Schludi for their comments, and Katy Hsieh and Jeanne Rasata for language corrections.

Notes

1 In September 1998, the SPD became the largest party in the Bundestag by receiving 40.9 percent of the vote and about 45 percent of the seats. Compared to 1994, it increased its vote share by 4.5 percent. Kohl's Christian Democrats, by contrast, lost a devastating 6.4 percentage points. For the CDU/CSU, it was the worst showing since the first federal election in 1949.

2 In September 2002, the SPD and the CDU/CSU each received 38.5 percent of the vote, the Greens 8.6 percent and the FDP 7.4 percent. Compared to 1998, the CDU/CSU regained 3.3 percentage points, primarily because of the CSU's strong showing in Bavaria, the home state of the Conservative's candidate for chancellor. This election result led to a very narrow majority of the SPD/Green coalition in the Bundestag. However, gains in regional elections in January 2003 by the CDU/ CSU mean that they can block Schröder's plans in the Bundersrat.

3 My analysis is based on numerous interviews with policymakers, many published documents and materials as well as on a large number of newspaper reports published in the Frankfurter Allgemeine Zeitung, Süddeutsche Zeitung and Frankfurter Rundschau. References for the newspaper reports used in this chapter are available from the author upon request (e-mail: hering@jhu.edu).

4 The SPD had major losses in three Länder. In the Saarland, the SPD was replaced by a CDU government. In Thuringia, the SPD was voted out of the governing coalition, and the CDU was able to form a single-party government. In Brandenburg, the election ended the SPD's single-party government. It had to enter a coalition with the CDU. The local elections in the state of North Rhine-Westphalia was a political earthquake for the SPD. The party lost majorities in many major cities of the Ruhr region, the heartland of German Social Democracy.

5 For an overview of the static nature of SPD social policy during its oppositional years, see Gohr (2001).

6 Interview with Rudolf Dreßler, Deutschlandfunk, 29 July 2000

7 Income replacement has been the most important guiding principle of post-war German pension policy. It means that pension benefit levels should enable a retired employee to maintain his standard of living achieved during his working life.

8 Interview with Gerhard Schröder, *Der Spiegel*, May 11, 1998; Associated Press Worldstream – German, 13 May 1997

9 The SPD's new center of decision-making consisted of Schröder, Müntefering, Steinmeier, Struck and Uwe-Karsten Heye, the chancellor's spokesperson.

10 Schröder's statement at the ÖTV congress gave rise to the term 'basta chancellor'. See Frankfurter Allgemeine Zeitung, 6 November 2000.
11 Several of the SPD's regional organizations passed resolutions against Schröder's pension reform plans, including Western Westphalia, by far the largest and most important SPD region.
12 On the strategy of policymakers to 'grandfather' in current beneficiaries, and on other blame-avoiding strategies, see Weaver (1986).
13 For a different view that conceptualizes ideas as weapons in political struggles, see Blyth (2002, Ch. 2).

References

Bannas, G. (1999) 'Die Sozialdemokraten haben die Seele der Partei verloren, doch die Zeit für Trauerarbeit ist schon vorbei', *Frankfurter Allgemeine Zeitung*, 18 March.

Bannas, G. (2000) 'Die Zwischenbilanz sollte bloss nicht von Übermut und Selbstzufriedenheit strotzen', *Frankfurter Allgemeine Zeitung*, 26 July.

Blair, T. and Schröder, G. (1999) 'Europe: The Third Way/Die neue Mitte', manuscript, (June), London: Labour Party.

Blyth, M. (2002) *Great Transformations: Economic Ideas and Institutional Change in the Twentieth Century*, Cambridge: Cambridge University Press.

Bundesministerium für Arbeit und Sozialordnung (1999) 'Eckpunkte für eine neue Altersversorgung', Manuscript, Bonn, 18 June.

Bundesministerium für Arbeit und Sozialordnung (2000a) 'Diskussionsentwurf zur Reform der gesetzlichen Rentenversicherung und zur Förderung des Aufbaus eines kapitalgedeckten Vermögens zur Altersvorsorge (Altersvermögensaufbaugesetz)', Manuscript, Berlin, 22 September.

Bundesministerium für Arbeit und Sozialordnung (2000b) 'Rentenreform 2000: Ein mutiger Schritt zu mehr Sicherheit', *Sozialpolitische Informationen Spezial* 34 (5).

Bundesregierung (1999) 'Deutschland erneuern: Zukunftsprogramm zur Sicherung von Arbeit, Wachstum und sozialer Stabilität', Berlin, 23 June.

Deutscher Bundestag (1997) 'Antrag der SPD Fraktion: Strukturreform statt Leistungskürzungen (Drucksache 13/8032)', 24 June.

Dreßler, R., Junker, K. and Mikfeld, B. (1999) 'Berliner Erklärung: Für eine Modernisierung der Sozialdemokratie', manuscript, Berlin, 28 November.

Gohr, A. (2001) 'Eine Sozialstaatspartei in der Opposition: Die Sozialpolitik der SPD in den 80er Jahren', in M. G. Schmidt (ed.), *Wohlfahrtsstaatliche Politik: Institutionen, politischer Prozess und Leistungsprofil*, Opladen: Leske + Budrich, 262–93.

Heclo, H. (1974) *Modern Social Politics in Britain and Sweden*, New Haven: Yale University Press.

Hombach, B. (1998) *Aufbruch: Die Politik der Neuen Mitte*, Munich: Econ.

Katz, R. S. (1997) *Democracy and Elections*, Oxford: Oxford University Press.

Kingdon, J. W. (1984) *Agendas, Alternatives, and Public Policies*, New York: Harper Collins.

Koalitionsarbeitsgruppe SPD und Bündnis 90/Die Grünen (2000) 'Deutschland erneuern: Rentenreform 2000', manuscript, 30 May.

Lafontaine, O. (1999) *Das Herz schlägt links*, Munich: Econ.

Majone, G. (1989) *Evidence, Argument and Persuasion in the Policy Process*, New Haven: Yale University Press.

Meng, R. 1999. Rasiert ist Riester auf jeden Fall: Der Arbeitsminister, das Rentenkonzept und die SPD. *Frankfurter Rundschau*, 19 June.

Nahles, A. (2000) 'Berlin-Erklärung: Zur Zukunft der Parteilinken', manuscript, Berlin, 16 June.

Nahles, A. (2001) 'Rentendiskussion endet mit Erfolg für die SPD-Linke', manuscript, (January).

SPD (1997a) 'Solidarität zwischen Alt und Jung: Sozialbeiträge stabilisieren, Renten sichern (Beschluss des Parteitags der SPD)', Hanover, 4 December.

SPD (1997b) 'Strukturreform statt Leistungskürzungen: Vorschläge der Alterssicherungskommission der SPD', Bonn, 17 July 1997.

SPD (1998) 'Arbeit, Innovation und Gerechtigkeit: SPD-Programm für die Bundestagswahl 1998 (Beschluss des ausserordentlichen Parteitags der SPD)', Leipzig, 17 April.

SPD (2000) 'Zur Rentenreform 2000 (Beschluss des Parteivorstands der SPD)', 3 July.

SPD (2001a) 'Sicherheit im Wandel (Beschluss des Parteitags der SPD)', Nuremburg, 19–22 November.

SPD (2001b) 'Wegmarken für ein neues Grundsatzprogramm: Sozialdemokratische Vorstellungen zur nachhaltigen Gestaltung der globalen Epoche (Zwischenbericht der Grundsatzprogrammkommission an den Parteitag der SPD)', Nuremburg, 19–22 November.

SPD (2002) 'Erneuerung und Zusammenhalt: Regierungsprogramm 2002–2006 (Beschluss des Ausserordentlichen Parteitags der SPD)', Berlin, 2 June, 2002.

SPD and Bündnis 90/Die Grünen (1998) 'Aufbruch und Erneuerung – Deutschlands Weg ins 21. Jahrhundert: Koalitionsvereinbarung zwischen der Sozialdemokratischen Partei Deutschlands und Bündnis 90/Die Grünen', manuscript, Bonn, 21 October.

Weaver, R. K. (1986) 'The Politics of Blame Avoidance', *Journal of Public Policy* 6 (4): 371–98.

7 The social and employment policies of the Jospin Government

Ben Clift

Introduction

This chapter assesses the discourse, the values, and the social and employment policy goals and instruments of the Jospin Government, exploring the viability of *Réalisme de Gauche* as a progressive political project. At the level of discourse and values, *Réalisme de Gauche* is built upon non neo-liberal economic foundations. The questioning of the received neo-liberal economic wisdom by the Parti Socialiste (PS) engendered a re-evaluation of the degree of *volontarisme* (policy or state activism) possible in today's international economic context. Rejecting accommodation with neo-liberal orthodoxy on the assumption that 'there is no alternative', there is an insistence upon the existence of room to manoeuvre, a concept central to *Réalisme de Gauche.*

Commentators 'read' the Jospin Government in different ways, depending on which policy areas they focus upon. Some point to almost Blairite 'modernisation' in the areas of privatisation, public–private partnerships employee saving schemes (Bouvet and Michel 2001), whilst others point to a distinctive 'left' redistributive agenda in social policy (Levy 2000, 2001, a, b). I argue here and elsewhere (Clift 2001) that Jospin's a relatively coherent and distinctive 'model' of Social Democracy, combining new ('employment centred') social policy thinking, constrained redistributive neo-Keynesianism, and activist state orchestrated employment policies.

Jospin's challenging of the dominant economic orthodoxy, and its corollary, the changing diagnosis of the economic problem, inform a particular set of employment and social policies. The Jospin Government's neo-Keynesianism dovetails with the insistence upon the 'active state'. Jospin asserts, 'we do not give in to the fatalistic idea that the neo-liberal capitalist model is the only one available. On the contrary, we can shape the world according to our values' (Jospin 1999: 10). Equality, social justice, and an active state are the values most consistently emphasized within the PS. Globalisation, according to Jospin, 'favours global growth, but is accompanied by growing of inequalities ... it liberates energies, but also negative forces which must be mastered'(2001: 33–4). Regulation is, Jospin argues, the 'political globalisation' required in this new context; 'wherever there is a risk that only the law of the strongest may apply, or where private interests threaten the general interest, or where the search for short term profit undermines social justice and damages the environment, States must define the "rules of the game"'(2001: 36).

We could, Jospin notes, 'let the supposedly natural laws of economics guide the evolution of our societies, and in so doing, abdicate our political responsibilities. On the contrary, we could seek to re-orient the forces at work in the globalisation of economic activity' (2001: 44). Whilst favouring the latter, nevertheless the abandonment of the Mitterrand experiment in 1983 enforced upon French Socialists recognition of external constraints and reduced room to manoeuvre in an international economic order where the 'embedded liberalism' of the Bretton Woods had ceased to insulate national economies (Hall 1986; Lordon 1998). The 'realism' and pragmatism that underpins the political economy of the Jospin Government (notably in its 'consolidation' of public finances) is testament to the integration of these 'limits of the possible' into its frame of reference.

Shifting the policy paradigm: from *Pensée Unique* to *Réalisme de Gauche*

In 1983, the *dirigiste* alternative was rejected in favour of an 'Ordo-liberal' policy paradigm, accepting EMS conditions for revaluation, and a German-influenced conception of sound policy and monetary policy making institutions. This engendered a paradigm shift of priorities in macroeconomic policy, relegating full employment to a distant future aspiration, and promoting tackling inflation to priority number one (see Lordon 1998).

The new hierarchy of priorities owed a good deal more to the (neo-liberal) new classical school than it did to Keynesian insights into the role of the state in maximising the level of employment within the economy. Competitive disinflation, as the new policy became known, was to an extent a reflection of changed international political economic realities. However, the new direction also reflected the singular reading of the implications of such changed realities by an elite in the capture of the *pensée unique*, the neo-liberal economic orthodoxy in its French articulation.

The flaws of competitive disinflation are demonstrated by its impact on French economy and society in the 15 years following the U-turn. Austerity dampened demand, meanwhile persistent high unemployment produced 'hysteresis' effects, with low activity and slow capital accumulation triggering bankruptcies, and destroying productive capacity. The market medicine was killing the patient. 'The strategy followed has been, quite simply, to achieve disinflation and increased competitiveness through higher unemployment' (Fitoussi *et al.* 1993: 18; Fitoussi 1995; see also Lordon 1998). The failure of the Bérégovoy government, like those before it, to deliver on its pledge to reduce unemployment, and the crushing PS defeat of 1993, led to a re-evaluation of Socialist economic strategy. Too much, it was felt, had been sacrificed at the altar of economic orthodoxy, with resultant gains in financial credibility and profitability, but not jobs.

The Bourget Conference text, written just months after the 1993 defeat, observes of the 1983 U-turn that; 'this choice did not instigate an authentic economic policy debate concerning the use of the available room to manoeuvre.'[1] The influence of neo-liberal economists (both supply-siders and monetarists) over what Moscovici titles the 'social-liberalism' of 1988–93, is, in retrospect, deemed questionable (1997: 43–4). Moscovici offers a periodisation of PS economic policy that applauded the measures of 1983–6 and 1988–91, but asserted that the policy of competitive disinflation was unnecessarily prolonged at great social cost. This forms the basis of the call to break with the orthodoxy of economic management.

Certain parameters for action, such as a commitment to monetary stability, are accepted, given the context of an interdependent and relatively open economy and deregulated financial markets. However, the precise location of the limits of the possible is contested. The need to be seen to be credible by investors and speculators does not rule out policy activism. Thus questioning of the dominant economic orthodoxy informs the philosophical foundation of the new strategy; an insistence upon the existence of *marges de manoeuvre*, and a belief that all the means of tackling unemployment have not yet been explored.

With the calling into question of competitive disinflation came also the questioning of its theoretical foundations, and the canon from which they are drawn. Indeed, within the neo-classical world-view, the *new* diagnosis of France's economic problem – a structural insufficiency of demand – is a theoretical impossibility. If Say's Law is to be believed, supply calls forth demand. The call for the use of automatic stabilisers to give a counter cyclical edge to budgetary policy betrays the renewed influence of economic thought of broadly Keynesian origin within the PS.

Although remaining within the framework of a commitment to macroeconomic stability, emphasis is placed upon 'solvent' levels of demand, mass consumption, and higher salaries. The increase in capital's share of added value, at the expense of labour that took place in the 1980s and early 1990s is seen as one cause of France's structural insufficiency of demand. This explains the commitment to *limited* redistribution from capital to labour, particularly towards those lower earners with a higher propensity to spend, albeit tempered by an appreciation of the importance of the profitability and competitiveness of firms. Whilst careful to point out that this is *not* a return to old-style Keynesian policies, the different ideological suppositions under-pinning this different view of the economy are explicitly highlighted (Moscovici 1997: 59–60).

Jospin rejects 'finding a middle way between Social Democracy and neo-liberalism'. The idea of capitalism as, 'a force that moves, but does not know where it is going' informs the view that, 'the regulation of capitalism is essential and requires an active state' (Jospin 1999: 4, 8, 7). The French state, institutionalising the values of solidarity, co-operation and inclusion should act, it is argued, as a counterweight to the market to promote social cohesion. Greater efficiency is called for in state redistribution policies, necessitating fundamental reform of the tax system 'to increase social justice, ceasing to privilege capital in order to favour labour, and to preserve solidarity' (Parti Socialiste 1996: 19). Thus *Réalisme de Gauche* reconciles an enduring *dirigiste* dimension with growing enthusiasm for the market. As Jospin notes, 'the concept of *volontarisme* (or an active state) does not set up the state in opposition to the market, but instead creates a new alliance between the two' (1999: 11). At the heart of *Réalisme de Gauche* is a more critical engagement with neo-liberal economic orthodoxy, and an unequivocal attachment to a recognisably Social Democratic role for state.

The social and employment policies of the Jospin Government

Despite the constraints of an increasingly open economy, the Jospin Government has sought to 'rehabilitate' activist economic policy. A broadly Keynesian rationale[2] underpins stimulation of purchasing power to increase the growth potential of the French economy, facilitating a boost in consumption and investment. This informs a set of redistributive fiscal measures, targeted social exclusion measures, and an activist employment strategy, all framed in egalitarian terms. The Jospin Government's redistribution, couched in republican discourse, continues to target both the working and the non-working poor. A recurrent guiding principle is, as Jospin's advisor Muet puts it, 'recasting the social contract of the work based society and restoring equality as one of its fundamental components' (2000: 9). The following three sections analyse the Jospin Government's policy record to establish degree to which these values and this discourse has fed through into actual policy outcomes. The first sets out the macroeconomic policy context. The second examines social policy measures, and the third focuses on employment policy.

Macro policy: 'chastened Keynesianism'[3]

The Jospin Government prioritises 'redistribution in favour of employment'. This involves fiscal redistribution in favour of lower earners to raise purchasing power, including tax reductions increasing households' disposable income. The Government actively advocates growth through expansion of demand, and the redistributing of added value in favour of salaried workers, since 1997 will, it is argued, further boost the 'dynamic' of purchasing power (Ministère des Finances 2001: 5). The Jospin Government emphasises the role of automatic stabilisers, and is keenly aware of the need to redistribute to lower income brackets with a higher propensity to spend as a means of keeping demand buoyant.[4] As Muet notes, 'macroeconomic policies are essential and play a key role in stimulating growth and jobs ... structural policies are only efficient in a context of rising demand. It is pointless to tackle unemployment with structural policies alone' (Muet 2000: 10).

Income and other tax cuts under Jospin disproportionately favoured low and non-earners.[5] Whilst the reorganisation of income tax 2000–03, included a reduction in income tax rates for all income bands – including the highest, the Jospin Government *has* made income tax more progressive, with the lightening of the load targeted particularly at the lower brackets (Ministère des Finances 2001: 21–2).[6] Taxes on small and medium-sized firms have also been reduced, with targeted tax-breaks introduced to boost job creation. Illustrating the pragmatism and commitment to macroeconomic stability of the Jospin Government, much of the redistributive reform has been achieved through fiscal 'cost-shuffling'. The 1998 budget, for example, involved a 'revenue neutral reform that shifted the burden from low-income groups to high-income groups (leaving business unaffected)' (Levy 2000: 340). Thus, redistributive commitments and egalitarian aspirations are tempered by 'realist' considerations, 'redistribution does not override other considerations ... for the fruits of economic growth to be redistributed, there must first be growth.' Such fruits have permitted tax cuts across the board. That said, progressive fiscal policy is constrained, not least because, 'in the new global market we must ... ensure that our production base is competitive' (Jospin 1999: 11).

The Jospin Government is best conceived as 'reluctantly post-Keynesian'. Their 'post-Keynesianism' owes more to the constraints of the Growth and Stability Pact given membership of the Euro than to a changed analysis of the economy. Even here, the Jospin Government seeks to explore any 'room to manoeuvre' created by flexible interpretation of the 'Growth and Stability' pact,[7] benignly viewed as a credibility-bolstering 'hedging' rather than a disciplinary 'binding' mechanism (Dyson 1999: 202). Furthermore, the 'soft' Euro and ECB interest rate decisions since 1999 have proved almost entirely consistent with the Plural Left Government's growth-oriented macroeconomic policy preferences.

Nevertheless, the 'external constraint' of the global political economic context engenders close attention to the *grands equilibres* of the French economy. Thus the 'medium term consolidation of the public finances' (moves towards budget balancing) remains a central objective. This is understood to necessitate public deficit reduction (down from 3.5 per cent of GDP in 1997 to 1.4 per cent in 2002), a reduction of public spending as a proportion of GDP (from 55 0 per cent in 1999 to 52.3 per cent in 2001), and a reduction of debt as a proportion of GDP (59.3 per cent of GDP in 1997, down to 56.3 per cent in 2002) (Ministère des Finances 2001: 6, 113). Such 'consolidation' does not mean the Jospin Government has ceased to be Social Democratic, or has 'swallowed' neo-liberalism. Rather, as Dyson notes, the French Socialists 'sought to draw a line between embracing rules of "sound" public finance and money and taking on the whole apparatus of neo-liberal and monetarist policy discourse' (1999: 202). That said, such budgetary constraints do have implications for the levels of redistribution achievable through Jospin's social policies targeted at the poorest groups in French society.

Social policy measures

A number of significant evolutions in the broad area of social policy have occurred under the Jospin Government. Jospin's egalitarian rhetoric, although not always matched by policy outcomes, should be set against the backdrop of French welfare provision that has sustained an ever-growing source of redistribution in terms of social welfare. France's welfare state is the largest outside Scandinavia. Social security spending was 30 per cent of GDP in 1995 (Levy 2001, 199). Household social welfare revenues have seen a trend increase, from 15 per cent of household budgets in 1960, to 27 per cent by 1998. (Gutman and Loyer 1998). The Jospin Government's welfare reforms seek to achieve *redistribution* to the poorest groups in society, but also has an employment policy dimension, with the Jospin Government pursuing 'employment centred social policy' *à la Française* (see later, and Clift 2001) is part of a wider aim to lower labour costs by reducing social security contributions, since costly social insurance inhibits job creation by increasing the cost, in particular, of low-skilled labour (Palier 2000).

Yet the Jospin Government's attempts to redistribute in favour of the poor is not easy to reconcile to a complex and historically social insurance based French welfare state that has tended to prioritise contribution-based income maintenance above universalistic redistribution (Palier 2000). The logic of the (limited) restructuring undertaken seeks to shift French *droits acquis* – or social rights – away from a 'Christian democratic' notion of entitlement based upon salary-linked contribution record, and towards a 'a logic of national solidarity' notion of social security as a right of each individual as a citizen (Gutman and Loyer 1998: 4–5). Accordingly such universal' (not contribution dependent, but often means-tested) benefits are funded increasingly through progressive general taxation.

Contribution Sociale Généralisée (CSG)

First introduced by the Rocard Government in 1991, reform to and augmentation of the role of the *Contribution Sociale Généralisée* (CSG) have been conspicuous mechanisms of the Jospin Government's redistributive agenda. This is part of the shift in the logic of welfare funding noted above. The CSG is *general* taxation applied to *all* earnings, levied on financial and capital revenues, and welfare benefits, as well as salaries. This shifting of the burden away from salary contributions to capital revenues is significant in the context of non-wage revenues becoming a more significant part of the household budget in the wake of the growth of French financial markets. More than 11 per cent of household income is currently derived from capital or property revenues (Gutman and Loyer 1998: 4).

There is some continuity with previous administrations. The Balladur and Juppé governments increased the role of the CSG, incrementally moving towards a more tax-financed welfare model. However, the Left and Right in France have had differing approaches to the *distributive effects* of CSG increases. The Left have used it as a means of shifting the burden from low-income to high income groups (Levy 2001a). The right, when augmenting the CSG, introduced two highly regressive dimensions, firstly by making new increments of the CSG tax-deductable, and secondly, the Balladur Government's increases in CSG were not off-set by reductions in other social charges (such as payroll taxes). Thus upshot of this was that, 'the 1993 (CSG) reform ultimately penalised low salaries more than higher salaries' (Gutman and Loyer 1998: 11).

The Jospin Government's significant augmenting of the CSG, however, has been underpinned by a different logic. Firstly, the additional increment was *non*-deductible (Levy 2001b: 282). This is highly significant because making the CSG increase non-deductible greatly increases its redistributive effects. Indeed, Gutman and Loyer show how a deductible CSG hike can be a highly regressive form of taxation (1998: 9–14). Secondly, it was offset by a shift in social charges. The 1998 budget increased the CSG from 3.4 per cent to 7.5 per cent, and at the same time decreased workers contributions to health insurance from 5.5 per cent to 0.75 per cent. According to Levy, 'although the fiscal yield was unchanged, the reform provided the average worker with a 1.1 per cent gain in purchasing power; conversely it added to the tax bill of those (primarily, the affluent) who derive earnings from property or capital' (2000: 340).

The CSG now contributes more to the French states coffers than does income tax (Gutman and Loyer 1998: 12–13). The increasing significance of the CSG to French welfare funding meant that, by 1999, the CSG provided more than 20 per cent of all social protection resources (Palier 2000, 130). Under the Jospin Government, the CSG not only became a more central feature of French welfare funding, but more progressive, too. The 2000–03 tax reforms envisaged reducing the CSG for low earners, exempting those on the minimum wage from the CSG by 2003.

Couverture Maladie Universelle (CMU)

The shifting of healthcare funding under the auspices CSG increase noted above, combined with the alleviation of healthcare contributions, created the conditions for citizen's rights based healthcare provision. One of the Jospin Government's biggest welfare achievement has been the establishment of universal health cover – *couverture maladie universelle* (CMU). The initial genus of this policy was contained in a commitment by the Juppé Government in 1995 to offer public health insurance to the 200,000 French citizens who have none to make the French healthcare system fairer. The Jospin Government has gone considerably further than Juppé, however. Not only has access to public health insurance been granted to those previously excluded, but also, Jospin's Government has addressed the problems of access to healthcare for those covered by public health insurance.

The 30 per cent of healthcare expenses that, under the French system, are subject to 'co-payment' (by the patient) can be prohibitively expensive. Roughly 85 per cent of French citizens have additional cover to pay these expenses. The disadvantaged 15 per cent of the population who do not enjoy insurance cover have been effectively excluded from all but the most urgent of treatments by the cost. Furthermore the trend increase in these healthcare costs was effectively excluding more and more lower income groups from health cover. Palier (2002: 252) notes charts a 'progressive reduction of social cover offered by the health assurance regimes, both in terms of numbers of people reimbursed, and amounts reimbursed' To counter this shortcoming, the Jospin Government provided 'free supplementary health insurance on a means-tested basis to an estimated 6 million people (those living on less than 3,500 francs per month for a single individual, 7,700 francs for a family of four)' (Levy 2001b: 198).

According to the Employment and social affairs ministry, 1.2 million people were benefiting from the CMU for their basic cover, roughly 2 per cent of the French population (Palier 2002: 252). Whilst this is a considerable achievement, the conception of universality underpinning the move must be distinguished from Esping-Andersen's 'Social Democratic' universalistic welfare model. The supplementary health cover is universal in the sense of being accessible to whoever needs it, with no reference to contribution record, but access is on a *means tested* basis. This means-tested dimension may, in time, compromise the legitimacy of a funding regime where those who pay (through the higher CSG) are not, on the whole, those who benefit. This contrasts with the logic of welfare programmes where contribution is seen as a forward payment on future services.

Family allowance reforms

Precisely such a dilemma of legitimacy has been faced by the Jospin Government in its attempts to render family allowance in France more redistributive towards poorer families. The logic underpinning family allowance in France has shifted in the last 20 years from a population-growth oriented policy towards redistribution from wealthy to poor (Levy 2001b: 197). In 1998, Jospin took the most significant leap to date in this direction by means-testing family allowances, aiming to exclude affluent families and focus limited resources upon the needy. Family allowances were eliminated for household incomes over 350,000 francs, and a 'nanny tax' introduced halving tax deduction for families who hire domestic child care.

However, in the wake of criticism from pro-family groups, and more generally from French citizens who saw family allowances as a citizenship right, the Government restored the benefit. In doing so, the Government 'retrieved the increased expenditure from the wealthy by reducing the maximum child income tax credit from 16, 380 francs to 11,000 francs' (Levy 2001a: 272). Thus the Jospin Government achieved, at the second attempt, its objective, by of increasing the tax burden of wealthier families rather than redirecting state resources towards more needy families.

Minimum incomes and minimum wage

The *Revenu Minimum d'Insertion* (RMI), a minimum income guarantee, was introduced by Rocard in 1988 to 'catch' those who slipped through the net of the entitlement-based welfare provision in France. It is a means-tested benefit, but non-contributory, and in that sense 'universal'. Eligibility is thus based on that 'logic of national solidarity', underpinned by the notion of social security as a right of each individual as a citizen. That said, the RMI involves a commitment on behalf of the recipient to 'reinsertion' (into society) activities such as re-training or job seeking. Initially envisaged to cover 300,000–400,000 people, by December 1998 1,112,108 people were claiming it. Including spouses and children affected, 2,117,000 people were covered by RMI, or 3.5 per cent of the French population. Furthermore, this is one of eight minimum income guarantees, covering 3.3 million households, or 10 per cent of the French population (Palier 2000: 129–30).

These highly significant social minima thus became a powerful tool for targeting those groups the Jospin Government most sought to help. In December 1998, the RMI and two similar minimum income guarantees were raised by 3 per cent, backdated a year. Such targeted redistributing of wealth to low and non-earners hinted at the 'neo-Keynesianism' of *Réalisme de gauche.* These state taxation financed, means-tested benefits which aim to tackle social exclusion are further evidence of a changing logic underpinning French welfare provision.

The redistribution and the consumption boost were given a further impetus by the Jospin Government's raising the SMIC (minimum wage) by 4 per cent (well above the rate of inflation) on entering office. However, the redistributive urges were kept within quite tight limits in the face of macroeconomic constraints. Indeed, Jospin's pragmatic realism held back SMIC increases to the legal minimum of 3.2 per cent in 1999 and 2000, despite strong economic growth. This is testament to the 'chastening' of Keynesian aspirations. The lower levels of minimum income guarantees relative to contribution-based benefits generated criticism of the Jospin Government (from both within and outside the Socialist Party) surrounded fears of a two-tier welfare system, with the 'included' workforce enjoying contribution-based benefits, whilst an excluded and insecure workforce relied on less-generous means-tested benefits. Significantly, the first commitment of the post-Jospin PS was to bolder increases in the minimum wage, and to boosting purchasing power of the poorest in society.

Pension Funds à la Française?

Pension reform has proved an intractable social policy problem, given the fragmented nature of the French pension system, the difficulty of achieving consensus between social partners[8] (who govern the numerous schemes) and the government, and the attachment of the French populace to cherished *droits acquis*. The expansive use of early retirement as a palliative to painful economic restructuring in the early 1980s has only exacerbated the pressure the French pension system is under (Levy 2000). Little has been achieved by the Jospin Government with regard to curtailing replacement rates or entitlements, or increasing contribution periods to address the shortfalls predicted to hit French public sector pension funds imminently (Palier 2002: 226–45).

In part to off-set this stasis, and testament to the pragmatism and eclectic ideological composition of French socialism, Fabius introduced the *épargne salariale* (employee savings) scheme in Spring 2001. The scheme allows companies to set up a series of tax-exempted savings funds for their workers, and extends the scheme to groups of smaller firms whose workers were previously denied access. These private savings schemes are envisaged as a means for individuals to offset anticipated shortfalls in pension provision. Although the term 'stock option' has been eschewed to avoid unpalatable Anglo-Saxon connotations, many see the scheme as an attempt to introduce pension funds under a different name, providing a source of fresh equity for companies, and increasing the liquidity of domestic markets. The move has the potential to dramatically expand the role of the private sector in French pensions provision.

Employment policy measures

The focus of French Socialist hostility to the *pensée unique* is its conception of the relative importance of inflation and unemployment which seemed to be excessively dominated by neo-liberal 'leave it to market adjustments on the supply side' assumptions. The Jospin Government sees the state's role as the guarantor of employment, and the PS recently affirmed a strong commitment to establishing 'a society of full employment and the amelioration of the quality of employment' (Parti Socialiste 2001: 38).

Employment policy is pursued on both national and European levels. European co-operation arguably offers a viable 'response' to globalisation. Pursuit of 'public goods' at EU level is exemplified by Delors 'Euro-Keynesian' White Paper, advocating co-ordinated European economic expansion, boosting employment across the continent (Delors 1993, see also Delors 1997). The Jospin Government has, with little success, championed such reforms, and sought to institutionalise more thoroughgoing employment goals to rearticulate Keynesian insights within the process of European construction. Jospin seeks a new path to full employment, a dual-level strategy combining national level reforms with a re-orientation of the process of economic integration towards greater emphasis on employment.

> As (Jospin) is often saying, the problems of growth and unemployment are also European problems . . . that is why the strategy for fighting unemployment has two facets: a national dimension, and a European one seeking to re-orient European construction in favour of jobs and growth.
>
> (Muet 1998: 85)

The aim is for a negotiated rebalancing of the policy mix, hoping to generate co-ordinated fiscal, monetary, and structural policies across the EU which would be geared towards jobs and growth (Moscovici 1997: 58). The strategy is one of continued critical engagement from within – arguing at every turn for reorientations, such as a European Jobs and Growth Pact (at Amsterdam), a European Growth fund (at Portschach) and the embryonic formulation of a common European employment strategy (at the Luxembourg and Cardiff jobs summits) (see Clift 2003).

This provides the context for the Jospin Government's 'domestic' activist employment policy. This multi-pronged strategy involves a state regulated reduction of the working week, expanding public sector employment for urban and environmental regeneration, and the shifting incentives in labour market through fiscal policy. Most of the tax and social security reductions outlined above (in particular tax and employer social security contribution reductions on low or modest incomes) have the dual aim of assisting employment creation as well as boosting purchasing power.

Fiscal measures: reducing disincentives to hire, and making work pay

The fiscal approach has both supply and demand side dimensions, both reducing the 'cost' of work for employers, but also increase revenues from work – to bring as many as possible back into employment. Reducing the cost of work (especially non-qualified work) through social security contribution reductions and exemptions has been reinforced by tax cuts lightening load on salaries, notably progressively exempting (lower) salaries from the *taxe professionnelle.* This cost the Jospin Government 3bn euros in 2001 (Ministère des Finances 2001: 9).

Perhaps the most significant new initiative in 'making work pay' is the *Prime pour l'Emploi* (PPE), a benefit of on average 144 euros (nearly 1,000 F) for all 'modest or medium' earners, be they salaried or 'independent' (traders, artisans, the 'liberal' professions), with 8.1 m households estimated to benefit in 2001. The PPE is presented as a means of 'compensating taxes on and contributions from workers income,' which aim both to 'aid return to work' and to provide 'maintenance in work'. Illustrating how this dovetails with other macro-policy objectives, the Finance Ministry notes that 'approximately 1.22 bn euros of purchasing power were distributed under the auspices of the PPE in 2001. Furthermore, the PPE is set to double in 2002 (Ministère des Finances 2001: 24–25).

The 35-hour week

Nowhere is the state's enduring role in the job creating strategy more in evidence than in the Jospin Government's state orchestrated shift to a 35-hour week, aiming to reduce unemployment and to have a redistributive effect between labour and capital. The French law emphasises job creation, with state aid in the form of reductions in social security contributions offered to firms creating new jobs as a result of the reduction of the working week. The fixed levels of these state financial aids means that they will be relatively more generous for lower earners. (Gubian 1998; Milner 2002)

In ideological terms, the 35-hour week policy is seen as a rejection of the neo-liberal interpretation of globalisation, and its implications for structural reform of labour market institutions. The 35-hour week is seen by the PS as an integral part of its own 'model' of capitalism, which prioritises employment, which it seeks to export. (PS 1996) Such new Social Democratic employment policies indicate an activist role for the state in a strategy compatible with an open economy in a globalising world. In terms reminiscent of Scharpf (1991) and Glyn (1995) the 35-hour week involves negotiated redistribution amongst workers as a means of furthering Social Democratic egalitarian employment policy. As Fitoussi (1998, 81) puts it, 'workers have to agree to share both their jobs and their salaries with the unemployed'.

Emploi jeunes

State-led employment creation and protection schemes have become a structuring feature of the French model (OFCE 1999: 58, 68; Levy 2001b: 195–6). In the run up to the 1997 election, the PS manifesto noted 'only an engagement of public power can triumph over massive unemployment. A master budget, re-orienting public expenditures towards employment, will be a powerful lever of action'.[9] 'Active' employment policy takes a number of forms, from apprenticeships, and work placements, to state-subsidised jobs, and employers' social security exemptions. There has been an increasing propensity to target particular groups 'excluded' from the labour market, notably the long-term unemployed, the uneducated, and young people. These groups have born the brunt of increased labour market flexibility in France.

The Jospin Government insists upon the role of the state as guarantor of employment, using public sector job creation to tackle unemployment. The resources devoted to employment policy have increased markedly, reaching 4.5 per cent of GDP in 2000 (Ministère des Finances 2001, 15).[10] French Socialist's *Plan Aubry* pledged to create 350,000 public sector jobs, which, it was anticipated, would be matched by 350,000 new private sector posts. The state's role as employer within an active employment policy remains central to the PS approach. The results of the *Plan Aubry* have been encouraging, with 274,900 jobs created in the public sector by March 2001, and a total of 308,000 private sector jobs under the Plan Aubry framework.[11] The 2001 Budget includes a number of measures further expanding state employment. In all, 25,000 new *emplois-jeunes* were created in 2001, with commitments to expansion in 2002 (Ministère des Finances 2001, 9).

Other significant labour market measures have also been undertaken, such as the introduction of a further 50,000 *Contrats emploi-solidarité* (a Youth employment subsidy scheme) in 2001. The Jospin Government's anti-exclusion employment measures (TRACE and *Nouveau Départ*) are expanding; nearly a million young people come under the auspices of the Nouveau Départ scheme each year. Meanwhile the number of people covered by the TRACE scheme is set to increase by 50 per cent in 2002 (Ministère des Finances 2001: 9). As Milner (2001, 333) notes, overall these 'anti-exclusion' employment measures 'costs 50 billion francs over two and a half years, with around 200 million francs coming from the European Social Fund'.

These measures, in conjunction with a favourable macroeconomic context provided by a 'soft' euro, enabled the Jospin Government to claim conspicuous successes on the employment front between 1997 and 2001. Unemployment fell below 10 per cent this year, with a total of 2,371,300 unemployed – down from 3.2 million (12.5 per cent) when Jospin took office.[12] Jospin and the PS talk of the creation of a full employment society

– something no one on the French left has done since the dramatic policy U-turn of 1983. Although, with the dip in the growth rate in late 2001, early 2002, the unemployment rate crept up slightly, healthy growth forecasts suggest unemployment could dip below 9 per cent by the end of 2003.

Conclusions

To what extent does the experience of the Jospin Government represent a new model of Social Democracy? The Jospin Government's record in office undermines the hubris surrounding the 'end' of Social Democracy. Jospin cites, 'determined efforts to combat unemployment, through economic growth, a negotiated reduction in the working week to 35 hours and a broad-ranging plan for youth unemployment ... laws we have passed to combat all kinds of exclusion and to establish universal health cover' as evidence of his Government's 'neo-Keynesian' approach (Jospin 1999, 6). A distinctive mix of policies has been pursued. The 35-hour week, for example, betrays recognisably *dirigiste* characteristics, embedded in the French 'social model,' whilst Jospin's employment centred social policy indicates some commonalities of approach with other European Social Democrats (Vandenbroucke 1999).

A partially activist fiscal policy has achieved limited redistribution through tax reforms and 'means-tested universal' benefits. The shift in welfare funding of towards general taxation, however, does raise questions. Firstly, it remains to be seen whether other social policy areas will face the same legitimacy problems that befell the means-testing of family allowance. Secondly, tax-financed welfare relies on government fiscal policy that is increasingly pressurised by macro-economic constraints imposed by the Growth and Stability Pact. Thus, these 'universal means-tested' benefits could, Palier (2002: 402–3) argues, 'progressively lose their universality, in order to make budgetary savings, and to concentrate public money on those in real need'.

The macroeconomic policy constraints, and the Jospin Government's self-imposed limitations on redistributive urges in a bid to reduce deficits, limit the degree of purchasing power redistributed in the interests of boosting demand. France's embedded welfare and labour market institutions continue to limit wage inequality, and offer relatively high minimum standards in terms, for example, of replacement rates. Yet such generosity does not extend to means-tested benefits, and overall the levels of redistribution are not comparable to the levels automatic stabilizers and transfers that characterised the French welfare state in its 'Keynesian' post-war expansion phase (Palier 2002: 148–50). The degree to which this has been constrained by a concern for sound public finances has been a source of auto-critique within the PS in the wake of Jospin's April 2002 defeat. Indeed, Palier (2002: 6–7) argues that targeting means-tested benefits suggest welfare reforms approaching a 'liberal' model of coverage for the poorest in society, rather than a more ambitious Social Democratic logic aiming to achieving equality.

This is particularly pertinent given the fragility of French Socialism's electoral base. Whilst Jospin reforms have clearly been informed by a redistributive and to an extent egalitarian logic, recent history has shown how the Right has used similar mechanisms to pursue a very different distributive agenda (Gutman and Loyer 1998, Levy 2001a). Increased reliance on means-testing makes it easier for the Right to move the goal-posts in the wake of their victory, confronting 'legitimacy' dilemmas by reducing entitlements, not increasing taxation, and introducing an anti-redistributive logic to French welfare reform.

In employment policy, the Jospin Government's commitment to an 'active state' exploiting room to manoeuvre and playing a central role in securing the widest possible access to employment feeds through into an eclectic strategy. Limited redistribution to boost purchasing power, and the macro-economic context of a soft euro, public sector employment expansion, and the 35-hour week, combine with new 'employment centred social policy' thinking – shifting incentives to hire and seek lower wage employment through the tax system. This has shown conspicuous successes between 1997 and 2001, reversing two decades of unemployment increases in France.

Jospin's Government sought to redistribute the fruits of growth, and ensure that France's growth was inclusive in employment terms. However, characteristic of Social Democracy's 'structural dependency' upon capitalism (Pzeworski 1985), the model is one of 'job-rich growth', thus economic growth is a pre-requisite of Jospin's employment strategy. Social democratic Governments reliant upon distributing the fruits of growth face dilemmas in 'hard times', as the sharp fall in France's growth rate in late 2001 demonstrated. This cost Jospin dear in the run-up to the presidential elections, with slight unemployment increases in early 2002, qualifying his government's employment achievements. A deeper flaw in Jospin's otherwise very creditable employment record is that aspirations for 'Social Democratic' macroeconomic co-ordination to boost jobs and growth, and defend the European Social Model, at the EU level has been undermined in the absence of widespread support.

The greatest threat to the 'Jospin model', however, is the lack of a secure electoral coalition underpinning the French 'plural left'. A 'neo-Keynesian' rationale dovetailed with pre-election tax-cutting *largesse,* but the groups targeted have not cohered into a stable electoral constituency. Unlike, say, Swedish Social democracy, the French Left has never enjoyed a reliable cross-class basis of support. Jospin himself concedes that the French Socialists have never been a mass party; 'we can experience wide-scale electoral successes followed by major setbacks because we do not draw our support from specific social foundations' (Jospin 1999: 5). This was eloquently demonstrated by Jospin's first-round elimination on

21 April 2002. The Socialists limited the damages in the June 2002 legislative elections, yet despite increasing their first-round vote share from 1997 (25–26 per cent), the PS lost 106 seats as the allied Left suffered a comprehensive defeat against a relatively united 'presidential' Right. This raises real questions as to whether the conditions exist to build a governing coalition of the Left in the French party system. Thus Jospin's 'model' of Social democracy is undermined not by internal programmatic contradictions, but by French Socialism's permanent electoral frailty, which could render some of the social and employment policy achievements of the last five years ephemeral.

Notes

1 *Vendredi* no. 212 (17/12/1993)
2 'Keynesianism' here refers not to precise mechanisms of fine tuning, or deficit financing, but to broader insights into the role of the state in the economy state, notably ensuring security of employment.
3 See C. Pierson (2001: 116).
4 Purchasing power as a proportion of household revenue increased by 16 per cent between 1997 and 2002 (the best 5-year performance in over 20 years) (Ministère des Finances 2001: 11).
5 In March 2000, a 10 per cent income tax cut was introduced for 5m lower earners, and 650,000 particularly low earners were exempted from taxation altogether. *Financial Times* (23 March 2000). In September 2000, income tax was further reduced. *Libération* (31 August 2000)
6 It should be recalled, however, that income tax represents a lesser proportion of the total tax take in France (24 per cent in 1999), than in, say, the UK (39 per cent in the same year) (Ministère des Finances 2001: 118).
7 Thus, the PS argue, in the event of a conjunctural down-turn, spending should not be changed even if it were to slightly overshoot the 3 per cent deficit target, allowing macro-policy to counter a crisis of insufficient demand as part of the job creating strategy (PS 1997; Moscovici 1997: 98).
8 Always a emphemistic term in the French context given the hostile climate of French industrial relations.
9 *L'Hebdo des Socialistes*, 9/5/97, p.4
10 Spending on employment policy increased by 13 per cent between 1997 and 2002.
11 Labour Ministry figures, see the website: www.nsej.travail.gouv.fr/actualite/bilan. Such results, however, must be placed in the context of a wider economic upturn, making the precise impact of the *Plan Aubry* difficult to discern.
12 In the first quarter of 2000, 140,000 new jobs were created in the private sector. In total, in the previous 12 months, 430,000 jobs were created. These increases are spread across all sectors, with service by far the most dynamic. See Robert Graham, 'France: Jobs Materialise at a Healthy Rate', *Financial Times*, 14 June 2000.

References

Bouvet, L and Michel, F. (2001) 'Pluralism and the Future of the French Left' in S. White (ed.) *New Labour: The Progressive Future?*, Basingstoke: Palgrave, 204–12.

Clift, B. (2001) 'The Jospin Way', *The Political Quarterly* 72 (2): 170–9.

Clift, B. (2004, forthcoming) *French Socialism in a Global Era: The Political Economy of the New Social Democracy in France*, London: Continuum.

Delors, J. (1993) *White Paper on Growth, Competitiveness and Employment*, EC.

Delors, J. (1997) *Comments and Proposals for a New Model of Development*, Paris: Notre Europe.

Dyson, K (1999) 'Benign or Malevolent Leviathan? Social Democratic Governments in a Neo-Liberal Area' *Political Quarterly*, 70(2): 195–209.

Fitoussi, J.-P. Atkinson, A., Blanchard, O., Flemming, J., Malinvaud, E., Phelps, F. and Solon, R. (1993) *Competitive Disinflation*, Oxford: OUP.

Fitoussi, J-P. (1995) *Le Débat Interdit: Monnaie, Europe, Pauvreté*, Paris; Arléa.

Fitoussi, J-P. (1998) 'Table ronde: Comment appliquer les 35 heures?', *Revue Politique et Parlementaire*: 73–91.

Glyn, A. (1995) 'Social Democracy and Full Employment', *New Left Review*, 211: 33–55.

Gubian, A. (2000) 'Les 35 heures et l'emploi: d'une loi Aubry à l'autre', *Regards sur l'actualité*: 259, 3–26.

Gutman, O and Loyer, A. (1998) 'CSG et Justice Sociale', *Regards sur l'Actualité*, (February), 3–16.

Hall, P. (1986) *Governing The Economy*, Cambridge: Polity.

Jospin, L. (1999) *Modern Socialism*, London: Fabian Society.

Jospin, L. (2001) 'Ma vision de l'Europe et de la mondialisation', *Notes de la Fondation Jean-Jaurès*, 25, Paris; Plon.

Levy, J. (2000) 'France: Directing Adjustment?' in F. Scharpf and V. Schmidt (eds), *Welfare and Work in the Open Economy: Volume Two*, Oxford: 337–44.

Levy, J (2001a) 'Partisan Politics and Welfare Adjustment: the Case of France', *Journal of European Public Policy* 8 (2): 265–85.

Levy, J (2001b) 'Social Policy in the Age of High Unemployment', in Guyomarch, A., Machin, H. *et al.* (eds), *Developments in French Politics 2*, Basingstoke; Palgrave, 191–210.

Lordon, F. (1998) 'The Logic and Limits of Désinflation Competitive', *Oxford Review of Economic Policy* 14(1): 96–113.

Milner, S. (2001) 'Globalisation and Employment in France: Between flexibility and protection?' *Modern and Contemporary France* 9(3): 327–38.

Milner, S. (2002) 'The Jospin Government and the 35 hour week', *Modern and Contemporary France* 10(3): 339–52.

Ministère des Finances (2001) *Project de Loi des Finances pour 2002 Les Notes Bleues de Bercy hors serie, Paris*; La Documentation Française.

Moscovici P. (1997) *L'Urgence: Plaidoyer pour une autre politique*, Paris: Plon.

Muet, P-A. (1998) 'Table ronde: Comment appliquer les 35 heures?', *Revue Politique et Parlementaire* 73–91.

Muet, P-A. (2000) *Achieving Full Employment*, London: Policy Network.

OFCE (1999) *L'Economie Francaise 1999*, Paris; La Découverte.

Palier, B. (2000) 'Defrosting the French Welfare State', *West European Politics* 23(1): 113–36.

Palier, B. (2002) *Gouverner la Sécurité Sociale*, Paris: P.U.F.

Parti Socialiste (PS) (1996) 'Final Text of the National Convention', *Mondialisation, Europe, France*, in *Vendredi* No. 276, 5 April.

Parti Socialiste (PS) (1997) *Changeons L'Avenir: Nos engagements pour la France* Paris; PS Presse.

Parti Socialiste (2001) *Pour de nouveax choix de société*, Text presented at the Conseil National of 17 November, Paris: PS.
Pierson, C. (2001) *Hard Choices: Social Democracy in the 21st Century*, Cambridge; Polity.
Przeworski, A. (1985) *Capitalism and Social Democracy*, Cambridge: Cambridge University Press.
Scharpf, F. (1991) *Crisis and Choice in European Social Democracy*, Ithaca: Cornell University Press.
Vandenbroucke, F. (1999) 'European Social Democracy: Convergence, Divisions, and Shared Questions', *Political Quarterly* 70(51): 37–52.

8 The Third Way in welfare state reform?

Social Democratic pension politics in Germany and Sweden

Karen M. Anderson and Traute Meyer

Introduction

The task of updating welfare state institutions to meet new economic and demographic pressures poses a major challenge to Social Democracy. This is especially apparent in the case of pension policy because of the size and cost of public pensions. Pensions are typically the largest component in public social budgets, and pensions constitute a classic case of path dependent change (Pierson 1994; Bonoli 2000; Myles and Pierson 2001). Benefit commitments made by governments over the course of many decades 'lock in' policies and make reform difficult. Under these circumstances are Social Democratic pension reforms destined to be simply pragmatic, defensive, *ad hoc* responses to demographic and fiscal pressures, or is there scope for the emergence of a 'Third Way' in pension politics?

This chapter investigates the role of Social Democratic parties and trade unions in pension reform politics in Sweden and Germany. We explore the extent to which both countries have modernised their pension systems, and the role of labour in this process. In Sweden, in 1994 the Social Democratic Party (SAP) co-operated in a structural overhaul of public pensions in order to guarantee their future sustainability. The reform strengthened market forces considerably but the state still plays a major redistributive role, and the system retains its core Social Democratic features. In contrast, the recent Social Democratic-led pension reform in Germany lacks a distinct Social Democratic profile and appears to be motivated mainly by cost containment. To explain this difference in outcomes, we argue that a crucial precondition for a Social Democratic pension reform is the emergence of party–union agreement about the content of reform.

The chapter is organised as follows. The first section identifies core features of Social Democratic pension policies. The next two sections discuss recent pension reforms under Social Democratic governments in Germany and Sweden. For each case, we examine the pressures that led to the reforms, the roles and behaviour of the major actors, and assess the extent to which each reform exhibits signs of Social Democratic renewal.

The final section compares the German and Swedish reform processes in order to identify the conditions that lead to the adoption of 'modernising' but still Social Democratic pension reforms in the latter and mainly to simple retrenchment in the former case.

Social Democracy and pensions policy

Is there a discernible 'Third Way' in pension policies that improves or adds to 'old' Social Democratic pension policies? This section draws on the literature on welfare regimes and Third Way debates in order to identify core Social Democratic features in pension systems. This provides the basis for determining the extent to which recent reforms in Germany and Sweden bear the imprint of core Social Democratic goals.

Esping-Andersen (1985, 1990) provides the most elaborated statement of the relationship between Social Democracy and social policy. According to him, Social Democratic social policy must promote three goals: solidarity, decommodification, and equality. First, *solidarity* is created and maintained through universal, public benefits and the marginalisation of the private pension sector. The participation of all citizens in the same system leads to the development of collective identity and loyalty to public schemes. *Decommodification*, refers to freeing citizens from the market imperative in securing basic needs, and is achieved through high replacement rates and generous qualifying rules in social insurance programmes. The third goal, *equality* implies the reduction of inequalities in status, income and wealth, and later came to include gender and race. These three goals were formulated before a modernised Social Democracy claimed a 'Third Way'. To what extent are they still valid today?

Green-Pedersen *et al.* (2001) argue that there is a coherent set of policy ideas associated with the Third Way or 'New Social Democracy.' New about them is their commitment to an active welfare state that promotes the creation of good jobs and high levels of labour market participation. At the same time, 'old' Social Democratic values of social justice and equality are not abandoned. The impetus for this policy re-orientation is the failure of existing policies to provide adequate welfare and employment in the context of fundamental economic and social changes, including globalisation, demographic trends, and changing patterns in everyday life. We examine the impact of each of these on social policy and the possible response of a New Social Democracy in turn.

Globalisation refers to increased economic integration, typically measured in terms of the increased mobility of productive and financial capital. Although the impact of globalisation on national welfare states is the subject of much scholarly disagreement (Hirst and Thompson 1999), Social Democratic theorists and politicians have been fairly clear about how globalisation affects the welfare state: capital mobility creates pressures for reducing taxation and non-wage labour costs, avoiding budget deficits and abolishing disincentives to paid employment. Rather than responding defensively to these shifts in the international economic environment, Social Democracy's task, according to Third Way theorists, is to embrace these changes and to adopt policies that minimise or cushion the effects of global economic forces (cf. Anderson 1998). One way to achieve this aim is to 'turn vices into virtues,' or pursuing policies designed to correct inefficiencies in the welfare state without significantly compromising commitments to disadvantaged groups (Levy 1999). This correction of programme weaknesses usually results in financial savings that can be used to expand commitments to disadvantaged groups.

Besides globalisation, Social Democracy must respond to changes in everyday life patterns, including the 'rise of individualism' (Giddens 2001: 5) and its impact on social risks. For example, many European welfare states were based on the male breadwinner model and lifelong employment. This assumption was gendered and biased towards white citizens from the very start; today, however, changes in the labour force, household structures and attitudes have substantially undermined its legitimacy (cf. Clarke and Newman 1997). To address these changes Third Way theorists advocate social policy reforms that assign more weight to individual instead of family income, and to variations in individual work patterns. Where possible, social policy should reinforce individual responsibility and respond to individuals' demand for choice and autonomy. This new emphasis does not mean, however, that the state should reduce its commitment to social justice achieved via social insurance (Giddens 2001).

Finally, demographic change, especially population ageing, creates pressures for policy change because the ratio of employees to pensioners in most Western European countries has decreased significantly and this trend is likely to become much stronger over time. This development threatens the financial sustainability of most pension systems because existing policy commitments imply future expenditures that are forecast to be much larger than corresponding revenues. Without major reform, most West European countries are likely to face major financial difficulties (cf. EC 1999).

What do the challenges discussed above mean for pension reform? Obviously, they do not apply uniformly to all pension systems, and the starting point for new thinking and possible reform strategies is always the existing pension system structure. Overall, however, the direction of reform aspirations is the following: a revamped pension system should promote the inclusion of new social risks, individual autonomy, and employment, it should be financially sustainable and intergenerationally fair, and it should not contribute excessively to non-wage labour costs.

So far our definition of 'new' Social Democratic policy goals is a general one and we have thus circumvented a methodological problem. How can we measure degrees of Social Democratic 'success' in different countries given their differing institutional starting points? In other words, is any Swedish reform process not automatically more Social Democratic in a sense than any German one could possibly be? It is difficult to escape this conclusion, considering the fact that the two welfare states have long been recognised as prototypes of the Social Democratic and the conservative model. We try to address this problem by using the institutional structure of each pre-reform pension system as the baseline for estimating the degree to which Social Democratic goals are promoted in the reformed pension system.

Pension reform in Germany

Core features of the German pension system until the reform in 2001

Germany is the prototype of Esping-Andersen's conservative welfare state not least because of the structure of its pension system. This system protected employees with life-long employment histories well but maintained status differences at the same time (Esping-Andersen 1990: 21–9). The level of state pension entitlement depended on occupational status – civil servants received better pensions than white-collar workers, on the level of income, and on the length of employment (Neumann and Schaper 1998: 158–73). Despite these differences until the most recent pension reform anyone with a full employment biography would have received a pension worth at least 70 per cent of their last net wage.

Citizens without lifelong employment were protected less well. A minimum pension did not exist. However, certain activities other than employment were recognised as if the person had paid contributions to the pension fund: phases of education, of military service, and of very low income, phases of childrearing, marriage (Neumann and Schaper 1998: 158–73). These rules modified the direct connection between labour market income and benefits but it is still fair to say that the quality of citizens' protection against loss of income after retirement was mainly determined by their former ties to the labour market.

Pensions were financed through a pay-as you go (PAYG) system, with the employer and employee each making mandatory contributions of 10.15 per cent of gross wages (January 1999 figure). The federal government contributed an additional amount, which during the eighties remained under 20 per cent of the pension providers' budget and rose to 24 per cent towards the end of the century (VDR 2001). All pensions were administered by corporatist bodies that were major players in pension politics (see below). However, it lay within the authority of the federal parliament to make final decisions about reforms. The pensions of civil servants were tax-financed.

The German pension system lacked central features typical for a Social Democratic programme. By reinforcing occupational differences and disadvantaging people with caring responsibilities, it reinforced social inequalities rather than *solidarity* and *equality* (cf. Meyer 1998). Furthermore, it did not provide citizens with a right to an income independent of the market, in other words the degree of *decommodification* after retirement depended on employment status. However, the system also had some Social Democratic characteristics, if not in form, then in outcome. First, it guaranteed a decent income after retirement for a large proportion of the population; since the mid-eighties old age poverty ceased to be a topic of political concern because pensioners' incomes had risen. Second, the high level of protection through state pensions kept the private sector very small; in the mid nineties about 85 per cent of all pension income was provided by the state system (OECD 1996: 68). Thus pension entitlements were determined by democratic institutions.

The political background of the reform by the Social Democrats

This conservative model was shaped mainly under the aegis of Conservative governments. Since 1949 a Conservative-Liberal coalition ruled (West-) Germany for 33 years.[1] Nevertheless, pension policymaking – due to the politically sensitive nature of pensions – was consensual (Rüb and Nullmeier 1991: 460; Schmidt 1998: 83). Until 1997 reforms were based on agreements between the major parties, the trade unions and employers (Schmidt 1998: 75–111; Schmähl 1999: 398). The participation of unions and employers was facilitated by their crucial role in the administration of employees' pensions. Pensions for blue- and white- collar workers are administered by corporations that are managed by equal numbers of employers' and employees' representatives. This function has given the corporations exclusive expert knowledge about citizens' employment biographies and retirement income. Their umbrella organisation, the Association of German Pension Providers (VDR) has thus been regarded as a central adviser by governments undertaking pension reforms.[2] This status has been reinforced by the fact that the VDR has traditionally and behind the scenes found a consensus between the unions' and the employers' position. The industrial peace in this area has been exceptional compared with other areas of social policy (von Winter 1997: 386). The stability of the 'conservative model' in Germany therefore cannot be attributed solely to the dominance of the Conservative party but must also be seen in the context of the support of the left.

Given this background, what was the likelihood for a left reform by the Social Democrats in 2001? On the one hand, tradition and the established links with the VDR strongly suggested a reform maintaining the structure of the existing system, in collaboration with the corporate actors of the pension policy network. On the other hand, the tradition of cross-party agreements had been broken for the first time in 1997. In the context of soaring expenses for unification, increasing unemployment figures and low financial reserves of the pension funds, the Christian Democrats initiated a reform that would have lowered the pension level from 70 per cent to 64 per cent of average net income by 2030 and restricted access to invalidity and early retirement pensions (Bundestagsdrucksache 13/8011). The Social Democrats voted against the bill because of its potential to cause poverty for a substantial share of the population (Deutscher Bundestag 1997a, b). With a general election coming up in 1998 the SPD attempted to boost its popularity by showing a traditional leftist profile.

After winning the elections, the SPD kept its promise and repealed parts of the pension reform, thus assuming responsibility for finding a better solution to the financial problems of the pension funds. This, however, was difficult, given that the two most obvious steps were equally unpopular: pension cuts or raising contributions.[3] Faced with these hard choices the minister in charge adopted a strategy that not only led to a reform without distinct Social Democratic imprints but that also leaves a considerable number of voters materially worse off.

Evaluating the Social Democratic content of the reform

The pension reform departs from existing policy in two fundamental respects: the introduction of across the board benefit cuts and the strong promotion of private pension provision, encouraged by tax incentives or subsidies. The main aim of the reform is to keep current contribution levels constantly under 22 per cent until 2030 – despite population ageing. This aim can only be achieved by the reduction of entitlements. The highest possible level of public pensions will be cut, to 64 per cent of last net earnings and widows' pensions were cut. Derived rights are thus unlikely to be sufficient for the surviving spouse. To counterbalance the cuts care-related pension rights have been extended for married couples; the VDR calculates that this extension will compensate for the losses mothers encounter through the levelling down of derived rights (Standfest 2001: 6).

To make up for these reductions citizens are strongly encouraged to invest in private or occupational pension schemes. Those who do receive state subsidies or tax exemptions, and parents are entitled to extra money for each child.[4] This is an individualisation of risks that disadvantages women and enforces class differences. Firstly, because women's life expectancy is higher than men's they will be required by private companies to pay higher contributions. Given their lower average incomes many will find this difficult; increased inequality is therefore likely (Langelüddeke and Rabe 2000a, b). Secondly, the reform enforces differences between households with lower and those with middle to higher incomes, since the latter group is eligible to the more favourable tax exemptions granted for investments in private pension schemes whereas lower incomes only receive the flat-rate subsidies (Fehr and Jess 2001: 11).

Citizens who acquire pension entitlements below the level of the means-tested income support will find it easier to make claims for this benefit. From now on the pension administrations are obliged to inform people about such entitlements and pass on their claims to the social welfare offices. In addition the means-test for income support in old age is less harsh than for younger citizens as close family members are not liable. However, means-testing remains the condition for receiving income support and people owning property or savings will not be able to claim it. Also, children or parents will still be asked to pay if the claimants are under 66 years old or if they have caused their dependency 'deliberately or by culpable negligence' (AVmG 2000: 72). Thus the minimum pension discourages early exit from employment; it is combined with social control and it penalises private savings and property ownership.

For employers the reform reduces mandatory contributions while they are under no obligation to pay for the private pension schemes; however, employees have the right to demand that employers deduct contributions from their payroll to go directly into an occupational or private pension fund. Employers have to provide this saving opportunity, but are allowed to choose the type they want to offer.

With the exception of the employers the reform does not produce many winners. Benefits for current pensioners will rise more slowly than before. Employees will continue to pay the same contributions to the public system, but their pension level will decrease. The private pensions will have to be financed with additional individual savings. So in order to receive the same pension all citizens and particularly women will have to pay more. Generations born after 1970 stand to gain the most; the Bundesbank calculates that their higher investment will lead to returns above 70 per cent of last earnings (Deutsche Bundesbank 2001: 57; cf. Fehr and Jess 2001). However, this does not affect large parts of the current population and it is doubtful whether it applies to all young citizens, given that a considerable number of them will not be pursuing the full-time, life-long career on which the calculations of the Bundesbank are based. Moreover, the private pension provisions are voluntary so there is no guarantee that all of those who are eligible will actually participate.

The new pension law exhibits few signs of Social Democratic renewal. The SPD's overriding strategy for meeting new social and economic challenges is to cut public spending and reduce non-wage labour costs. In this sense, the reform reflects Social Democracy's current emphasis on reforms that improve the financing side of public pensions. The introduction of financial incentives for private and/or occupational pension savings to supplement public benefits might also be considered to respond to Third Way theorists' call for more individual responsibility and choice in social policies. However, the reform does not fare well regarding the goal of social inclusion for the groups most exposed to social risks. With the shift to private pensions the existing degree of employers' obligation towards employees is weakened, differences between pension levels of lower and middle income groups are enforced, and the legally guaranteed *solidarity* between men and women is reduced, expressed by equal contributions despite women's greater life expectancy. The reform is therefore likely to lead to greater gender *inequality* and generally to higher pension differentials. Its strongest Social Democratic hallmark concerns *decommodification.* By making it easier for citizens with very low pension entitlements to claim income benefit the reform does provide a minimum protection against market failure and family breakdown. However, because this provision is low and means-tested it is still a far cry from the original Social Democratic concept of decommodification.

Analysis of Reform Process[5]

From the outset the reform process was characterised by acute conflict and latent tension among the central actors in the pension policy network. When the SPD-Green government took office in September 1998, parts of the previous government's pension cuts were reversed. Beyond this, however, the new government had few concrete ideas about comprehensive reform. The SPD's coalition agreement with the Greens, however, included plans for the introduction of some sort of private pension provision, and the government had committed itself to the stabilisation of contributions. These two principles formed the basis for the proposed reforms.

In summer 1999 government released a reform draft aimed at an immediate slowdown of pension rises, which would also affect the income of current pensioners. Despite criticism from all sides, the government stuck to its plan for an immediate slow down while working on a draft for long-term reform. This draft was released in May 2000; at its centre were incentives to build up private pensions gradually while at the same pace reducing the level of public pensions. This draft was instantly rejected by the leaders of the German Trades Union Association (DGB) and by all other large unions, who threatened the minister with industrial action. Within the SPD the traditional wing and the head of the Social Democratic employees expressed their criticism. The Christian Democrats – whose consent the government was seeking – also rejected the plan. Moreover, the corporate Association of German Pension Providers feared that the reform would replace a system based on earnings-relatedness by one merely ensuring a minimum pension (VDR, 2.6.2000). The almost equally powerful Insurance Institution for Employees (BfA) warned that the reform would lead to increased poverty (BfA 28.6.2000). Shortly after this public relations disaster the minister in charge revised his plan, ensuring that public pensions could not drop below the level of 64 per cent by 2030. This met with only little more approval.

The board of the SPD – grudgingly – accepted the new proposal, against some internal opposition. The CDU continued their criticism and threatened to lead a 'pension election-campaign' in 2002. The IG-Metall remained opposed and started a campaign against the reform. Only the public sector union (ÖTV) and a few smaller unions became more sympathetic on the grounds that the long-term problems of the pension fund needed to be solved together. The leader of the DGB initially showed willingness to find a consensual solution (einblick 14/00), but by the time the bill was given a first reading in parliament in November 2000 that willingness had evaporated. The main criticism of all these actors remained the planned reduction of the pension level.

The SPD leadership clearly underestimated the opposition of unions to their reform plans. Likewise, the unions were surprised at the magnitude of the proposed cuts given that the SPD had just fought an election campaign on precisely this issue. The DGB's initial strategy was to try to block the reform, and when this failed, they joined with the VDR and the left wing of the SPD in pressuring the government to modify its proposal. The DGB's strategy was mostly defensive; it had no reform alternative of its own and pushed for smaller benefit cuts and a larger role for unions in the implementation of the private pension provisions. The VDR advocated a generation-neutral solution that would not threaten the long-term sustainability and legitimacy of the public pension system, and the SPD Left pressed for a reform that would not burden younger generations and would provide better entitlements for combining child rearing with part-time work.

The Association of German Pension Providers suggested an alternative method of reducing pensions (VDR, 1.12. 2000). By spreading the financial burden to more people, including current pensioners – albeit more moderately than originally planned by the SPD, contributions could be contained while the pension level would not drop below 67 per cent of the last net wage.[6] During a public hearing of a parliamentary committee in December 2000 the proposal was endorsed by all invited representatives from the pension policy network and by academic experts, all of whom criticised the government's reform.

Faced with such strong disapproval and an internal party revolt the government yielded and integrated the VDR's proposal into their bill. The reform was passed in parliament with the votes of the Social Democrats and the Greens in January 2001. However, the federalist system offered the opposition another veto-point that yet again changed the reform. Because some parts of the legislation needed the consent of the *Länder*-Parliament, the *Bundesrat*, in which the SPD in May 2001 did not have the majority, but both big parties were equally strong (www.bundesrat.de), the Conservatives had another chance to influence the final result. Their campaign against the hollowing out of the widows' pension contributed to the government's decision to take back the cuts widowed mothers would have suffered. Despite this Conservative success, when the final version of the reform passed the *Bundesrat* in May 2001 the CDU in the *Bundestag* still opposed the reform.[7]

In the end the SPD–Green government adopted a reform solution influenced at the last minute by the combined pressures of the VDR, the unions and the left wing of the SPD. Even though the government sidestepped the pension policy network throughout the reform process, eventually they could only fashion a feasible reform with the help of these actors.

Pension reform in Sweden

Core features of the Swedish pension system before the 1994 reform

Sweden is the prototype of Esping-Andersen's Social Democratic welfare state. As in Germany the structure of its public pension system is one of the reasons why Sweden was put into that category. In 1990, this system consisted of two tiers: the flat-rate basic pension (folkpension) and the national supplementary pension (ATP). Both tiers operated as PAYG systems financed by earmarked employer contributions. In 1990, the basic pension contribution (7.45 per cent of payroll) financed 85 per cent of benefits (the state paid the rest), while the ATP contribution (13.5 per cent of payroll) financed both current benefits and the accumulation of savings in the AP funds. For retirees with few or no ATP pension credits, the basic pension system provided a flat-rate benefit while the ATP system provided income-related pensions calculated according to 'defined benefit' principles. A full ATP pension pays 65 per cent (with the basic pension) of average income for the best 15 years of at least 30 years of labour market participation, up to the benefit ceiling. Both the basic pension and the ATP pensions were indexed to inflation every year.

The pension system is the largest government programme in terms of spending, and in 1992 accounted for 12.2 per cent of GDP. In 1992, the publicly controlled pension funds (AP Funds) stood at 512 billion Swedish Kronor (SEK), or 35 per cent of GDP (Proposition 1993/94: 250, p. 16). Private pensions in Sweden play a minor role; collective agreements pay about 10 per cent of the terminal salary for 90 per cent of the labour force.

How is this system Social Democratic? First, *solidarity* is promoted by the existence of one public pension system for all citizens, regardless of socioeconomic status. The role of private and occupational pensions is small, employers finance benefits, and substantial pension capital is accumulated in publicly controlled pension funds. Second, *decommodification* is promoted by the provision of a flat-rate pension that ensures an adequate minimum standard of living in old age. Entitlement is based on citizenship, thus avoiding the stigma of means-testing and permitting private savings. Most pensioners also have earnings-related ATP benefits. Finally, income *equality* is promoted by the redistribution of income from high earners to low earners through the basic pension, pension supplements, and the ATP system. Gender equality is also promoted by the absence of qualification rules related to gender, marital status, and hours worked.

The political and economic background of Social Democratic participation in the pension reform

The electoral hegemony of the SAP has heavily influenced the design of the pension system.[8] Although the non-socialist parties opposed the 1959 ATP reform, political necessity led them to grudgingly accept the basic features of the pension system. Before 1990 major pension reform was never seriously attempted even though pension expenditures increased significantly during the previous decade.

The rapid deterioration of the Swedish economy in the late 1980s dramatically changed this outlook. In the wake of stagnant economic growth and rapidly rising levels of unemployment, the pension system faced the twin shocks of shrinking tax revenues and increasing expenditures because of the growing number of retired persons. Between 1990 and 1993, Sweden went from budget surplus to recording a deficit of 12.3 per cent of GDP. During the same period, open unemployment climbed from 1.7 per cent to 8.2 per cent. The recession undermined two crucial preconditions of the Swedish welfare model – full employment and stable growth – and prompted massive reductions in public spending (Pontusson 1992; Huber and Stephens 1998).

The economic crisis exposed the instability of the pension system. The design of the ATP system assumes a stable annual economic growth rate of 3–4 per cent and full employment. When inflation began to exceed real wage growth in the 1980s, the indexing mechanism resulted in rising pension costs relative to payroll tax revenues, raising the spectre of trust fund reduction. In 1982, the number of years the AP funds can finance benefits was 7.4 and had declined to 5.1 in 1992 (Riksförsäkringsverket 1994). Since 1982, ATP contributions have not covered expenditures, and the gap has increased because of the economic crisis. Revenue shortfalls in the basic pension system also exacerbated central budget deficits as the state absorbed higher proportions of program financing (Riksförsäkringsverket, various years).

The economic crisis made pension reform a political priority. The shift to the right in electoral politics in 1991 gave the non-socialist government the legislative initiative, but both political blocs struggled to control the pension reform.[9] For the non-socialist parties (and their allies in organised business), their tenure in office during an economic downturn provided the strategic opportunity to advocate changes only recently considered politically impossible. The maturity of the system made radical privatisation impossible, but reform offered the promise of trimming the

Social Democratic excesses from the system, especially the perceived disincentive to work and the accumulation of large public pension funds. However, reform was impossible without the participation and substantial influence of the SAP, which was still the largest party in parliament and occupied a veto player position. For the SAP, retrenchment has been both a painful necessity brought on by the severe economic crisis and an opportunity to preserve the basic structure and scope of the pension system by correcting its perceived weaknesses.

Evaluating the Social Democratic content of the reform

The SAP co-operated with the four main non-socialist parties on a far-reaching pension reform that resulted in the passage of framework legislation in the Spring of 1994. Between 1994 and 1998, the same parties in Parliament passed follow-up legislation to fill in the details of the reform.

The new system departs from the existing system in several fundamental respects. First, ATP benefits will be based on lifetime earnings rather than the best 15 years of 30. Thus the link between pension contributions and benefits is made explicit, and the new system will lose much of its redistributive character. Second, pension contributions will be evenly divided between employers and employees. The switch to employee payroll taxes is intended to increase public awareness of the costs of retirement. Third, a new index will link benefits to wage developments and real economic growth. Pensions will also be adjusted if average life expectancy changes. These changes mean that the pension system will be more resistant to economic swings and it will be self-financing regardless of the state of the economy. Fourth, pension rights may be shared by spouses, and pension points will be earned for military service, child rearing, and education. Finally, the new system contains a premium reserve; of the total 18.5 per cent in pension contributions, 2.5 per cent will be placed in an individual investment fund. The system is also designed to be transparent in that individuals receive an annual statement about the size of their projected pension. In addition, the old basic pension and pension supplement will be replaced by a higher guaranteed pension for those not eligible for income-related benefits. The transition to the new system will take 20 years (*Proposition 1993/94*: 250).

The pension reform reflects the nature of compromise among five parties. The Christian Democrats and Centre Party wanted shared pension rights for spouses, and the Centre Party also advocated the higher guarantee pension. The SAP wanted to retain the obligatory system with high replacement rates, while the Liberals and Conservatives wanted a more explicit link between contributions and benefits, the premium reserve, and the elimination of contributions above the ceiling. All of the political parties advocated the introduction of real wage indexing. Although the influence of the SAP in the reform process has been substantial, they have acquiesced in three main areas: contributions above the ATP ceiling, shared pension rights, and the premium reserve system. The switch to visible individual contributions was also a concession by the SAP.

Has the revamped pension system retained its core Social Democratic features? There is no doubt that the new system is a major departure from existing pension policy. In particular, the switch from defined benefits to defined contributions in the ATP system is a radical change. In order to receive the same pension benefits under the new system, at least 40 years are required. A study conducted by the National Insurance Board estimated that 2/3 of those studied would be worse off in the new system, mainly TCO members and women who work fewer than 40 years (Statens Offentliga Utredningar 1994: 21, bilaga A). The biggest winners are those who work less than 20 years and receive the new higher guaranteed pension.

These losses must be considered in the context of the improvements introduced by the reform. First, the new pension system is much more resistant to economic and demographic shocks so its long-term stability is vastly enhanced. Second, the new indexing rules will stop the erosion in the value of ATP pensions. The old index rules meant that more and more workers earned income above the pension-qualification ceiling, for which they accumulated no pension rights. This trend threatened to transform the ATP system into a bigger basic pension, a development that posed a serious threat to the legitimacy of the system. Third, the new system corrects the unintended redistribution from lower income groups to higher income groups because of the best 15 years of 30 year benefit rule.

Although the overall impact of the reform is to reduce the degree of decommodification in the pension system, we argue that it still retains its core Social Democratic features. The state remains responsible for a minimum level of provision for all citizens, and this commitment is strengthened with the new guarantee pension. The earnings-related pension is now less generous, but this type of pension remains firmly within the public sector. Moreover, the reduction in generosity for white collar workers is still in line with traditional Social Democratic policy, since this is accompanied by improvements for most blue collar workers who tend to have longer employment histories and those with atypical risk profiles. The introduction of the premium reserve amounts to partial privatisation, but this will be carried out under tight public regulation.

The pension reform also demonstrates some renewal in Social Democratic thinking. Changes in the financing structure and indexing mechanism will reduce the pension system's pressure on central government finances, contribute to reductions in non-wage labour costs, and reduce the tax wedge. The new guarantee pension results in greater protection for vulnerable groups and increases the pension systems' responsiveness to new social risks. Finally, the new system significantly increases work incentives with the introduction of a more actuarial benefit formula, and the premium reserves enhances individual choice in pension planning.

Analysis of the reform process

The non-socialist government took an unusual procedural approach to negotiating the pension reform with the SAP. In 1991, the government appointed a working group composed of representatives from the five main parliamentary parties, including the opposition SAP, to formulate reform legislation. Unlike earlier pension investigations, the working group excluded members of the interest groups, such as the trade unions. The Confederation of Professional Associations (SACO), the Confederation of White Collar Unions (TCO) and the Confederation of Blue Collar Unions (LO) were still consulted and their views were well known, especially to the SAP, but they could not directly influence the content of the reform. The working group issued a comprehensive report in early 1994, and parliament passed the initial reform legislation in June 1994. Between mid-1994 and 1998, an implementation group worked to finalise the details of the reform. By early 2001, nearly all aspects of the reform had been implemented.

Unions' responses to the 1994 proposals ranged from cautious acceptance to strong criticism. The LO's main concern was the retention of a publicly financed, income-related system, so it accepted the main features of the reform in return for improved stability in the system. However, the LO had to compromise on two central issues: the premium reserve and, especially, shared employer–employee financing (Landsorganisationen, 1994). In contrast, TCO and SACO accepted the necessity of reform but argued strenuously that pension points for education were entirely too low. Both union confederations demanded the postponement of the reform until this issue was resolved (Tjänstemännens Centralorganisation, 1994; Sveriges Akademikers Centralorganisation, 1994). TCO and SACO also opposed the switch to shared financing. Significantly, LO declined to join with TCO and SACO in their opposition to the proposed method of pension credits for education. The Employers Organisation cautiously supported the legislation.

Despite their non-participation in government until 1994, pension reform has occurred more or less on SAP terms. The SAP dominated the process, with the LO and to a lesser extent the TCO and SACO acting as junior partners. The institutionalisation of the existing system and the magnitude of existing pension commitments precluded radical privatisation.

Conclusions

Our case studies show that in the face of programme weaknesses and huge financial problems the Swedish pension reform exhibits more signs of

Social Democratic renewal than does the German reform. Both reforms led to an improvement of the financing side of public pensions and both strengthened the link between earning and pensions. However, their potential for social inclusiveness differs. In Germany the SPD failed to improve pension entitlements of the groups most exposed to social risks, except perhaps for mothers who work part time. Despite this, the reform is likely to lead to greater gender inequality and favours the young middle classes. In contrast, in Sweden the reduced overall generosity of the earnings-related pension is accompanied by improvements for blue-collar workers and those with atypical risk profiles. In addition the new guarantee pension results in greater protection for vulnerable groups and increases the pension system's responsiveness to new social risks. When taking each pre-reform pension system as the baseline for estimating the degree to which Social Democratic goals are promoted we thus conclude that the Swedish reform fares better.

The conflictual nature of the German reform process stands in sharp contrast to the more consensual Swedish approach. We argue that this difference, and primarily the success or failure of coalition-building on the left, explains the difference in outcomes.

The Swedish SAP was able to dominate the reform negotiations and to build union support for the reform. This union-party co-operation functioned reasonably well in the 1990s because the unions had gone through a process of modernisation. In the late 1980s, internal conflict within the LO, the SAP, and between the LO and SAP resulted in the victory of the modernising wing of the party and union federation, whose influence was arguably consolidated by the economic crisis in the early 1990s. Moreover, the SAP's election failure in 1991 contributed to the strength of the modernisers.

In contrast, the political goals of the German Social Democratic government were hard to reconcile with the traditionalist outlook (e.g. Koch-Baumgarten 1997) of the largest German unions. Because the age structure of unions is biased towards older male workers, the policy preferences of the German Trades Union Association largely reflect the interests of this group at the expense of younger or part-time workers. Therefore the DGB would be expected to oppose any type of reform that would mean cuts for core segments of its membership. Given these constraints, isolating the unions was a plausible strategy for a minister who wanted a structural reform. However, by doing that, and by sidelining the traditionalist left wing of the SPD, sorting out the financial problems of pensions became government's paramount goal, and social inclusion was neglected. This lack of societal 'grounding' contributed to the weaknesses of the reform, weaknesses that have become even more apparent two years later.

Social Democrats in both Germany and Sweden faced tough re-election campaigns in late Summer 2002. The Swedish SAP strengthened its hold on power, gaining 39.9 per cent of the vote in the September 15 election, up from 35.1 per cent in 1998. The German SPD had more difficulty convincing voters to return them to office. The SPD's share of seats in the Bundestag declined from 44.5 per cent to 38.5 per cent in the September 22 election, but the gains of their coalition partner, the Green Party, provided a razor-thin margin of victory for the coalition. Whereas pension reform was virtually a non-issue in the Swedish election campaign and afterwards, the continuing problems of the German social insurance system, and particularly pensions, forced themselves onto the agenda of the new government. Shortly after taking office again in September 2002, the SPD announced that due to consistently high unemployment it would have to increase pension contributions from 19.1 per cent of qualifying income to 19.5 per cent in order to meet benefit obligations. This surprised and infuriated many members of the Green Party, and some SPD MPs even voiced their concern. Nevertheless, government passed a 'protection of contributions law' that raised pension contributions by 0.4 percentage points and increased the income threshold for contributions by January 2003 (Bundestagdrucksache 15/28). At the same time a commission of experts and members of corporate bodies was set up whose mission it is to design a scheme for a complete overhaul of the social insurance systems (www.spd.de). This shows that the search for a more viable solution for the public pension system is far from over – whether it also means a turning away from the confrontational style of politics and an opportunity for a greater degree of inclusiveness remains to be seen. Large parts of the public at least seem to have lost their faith in the Social Democrats.[10] The Social Democrats suffered losses in regional elections in January 2003, which meant that the Christian Democrats could block legislation in the Bundersrat.

Finally, we return to the central themes discussed in Chapter 1. It is striking that in both Sweden and Germany, 'the Third Way' as such rarely entered pension policy discourses. As the most successful Social Democratic party in the world (in terms of tenure in government), Swedish Social Democrats had already implemented their own 'Third Way' (tredje vägen) in the early 1980s and had moved beyond it. By the 1990s, the discourse of the SAP emphasised Social Democratic renewal in the pursuit of the traditional goals of equality, security, and solidarity. In addition, many more policy means were considered compatible with the pursuit of these goals, including publicly regulated privatisation, an enhanced role for the market, and less redistribution. As Steinmo (1988) argues, the Swedish SAP owes its success in part to its potential to adapt to changing political and economic circumstances. This is still true.

The concept of the 'Third Way' entered the German political debate in the spring of 1999 with the Blair-Schröder paper calling for a 'New Middle.' Reactions were less than enthusiastic to this initiative, especially within the SPD and unions, and the issue soon lost importance. If anything, German Social Democrats probably tried to avoid referring to the Blair-Schröder Paper or Third Way ideas because they were seen as politically dangerous. Thus, like their Swedish counterparts, the German SPD preferred to refer to their reforms as attempts at modernisation, rather than linking them to any other developments on the European Left, including the emergence of the Third Way debate in Britain.

Notes

1 From 1949 to 1965 and from 1982 to 1998, including 9 years after unification. Since 1998 the Social Democrats and the Green Party have formed the governing coalition (Bundeszentrale für politische Bildung 1996: 27–36).
2 Rüb and Nullmeier went as far as calling it a 'competing legislator' (1991: 457).
3 The acute problems of the low financial reserves of the pension funds had been solved by a considerable increase in the state's subsidy in 1998 and 1999. However, this left the root of the problem untouched (VDR 2001).
4 The flat-rate subsidies start 2002 and will increase gradually until 2008 when they will comprise 154 Euro yearly, fully payable only to citizens who invest 4 per cent of their gross wages in private pension funds. In 2008 parents will receive 185 Euro yearly for each child.
5 Unless indicated otherwise this analysis is based on the press coverage of the reform process in the most important German papers: the Süddeutsche Zeitung, the Frankfurter Allgemeine Zeitung, der Spiegel, die Zeit as well as on a number of expert interviews with representatives from the DGB, the SPD and the administration of the Federal Ministry for Employment, undertaken by Karen Anderson in June 2001.)
6 By that point a semantic consensus had been built. Despite the fact that the state pension level will be only around 64 per cent of today's net wage all major participants in the process had adopted the government's interpretation.
7 The Federal parliamentary CDU was seen to have refused its consent because it wanted to have the option to make pensions yet again an election issue in autumn 2002.
8 The SAP has governed Sweden from 1933 to 1976 (sometimes in coalition with the Farmers' Party); 1982–91; and 1994–present. For a more detailed analysis of the pension reform, see Anderson (2001; 1998).
9 The SAP served as a minority government from 1982 to 1991 when a multiparty non-socialist coalition composed of the Conservatives, Liberals, Christian Democrats, and Center Party led by the conservative party took power (1991–94). Despite the change in government, the SAP was the largest party in parliament.
10 Opinion polls showed a very fast decline in the SPD's popularity after the election. Citizens blamed the party for a dishonest campaign during which the real problems were kept secret (zdf politbarometer, 20.1.2003: http://www.zdf.de/ZDFde/inhalt/0,1872,2022974,FF.html).

References

AVmg (Altersvermögensgesetz) – Bundestagsdrucksache 14/4595: *Gesetzentwurf der Fraktionen SPD und BÜNDNIS 90/DIE GRÜNEN: Enwurf eines Gesetzes zur Reform der gesetzlichen Rentenversicherung und zur Förderung eines kapitalgedeckten Altersvorsorgevermögens.* 14.11.2000

Anderson, K. (1998) 'The welfare state in the global economy. The politics of social insurance retrenchment in Sweden 1990–1998'. PhD dissertation, University of Washington.

Anderson, K. (2001) 'The politics of retrenchment in a Social Democratic welfare state. Reform of Swedish pensions and unemployment insurance', *Comparative Political Studies* 34, (9), 1063–91

BfA (Bundesversicherungsanstalt für Angestellte) *Bericht des Vorsitzenden des Vorstandes anlässlich der Vertreterversammlung der BfA am 28.06.2000 in Bremen.* http://www.bfa-berlin.de.

Bonoli, G. (2000) *The Politics of Pension Reform.* Cambridge: Cambridge University Press.

Bundestagsdrucksache 13/8011: *Gesetzentwurf der Fraktionen der CDU/CSU und F.D.P: Entwurf eines Gesetzes zur Reform der gesetzlichen Rentenversicherung (Rentenreformgesetz 1999 – RRG 1999)* 24.6.97

Bundestagsdrucksache 15/28: *Gesetzentwurf der Fraktionen SPD und BÜNDNIS 90/DIE GRÜNEN: Entwurf eines Gesetzes zur Sicherung der Beitragssätze in der gesetzlichen Krankenversicherung und in der gesetzlichen Rentenversicherung (Beitragssatzsicherungsgesetz – BSSichG).* 5.11. 2002

Clarke, J. and Newman, J. (1997) 'From the cradle to the grave: the crises of the post-war welfare settlements', in Clarke, J. and Newman, J. (eds), *The Managerial State: Power, Politics and Ideology in the Remaking of Social Welfare.* London: Sage Publications, 1–17

Deutsche Bundesbank (2001) Änderungen im Rentenreformkonzept und Auswirkungen auf die 'Rendite' der Altersvorsorge. *Monatsbericht,* Februar: 57

Deutscher Bundestag (1997a) *Stenographischer Bericht* Plenarprotokoll 13/185, Bonn.

Deutscher Bundestag (1997b) *Stenographischer Bericht* Plenarprotokoll 13/198, Bonn.

einblick 14/00: Riester nicht kompromissbereit', *einblick – Gewerkschaftlicher Info-Service,* 17.7. 2000: 1

Esping-Andersen, G. (1985) *Politics Against Markets. The Social Democratic road to power.* Princeton: Princeton University Press.

Esping-Andersen, G. (1990) *The Three Worlds of Welfare Capitalism.* Princeton: Princeton University Press.

European Commission (EC) (ed.) (1999) *Rebuilding Pensions. Security, Efficiency, Affordability. Recommendations for a European Code of Best Practice for Second Pillar Pension Funds.* Brussels.

Fehr, H. and Jess, H. (2001) 'Gewinner und Verlierer der aktuellen Rentenreform', *Die Angestelltenversicherung* 5 (6): 1–12

Giddens, A. (2001) 'Introduction', in Giddens, A. (ed.), *The Global Third Way Debate.* Cambridge: Polity Press.

Green-Pedersen, C., van Kersbergen, K. and Hemerijck, A. (2001) 'Neo-liberalism, the 'Third Way' or what?: recent Social Democratic welfare policies in Denmark and the Netherlands', *Journal of European Public Policy* 8 (2): 307–25.

Hirst, P. and Thompson, G. (1999) *Globalization in Question: the International Economy and the Possibilities of Governance.* Malden: Polity Press, 2nd ed.

Huber, E. and Stephens, J. D. (1998) 'Internationalization and the Social Democratic model: crisis and future prospects', *Comparative Political Studies,* 31, 353–97.

Koch-Baumgarten, S. (1997) 'Die selbstverständliche Dominanz der Männer' in der (Gewerkschafts-)Öffentlichkeit. 'Überlegungen zur geschlechtsspezifischen Selektion von Interessen im politischen System', in Kerchner, B. and Wilde, G. (eds), *Staat und Privatheit*. Berlin: Leske und Budrich, 259–84

Levy, J. (1999) 'Vice into virtue?: progressive politics and welfare reform in continental Europe', *Politics and Society* 27: 239–73.

Landsorganisationen (1994) 'Yttrande. Reformerat pensionssystem' (Comment. Reformed pension system). Stockholm: Landsorganisationen.

Langelüddeke, A. and Rabe, B. (2001a) 'Rentenreform 2000: Verbesserung der eigenständigen Alterssicherung von Frauen?' *Sozialer Fortschritt* 1, 6–12.

Langelüddeke, A. and Rabe, B. (2001b) 'Auswirkungen der Rentenstrukturreform auf die Alterssicherung von Frauen', *femina politica* 1/2001.

Meyer, T. (1998) 'Retrenchment, reproduction, modernisation. pension politics and the decline of the German breadwinner model', *European Journal of Social Policy* 8 (3): 212–27.

Myles, J. and Pierson, P. (2001) 'The comparative political economy of pension reform', in P. Pierson (ed.), *The New Politics of the Welfare State*. Oxford: Oxford University Press, 305–33.

Neumann, L. and Schaper, K. (1998) *Die Sozialordnung der Bundesrepublik Deutschland*. Frankfurt a. M.: Campus.

OECD. (1996) *Economic Surveys. Germany*. Paris: OECD.

Pierson, P. (1994) *Dismantling the Welfare State? Reagan, Thatcher, and the Politics of Retrenchment*. Cambridge: Cambridge University Press.

Pontusson, J. (1992) 'At the end of the third road: Swedish Social Democracy in crisis', *Politics and Society* 20: 305–32.

Proposition 1993/94: 250 (Swedish Government Bill 1993/94, no. 250).

Riksförsäkringsverket. *Social insurance statistics. Facts*. Stockholm: Riksförsäkringsverket, various years.

Rüb, F. and Nullmeier, F. (1991) 'Alterssicherungspolitik in der Bundesrepublik Deutschland', in Blankert, Bernhard and Wollmann, Hellmut (eds), *Die alte Bundesrepublik – Kontinuität und Wandel*. Opladen: Westdeutscher Verlag: 435–62.

Schmähl, Winfried (1999) An der Schwelle zum neuen Jahrhundert – vor Weichenstellungen für die Alterssicherung in Deutschland, *Die Angestelltenversicherung* 46 (9): 397–412.

Sveriges Akademikers Centralorganisation. (1994) *Remissvar. Reformerat pensionssystem* (Official comment. Reformed pension system). Stockholm:

Schmidt, M. G. (1998) *Sozialpolitik in Deutschland. Historische Entwicklung und internationaler Vergleich*. 2. Auflage. Leske und Budrich: Opladen, 2nd rev. edn.

Standfest, Erich (2001) *Mitgliederversammlung am 15. Mai 2001 in Berlin. Bericht des Vorstandsvorsitzenden des VDR*. http://www.vdr.de (on 15.11.2001)

Statens Offentliga Utredningar (Official Commission of Inquiry) (1994) *Reformerat pensionssystem. Kostnader och individeffekter. Bilaga A* (Reformed pension system. Costs and individual effects. Appendix A). Report no. 21.

Steinmo, Sven. (1988) 'Social Democracy vs. Socialism: Goal Adaptation in Social Democratic Sweden', *Politics and Society* 16(4): 403–46.

Tjänstemännens Centralorganisation. (1994) *Yttrande. Reformerat pensionssystem* (Comment. Reformed pension system). Stockholm: Tjänstemännens Centralorganisation.

VDR (Verband Deutscher Rentenversicherungsträger) (2001) *Kenngrößen und Bemessungswerte: Entwicklung des Standardrentenniveaus – ArV + AnV.* http://www.vdr.de.

VDR, 2.6 (2000) VDR Geschäftsführer befürchtet Systemwechsel durch Ausgleichsfaktor. Informationen aus der gesetzlichen Rentenversicherung. http://www.vdr.de.

VDR, 1.12 (2000) *Stellungnahme des Verbandes Deutscher Rentenversicherungsträger vom 1.12.2000 für die öffentliche Anhörung durch den Ausschuss für Arbeit und Sozialordnung des Deutschen Bundestages von Montag, den 11.12.2000, bis Mittwoch, den 13.12.2000, zum Entwurf eines Gesetzes zur Reform der gesetzlichen Renten-versicherung und zur Förderung eines kapitalgedeckten Alters-vorsorgevermögens* (BT-Drucks. 14/4595) http://www.vdr.de.

Winter, T. von (1997) *Sozialpolitische Interessen. Konstituierung, politische Repräsentation und Beteiligung an Entscheidungsprozessen* Baden-Baden: Nomos.

9 Why do Social Democratic parties change employment policy positions?

A comparison of Austria, Germany and the United Kingdom

Monika Feigl-Heihs

Introduction

In the prosperous period after World War II Social Democrats in Europe were engaged in expanding the welfare state in order to raise the living conditions of all people. For that purpose full employment represented the crucial concern for these parties as it was estimated to maintain the political and social stability of a country. The interest in creating jobs linked the working-class to the Social Democrats. However, the economic crisis of the 1970s leading to increased unemployment challenged Social Democratic parties to combat unemployment and high inflation through Keynesian demand management. As at the beginning of the 1980s cost-push inflation and demand-gap unemployment (stagflation) occurred simultaneously Keynesian strategies 'were no longer able to ensure acceptable outcomes' (Scharpf and Schmidt 2000b: 4) on these economic numbers. Social Democratic parties found themselves in an economic situation where the foundations for everlasting prosperity (Lutz 1984) began to crumble.

As unemployment became a mass phenomenon one can be interested in the question of how Social Democratic parties in various countries have dealt with that problem since the late 1970s. The chapter examines the period of the 1980s and 1990s when the employment positions of three Social Democratic parties, the Social Democrats in Germany (SPD), the British Labour Party and the Austrian Social Democrats (SPÖ) changed decisively. In the first part programmatic positions rather than actual policies are analysed as the SPD and the Labour Party were not in office until the late 1990s. In contrast, the SPÖ was the leading party in government from 1970 to 2000, building a coalition government in the mid 1980s with the FPÖ and later with the ÖVP. Therefore I refer to the party manifestos representing the policy premises of the party as a whole. Although party manifestos are often estimated as being without relevance for the political behaviour of parties, several studies have demonstrated that they are strongly related (Ginsberg 1982; Rallings 1987). The analysis of the changing employment policy concepts of the SPÖ, the SPD, and the Labour Party will show that all three parties replaced the Keynesian macro-economic approach by supply-side policy and at the same time strengthening the importance of active labour market measures. This major change breaking with traditional Social Democratic tradition took place at different points in time in the three parties.

The chapter then goes into more detail on the question of what caused these parties to change their concepts. Three conditions for party policy change are elaborated for each party: the economic performance and the debate about the appropriate economic approach; the situation of the electoral market; and the question of party cohesion. Finally, the conclusion picks up the questions raised in this section.

From Keynesian employment policy to supply-side policy

The so-called 'golden age' of Social Democracy with its high economic growth and national control over financial markets allowed Social Democrats to enlarge the welfare state and maintain full employment through Keynesian policies. Keynesian demand management policies were designed to stimulate the economy through government spending that would increase private demand sufficient to lower unemployment. At the beginning of the 1980s Keynesian strategies were no longer able to ensure low inflation and unemployment under the condition of stagflation. In that time especially Conservative parties emphasised supply side strategies which consist of reducing taxes in order 'to encourage private savings, boost private investment, and accelerate the rate of growth' (Boix 1998: 3). The state is responsible for creating a competitive market framework through liberalisation of trade and business barriers. In addition a third strategy aims at investing in human capital in order to foster the employability of the people. Active labour market policies offer unemployed people training, skills and qualifications for the labour market.

At the end of the twentieth century supply side measures became part of the Third Way project of Social Democratic parties (Blair and Schröder 1999). The Third Way suggests a combination of demand and supply side measures as well as active labour market policies for reducing unemployment and for promoting the whole economy. It is argued that tax and labour cost reductions are directed towards increasing public investment of both target groups: the companies and the private households. Public welfare to work programmes should be instrumental not only in higher incomes but also in improving 'the supply of labour available to employers' (Blair and Schröder 1999: 7). 'New' Social Democracy views these three approaches as complementary and not as mutually exclusive. The following part shows in which way the SPÖ, the SPD and the Labour Party embedded in specific economic situations of their countries changed their programmatic employment positions with respect to the above mentioned strategies.

In the 1970s the Austrian Social Democrats practised and praised an 'Austro-Keynesian' economic and employment strategy by means of public demand management. Public money was invested in infrastructure, housing, etc. in order to combat unemployment and to stimulate economic growth. As unemployment remained below two per cent until 1981 (Scharpf 1987: 66) economic growth was relatively satisfactory, and inflation increased only moderately, the strategy of the SPÖ seemed to be rather successful (Müller 1988: 104; Merkel 1993: 247).

At the beginning of the 1980s the formerly hidden costs of this political strategy (national debt, structural problems) became visible, while at the same time macro-economic performance deteriorated and the scope for fiscal action was constrained (Talos 1987: 118; Merkel 1993: 245). The SPÖ intended to reduce growing unemployment by continuing its deficit-spending strategy and special employment programmes through the efforts of nationalised firms. The Keynesian employment policy was justified by the argument that unemployment causes higher expenditure for unemployment benefits, decreasing tax revenue and consumption. Therefore, the state should invest in employment accepting a higher budget deficit (SPÖ 1983).

In the UK and in Germany the world economic crisis in the mid-1970s led to a decrease in the economic growth rate, while unemployment and inflation increased, especially in the UK (Scharpf 1987: 65–6). As the Labour government was forced to request an IMF loan in the mid-1970s, it had to cut public spending and to pursue monetarist goals, which fulfilled the IMF's conditions. With these policies the Labour Party threw overboard programmatic key elements of their policy programme. At the same time, the voters lost confidence in the party's capacity to govern. This lead to Labour's defeat in the 1979 general elections (Shaw 1994a: 7, 23; Schmucker 1997: 57).

In Germany economic performance deteriorated strongly in 1982 (the GDP per capita declined by one per cent). Because of the different options of the two parties in power, the SPD and the FDP, the government could not find a coherent strategy to address that problem. The FPD opposed expansionary public investments and tax increases – the SPD's recommendation for reducing unemployment. Eventually, the SPD agreed to introduce cuts in welfare benefits and was seen responsible for the increase in unemployment by many voters. For electoral and policy reasons the SPD ended its coalition with the SPD in 1982 (Scharpf 1987: 192; Borchert 1995: 118).

In the late 1970s and the early 1980s the Labour Party and the SPD, now in opposition, still praised Keynesianism despite their former governmental practices (Shaw 1994a: 13; Heath *et al.* 2001: 83). The Labour Party (1979; 1983) and the SPD (1983) suggested public employment and investment programmes to combat unemployment. In addition, Labour and also the SPÖ put emphasis on state-owned enterprises. Labour even advocated the expansion of nationalised firms, planning agreements between the state and the enterprises, and the restriction of imports to the UK. The demand to reduce labour supply through longer holidays, earlier retirement, and the move to a 35-hour working week fits into the macro-economic orientation of the SPD (1983, 1987), the Labour Party (1979, 1983, 1987) and the SPÖ (1983). Active labour market policy such as Labour's plans for subsidies to employers who employ long-term unemployed or the SPD's employment training and direct job-creation ambitions played only a minor role in Social Democratic employment policy at that time.

Besides this Keynesian approach the SPD started to take into account supply-side economic policy as a means to reduce unemployment. If the competitiveness of the companies is increased through public support, private firms will create jobs. However, in the 1980s these plans were rather vague (SPD 1983; 1987).

In the second half of the 1980s Labour and the SPD still stuck to their Keynesian preferences. It was the SPÖ, which came forward with the most radical break of its employment concepts happening with the 1986 electoral platform. The SPÖ formulated the goal of promoting the Austrian economy by means of supply-side policy and promised the privatisation of nationalised firms (Müller 1988: 108; Meth-Cohn and Müller 1994: 165). The promotion of an internationally competitive economy through state aid for technology, environmental protection and so on should increase the level of employment. The most drastic innovation was the refusal of public demand management policy, or more, specifically, Keynesian policy (SPÖ 1986; Talos 1987: 143).

Later on the SPÖ pursued a double strategy. One strategy consisted in intensifying active labour-market policy. In the 1980s subsidies to employment, payable to employers, and job-search assistance were in the centre of this measure, while in the 1990s the SPÖ shifted its emphasis to employment training, especially for young people and women. The second main feature of the SPÖ strategy was to strengthen the competitiveness of Austrian enterprises, as a prospering economy is necessary for increasing the tax revenue and for creating jobs (SPÖ 1990, 1994).

In the late 1980s the Labour Party still supported social ownership, reduction in labour supply, and investment in high technology for nationalised enterprises (Labour Party 1987). At the beginning of the 1990s Labour – following the SPÖ's track of the 1980s – shifted to supply-side economic policy and focused on the improvement of the competitiveness of private enterprises. The arguments for employment policy by the way of supporting the private economy, as stated in the 1992 election manifesto, are related to increased worldwide competition and the necessity to improve the performance of the UK as location for enterprises. The reason for these changing priorities can be seen in the idea that steady and sustained economic growth, which benefits private companies, generates long-term jobs (Labour Party 1992).

At the beginning of the 1990s the SPD (1990) introduced a strong environmental element to its demand side employment strategy. Thus, German's Social Democrats combined environmental protection with combating unemployment. Ecological investments in traffic and housing through the public and the private sectors and reductions in working hours represent the macro-economic side of SPD's employment policy.

In contrast to the SPÖ and the Labour Party, the SPD did not emphasise the economy and prosperous companies as strategies for reducing unemployment before the mid-1990s. Then the supply-side measures, including the reduction of bureaucratic obstacles to competitiveness and of add-on costs, were complemented by demand-side arguments. The claim to reduce employment and income tax is based on the idea for fostering the demand of private households, as they have more money at their disposal (SPD 1994). At that time the SPD abandoned the conventional methods of Keynesian policy such as public employment programmes. However, some elements of or arguments for a macro-economic approach were reinstated in the 1990s.

All three parties ascribe more significance to active labour market policies in the late 1990s. The new policy of Labour (1992, 1997) encapsulated in the welfare-to-work scheme includes training programmes, subsidies to employers and obliges the unemployed either to find a job or

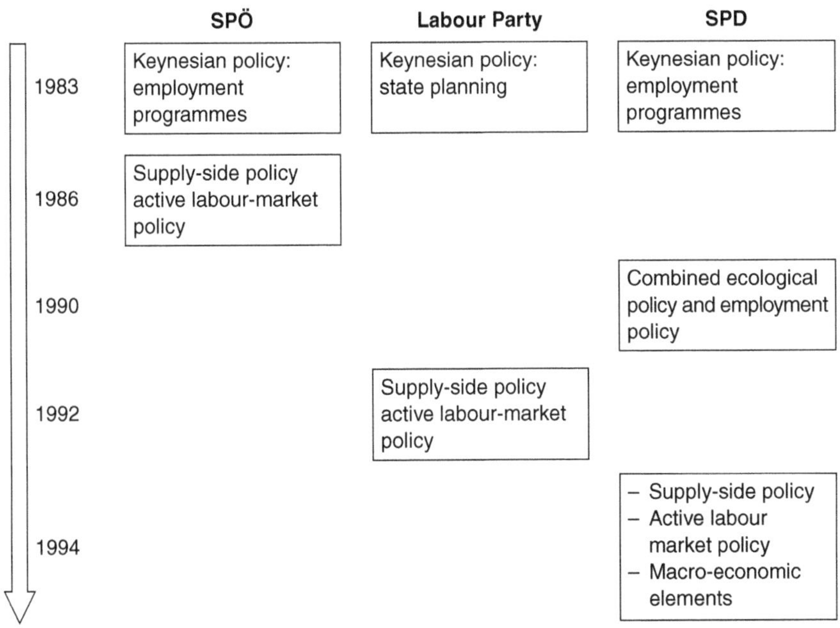

Figure 9.1 Changing conceptions of employment of the SPÖ, the SPD and the Labour Party.

to take part in a training programme. The goal of this initiative is to reduce the public expenditures for social security in order to achieve a low budget deficit. Labour puts emphasis on 'the supply-side aspects of employability primarily through redressing the inadequacies of the unemployed, training them into appropriate skills in demand, and discerning what labour market employment trends need to be met' (Cressey 1999: 176).

Similar to the welfare-to-work programme of the Labour Party, the SPD (1998) aimed at bringing the long-term unemployed back to the labour market through subsidies to employers. While New Labour is not entirely clear about what will happen to people who do not find a job, the SPD indicates cutting benefits when a job is refused for no obvious reason.

Already in the late 1980s the SPD (1987) identified the EU as an appropriate level for solving the unemployment problem. Later, the SPÖ (1994) and the Labour Party (1992) also incorporated this idea into their employment policy conceptions, while in the mid-1980s Labour (1983) had demanded Britain's withdrawal from the EU.

By the end of the 1990s, the SPÖ (1999), Labour (1997) and the SPD (1998) articulated their new economic and employment policies: flexibility, improvement of the competitiveness of enterprises, deregulation of anti-competitive practices, increased flexibility for the labour market, and cutting labour costs. In contrast to the Labour Party and the SPÖ, the SPD (1998) still maintained the reduction of working time and some macroeconomic ideas as solutions to the unemployment problem. Thus, German's Social Democrats proposed a mix of supply-side as well as demand-side measures in their employment policy concepts (see Figure 9.1).

The strategic shift from Keynesian to supply-side politics constitutes the fundamental change of Social Democratic employment concepts – especially the SPÖ's and the Labour Party's. While in a Keynesian understanding the employment problem is dealt with on the collective level, supply-side measures start from an individualistic perspective. In this latter approach the role of the state aims at the creation of the most efficient conditions for enterprises and employability. By promoting employers in order to stimulate economic growth and to create jobs, Social Democratic parties give up – strictly speaking – a part of their traditional identity as labour movement.

Reasons for the changes in employment policy

Three aspects seem particularly relevant to explain the observed policy changes: First, the changing economic environment provides the wider context for the changes in the parties' employment positions and can be described as the 'ultimate source' for party change (Katz and Mair 1990 quoted in Harmel and Janda 1992: 8; Müller 1997: 294; Kitschelt 1999:

321). The altered economic conditions are linked to the struggle for votes in the party competition and the mobilisation for support inside Social Democratic parties or more general party cohesion.

Economic environment

Some authors (e.g. Merkel 1993; Kitschelt 1999) emphasise a general crisis of Social Democracy as a result of social and political changes beginning in the late 1960s. Social class erosion, seemingly unmanageable economic crisis, problems with the welfare state, new political values, and rejuvenated conservative rivals have shaken Social Democratic parties across western Europe. As a result of the economic crisis in the 1970s the governments in Austria, the UK and Germany put their main emphasis on reduction of the public deficit. The full-employment doctrine was pushed into the background. Alternative supply side conceptions were suggested and accepted by a majority of voters, leading to shifts in the party composition of government in the UK and Germany, where the Conservative parties occupied offices in the 1980s and nearly all of the 1990s (Borchert 1995: 16; Scarrow 1999: 85; Webb 1999: 41). These parties carried out shifts in budgetary priorities, cuts in welfare benefits, substantial tax relief and privatisation of nationalised firms. In Austria the SPÖ occupied the economically most relevant departments of the government that also carried out similar reforms. In the long run the neo-liberal priorities came to be considered the only possible economic strategy in order to maintain international competitiveness. As long as this remained the general attitude of the majority of voters and the SPD and the Labour Party held on to their traditional state-interventionist policies there was no chance for a return to government.

Moreover, the collapse of communism in eastern Europe in 1989 seemed to demonstrate that state ownership and centralised planning were incapable of matching the economic performance of market economies. From that time on socialist elements of economic policy such as centralised planning were despised in the capitalist world. Especially the Labour Party, which still believed in public companies and planning agreements in the late 1980s, had to adapt to that new situation (Shaw 1994a: 154).

In a more general perspective the changing economic situation consisted of globalisation, the decline of traditional industry and industrial employment and pressure toward flexible production (e.g. Held *et al.* 1999). The widening, deepening, and speeding up of global interconnectedness led to a debate about the efficacy of the nation states. The shrinking scope for national actions also referred to the question how unemployment can be fought most successfully. In this context, the SPÖ, SPD, and the Labour Party included in their proposals the arguments of an increased worldwide competition and attached importance to the EU as a potential solution for this problem. Policies designed and decided at European level were seen as a means for reducing unemployment and to ensure economic prosperity.

Electoral arena

In 1983 when the SPÖ lost its absolute majority the party accounted socio-economic changes for this electoral defeat. After twelve years of governing with an absolute majority the SPÖ formed a coalition with the FPÖ. Because of many problems in the context of a deteriorating economy the SPÖ-FPÖ coalition became very unpopular. The ÖVP benefited form this constellation and seemed to be the likely winner of the next elections as revealed by opinion polls. When Jörg Haider became the FPÖ party leader in the autumn of 1986 his party moved away from its more or less liberal course. Because of Haider's election to the leadership, Franz Vranitzky, the new chancellor, broke with the FPÖ and called early elections. As the SPÖ had decided not to renew its coalition with the FPÖ and wanted to prevent an ÖVP–FPÖ coalition to be formed, the SPÖ needed the ÖVP as its partner in government. The changing economic strategy of the SPÖ in its 1986 electoral platform was primarily designed to attract voters and to win the ÖVP as coalition partner (Luther 1987: 392; Meth-Cohn and Müller 1994: 165).

After the elections of 1986 the SPÖ remained the strongest party in parliament (80 seats) but had to cope with losses:

> One reason for the SPÖ once again being the strongest party was that it had more or less adopted the ÖVP's economic policy, thus taking the wind out of the latter's sails. The two parties decided to form a grand coalition government with the declared intention of implementing structural reforms to deal with the deep-seated economic problems that had become evident in the first half of the 1980s.
>
> (Meth-Cohn and Müller 1994: 196)

As the SPÖ has been able to maintain its plurality despite substantial electoral losses of almost 8 per cent in the 1994 elections and could successfully defend its leading role in government in the 1980s and 1990s, the party saw decreasing electoral results as a communication problem between the party elite and the people. Therefore it put its main emphasis on improving communication structure and election campaigns. The 1994 elections revealed, however, that the SPÖ was very much challenged by the FPÖ breaking into its core segment – the workers. Nevertheless, the SPÖ was able to achieve its primary goal – control of the government – until 2000 (Müller *et al.* 1999: 212, 215).

After the 1987 elections the Labour Party was devastatingly disappointed because of the weak election results. In contrast to the 1983 elections – the worst for the party – Labour won votes and seats, but the party had expected even greater success (see Table 9.1). The party leadership concluded that the economic policies pursued by Labour in the late 1980s, however valid in themselves, were politically no longer feasible. If the party wanted to attract more voters it had to discard the unpopular policies and adopt those aspects of the Conservative policies that were well accepted by the people. Shortly after the 1987 elections the Labour Party began to analyse its election defeat and asked the question of why it had not attracted that many voters. The analysis pointed out that the people did not trust Labour's ability to effectively cope with the changing economic and social environment. Thus, Labour started a far-reaching policy review, trying to adapt the party to the new social, economic, and cultural realities of Britain in the 1990s. One part of the shifting policy proposal included the retreat from Keynesianism. With respect to the economic environment Labour no longer believed that full employment could be achieved by demand management and deficit spending. The problems of such a policy could be an increase in inflation and pressure on the pound. Labour concluded that the only option was to rely on the private sector to raise investment and output. From the party's point of view the task of public policy was to create the conditions which would give business the confidence to invest (Shaw 1994a: 84; 1994b: 161; Webb 1999: 58; Heath *et al.* 2001: 101).

In the eyes of the electorate Labour was seen as tax-and-spend party whose economic incompetence would lead to massive tax increases. As this kind of policy was very unpopular Labour was perceived as old-fashioned and incapable of understanding the aspirations of the people in a changing society. The party recognised that the change in the social structure led to new needs of the people that it did not address in the 1980s. Opinion polls showed that even those voters who favoured Labour's position on individual issues had considerably more confidence in the Conservative government. These perceptions were reflected in the

Table 9.1 Election results of Social Democratic parties in Austria (SPÖ), Germany (SPD) and Britain (Labour Party), 1983–99, votes (%) and seats (N).

SPÖ	*%*	*N*	*SPD*	*%*	*N*	*Labour*	*%*	*N*
1983	47.6	90	1983	38.2	193	1979	37.0	269
1986	43.1	80	1987	37.0	186	1983	27.6	209
1990	42.8	80	1990	33.5	239	1987	30.8	229
1994	34.9	65	1994	36.4	252	1992	34.4	271
1995	38.1	71	1998	40.9	298	1997	43.2	418
1999	34.6	65						

Sources: Austria: Müller/Plasser/Ulram 1999; Germany: http://www.wahlrecht.de/ergebnisse/bundestag.htm, retrieved on 1999–08–28, created on 1999–06–15, Britain: Webb 1999.

electoral success of the Conservatives in the years 1979, 1983 and 1987 and built the starting point for Labour's policy review after the 1987 elections (Shaw 1994a: 157; Webb 1999: 58). Poor electoral performance in the 1980s and the party's analysis of the electoral market urged Labour to change its policy proposals in order to bring it back to government.

Various analyses of the SPD's election defeats in the 1980s (see Table 9.1) stressed the fact that the party's future would depend on its ability to assimilate post-materialist interests with the party's traditional concerns. The SPD could not hope to return to government – the party's primary goal – unless it took votes from the Greens and to a much larger extent from the CDU/CSU (Scarrow 1999: 81).

The effort to form an electoral alliance between the 'old' and the 'new' left eventually lead to the 1990 manifesto, which was based on the Berlin Manifesto of 1989. The combination of environmentalist concerns with the question of unemployment constituted a new policy statement of German's Social Democrats. This new issue constituted a signal to the people who were attracted by the Greens but shared the Social Democratic values. However, as unification became the dominant topic in the 1990 elections, the SPD's ecological policy played only a minor role and the CDU/CSU–FDP coalition was returned to office (Padgett 1994: 22; Leif and Raschke 1994: 92).

As the concern about the Green challenge diminished within the SPD at the beginning of the 1990s, the party put more emphasis on its right wing in order to win votes from the CDU/CSU. By adopting supply-side employment policy concepts the SPD tried to move towards the centre and simultaneously maintained the traditional idea of a macro-economic approach. These two policy shifts that informed the 1990 and 1994 election manifestos make clear that the SPD was encouraged to respond to the electoral arena (Scarrow 1999: 82–3).

To sum up, 'external shocks' (Harmel and Janda 1994: 267) from the electoral market that is electoral losses, had an enormous impact on the policies of the SPÖ, SPD and the Labour Party. The SPD and Labour tried to react to the voter's preferences in the 1980s by changing their policies only after several election defeats. The fact that the SPD and the Labour Party were not able to return to government until the late 1990s was a great challenge to them.

Party cohesion and party leadership

Besides the environmental conditions – in particular the electoral arena – the parties' internal life is crucial for understanding party position change. In 1986, when Franz Vranitzky became chancellor, the SPÖ struggled to recover from a crisis of electoral support as revealed by opinion polls. The party leadership decided to change the party's policy proposals in a supply-side direction in order to convince the voters of the SPÖ's capacity to govern. Franz Vranitzky, a pragmatic politician with a business background and no typical party career, was very much in favour of a grand coalition with the ÖVP and hence favoured policies that were compatible with this choice of partners. The threat of likely electoral defeat silenced most critics of this change within the party. Opposition to a new policy direction within the party was relatively moderate. Therefore the proposed employment policy changes that contained a major break with earlier concepts could be implemented without considerable resistance in the 1986 electoral manifesto (Müller 1988: 109; Meth-Cohn and Müller 1994: 165; Dachs 1996: 293).

From a party perspective the policy change had to be assessed in comparison with its alternatives:

> If the party stuck to its previous policy it is very likely that it would have suffered electoral defeat and not be included in a government coalition. However, participating in government and in particular being the leading force there and occupying the economically most relevant departments is giving the Social Democrats the chance to influence a process which cannot be held up totally.
>
> (Müller 1988: 113)

Although Vranitzky became chancellor in 1986, Fred Sinowatz, the former chancellor, remained party chairman. Initially, the party officials expressed their scepticism of Vranitzky because of his business background and his relative distance from the grassroots Social Democratic organisation. However, Sinowatz acted very cleverly as a mediator between the party in public office and the party organisation and managed to maintain party cohesion. In the meantime Vranitzky won confidence within the party because of his popularity, electoral success, and his rejection of Haider's FPÖ. In 1988 Vranitzky took over a cohesive party and held the offices of chancellor and party chairman until 1997. He could rely on a disciplined party that the former party chairman, Sinowatz, had guaranteed and hence had the chance to introduce party policy change (Luther 1987: 392; Campbell 1995: 530; Müller *et al.* 1999: 231).

Formal powers and real power within the Labour Party were distributed amongst a range of institutions in the early 1980s. When Neil Kinnock became party leader in 1983 Labour was a deeply polarised party between hard left and right activists. Kinnock belonged to the soft leftist block and could also find support from the right wing of the party. At the beginning of his leadership his capacity to produce major organisational and programmatic change was therefore limited.

One of the most crucial developments in the internal politics of the party has been the loss of influence of the hard left as a consequence of the succession of electoral defeats. The 1983 election Manifesto, said to be the farthest left election programme the party ever had presented, resulted in its worst performance since 1900. This disastrous defeat discredited hard-left policies. After the 1987 election many party activists lost confidence in the ability of Labour to win unless it changed its policy proposals. Most important was that former hard-left officials changed their minds either because of the conclusions they drew from the election defeats in the 1980s or because they no longer believed that the policies they advocated earlier were workable, politically viable, or electorally acceptable. The most obvious factor explaining the altered attitude with respect to changing policies was the desire for electoral victory (Shaw 1994a: 161; Webb 1999: 57–8).

In the mid-1980s Labour's leadership could fill important policy positions with its allies and rely on a majority within the party in the struggle against the hard left. Hence, the soft left had occupied the strategic power position in the Labour Party that allowed subsequent policy change. Another important power shift by the end of the 1980s can be observed. The traditional right fully recovered and formed the dominant axis within the party together with the pragmatic centre. This gave Kinnock the power basis to succeed with organisational transformation via the strategies of centralisation and direct membership enfranchisement. In combination with marginalisation of the hard left and the broader organisational changes the new institutional setting at the end of the 1980s provided the leader and his allies with an enormous amount of power in formulating the new policy. 'The deep yearning to rid Britain of the much reviled Thatcherite Government fed a growing disposition to compromise and swallow unpalatable leadership decisions if this facilitated victory at the polls' (Shaw 1994b: 166). At the same time, a new generation of pragmatists such as Gordon Brown and Tony Blair emerged and influenced the party. Their political approach directing towards winning elections and gaining office again since 1979 contained the repudiation of the old conflicts between state and market, public and private sector, and labour and capital. Generally, 'a spirit of sombre realism now pervaded the party' (Shaw 1993: 128) putting individualistic values in the core of Labour's policy.

These reforms made Labour attractive for the voters and indirectly forced the Conservatives to replace Margaret Thatcher by John Major who won the 1992 elections by a relatively small margin. Labour continued Kinnock's way under his successor John Smith. When Tony Blair became party leader in 1994, after Smith's sudden death, he proclaimed that the party represented a united organisation that had undergone major organisational and policy changes in the 1980s. The stable and long lasting party leadership of Neil Kinnock from 1983 to 1992 provided the foundation to overcome internal resistance to proposed changes. Eventually, party officials were willing to accept the leaders' policy proposals in order to win elections.

After being voted out of office in 1982 power in the SPD was distributed among a hydra-headed leadership consisting of Willy Brandt as party chairman, Hans Jochen Vogel as the leader of the party in parliament, and Johannes Rau as the chancellor candidate for the 1987 elections. A number of party officials stood up for tightening the party leadership, which represented the old guard of the SPD at that time. In the first years of opposition the left within the party gained influence. But the left was not a cohesive group, as it was divided into an old left representing orthodox Social Democracy and a new left oriented towards post-materialist values. Because of these distinctive groups there was no common understanding of the socio-economic changes and the factors responsible for electoral defeat in the 1980s. One faction advocated traditional Social Democracy, another faction stood up for neo-liberal modernisation, and another one proclaimed post-materialist values. Considering this situation, the creation of a strategic response towards the electoral and economical challenges was rather uneven (Lösche and Walter 1992: 187; Padgett 1994: 21; Scarrow 1999: 82).

One result of or one condition leading to the breakdown of cohesion was the instability of the party leadership. After the 1987 elections Willy Brandt, who had been the party leader for twenty-three years, resigned from leadership because of internal tensions. The disputes about the prospective direction and identity of the SPD started immediately after the election defeat in January 1987 (Padgett 1987: 348).

In a short period of time the SPD replaced its party leaders. Hans-Jochen Vogel (1987–1991), Björn Engholm (1991–93), Rudolf Scharping (1993–1995), and Oskar Lafontaine (1995–99) represented the party for a few years. In addition the party nominated for each election a new chancellor candidate who was – with the exception of the 1994 elections – not identical with the party chairman (see Table 9.2). The fractionalisation of the party and the frequent change of party chairmen accounted for the failure of the party leaders' attempt to unite the party and to give it a clear policy direction (Padgett 1994: 26–7; Leif and Raschke 1994: 150; Walter 1998: 92, 107).

Table 9.2 SPD: Candidate for chancellor and party chairman (1983–)

Parliamentary elections	*Chancellor candidate*	*Party chairman*
1983	Hans Jochen Vogel	Willy Brandt (1964–87)
1987	Johannes Rau	
1990	Oskar Lafontaine	Hans Jochen Vogel (1987–91) Björn Engholm (1991–3)
1994	Rudolf Scharping	Rudolf Scharping (1993–5)
1998	Gerhard Schröder (also Party chairman since 1999)	Oskar Lafontaine (1995–9)

Since the beginning of the 1980s the SPD elaborated a new party programme that was adopted in 1989. This new programme as well as the 1990 election manifesto reflected the concerns of the various intra-party groups containing a mixture of old left and new post-materialist policy statements. Within these programmes ecological policy was the only issue the traditional left and especially the trade unions permitted out of the proposals the new left had developed. This new generation within the party coming from the Land level also suggested breaking with traditional policies such as rigid labour market conceptions but could not succeed (Padgett 1993: 20; Gohr 2001: 270).

On the federal level the SPD failed to win government office until 1998. But at the Land level several SPD politicians had landslide victories (e.g. Lafontaine, Scharping, Schröder). These Länder represented an important recruitment ground for the SPD at the national level. The new generation of politicians were endowed with pragmatism and strategic flexibility. Their advance and success at Land level increased their weight in the central party organisation, but also fostered their independence from the party and allowed them to take stands which did not reflect the 'official' party position on many issues. 'These tendencies in the SPD elite had the effect of reducing the internal cohesion of the party, giving free reign to policy differences' (Padgett 1994: 21).

To sum up, the frequent change of party chairmen did not allow for a high degree of party cohesion. The dilemma of the SPD in the 1980s and 1990s is reflected by the attempt to satisfy old and new left policy. After Lafontaine's resignation from the office of party chairman in 1999 chancellor Schröder also assessed this position. In the beginning of his leadership the SPD remained divided (Scarrow 1999: 84) but especially in recent times Schröder could consolidate his power basis and seems to have a stronger grip on the party now (see Hering, this volume).

Conclusions

The changing economic situation and the dominance of neo-liberal politics since the 1980s has challenged Social Democratic parties in Europe. At the end of the 20th century, the SPÖ, SPD and the Labour Party represent converging employment policy conceptions that displayed central features of neo-liberal supply-side policy. The retreat from Keynesian policy shows that all three parties have reacted to the changing economic situation, in which a low public deficit has become the primary goal. Social Democratic parties adopted the common neo-liberal argument that unemployment can no longer be effectively fought by deficit spending and public expenditure. As the macro-economic Keynesianian approach and supply-side policy viewing from a micro-perspective are based on different economic and ideological ideas, this policy shift observed in the SPÖ, Labour and to a lesser extent in the SPD indicates a transformation of traditional Social Democracy. Eventually, all three parties move towards the centre of the party spectrum by adopting supply side proposals. They did not create a new policy approach but made use of supply-side concepts and strengthened active labour-market policy.

Nevertheless, adaptation to the changing environment did not happen inevitably, but resulted from party competition and internal party politics. Before the SPÖ shifted to supply-side policy in its 1986 manifesto, it lost its absolute majority in 1983 and was represented by a new chancellor, Franz Vranitzky. The analysis showed that Vranitzky played the key role for party policy change. His pragmatic approach towards solving the economic problems and his preference of a coalition with the ÖVP were decisive for the shift in economic policy. The possible electoral defeat, as predicted by opinion polls, was the crucial factor for convincing the party to submit to the suggested policy plans. Possible resistance to the new policy from within the party was diminished initially, because of the weak electoral predictions for the 1986 elections and afterwards because of the relative success at the 1986 elections when the SPÖ was able to defend its relative majority and remained the senior partner in government. It was obvious that the policy shift had accounted for much of the relative electoral success of the party in 1986.

In 1992 when the Labour Party changed its employment policy conception to a supply-side policy Neil Kinnock had been the party leader since 1983. During his leadership he tried to unite and modernise the Labour Party and had started with organisational reforms. These reforms were decisive for consolidating his power base and establishing the necessary structures for policy change. Opinion polls in the 1980s showed the people did not trust Labour because of its image as a tax-and-spend party. A succession of electoral defeats (1979, 1983 and 1987) leading to a loss of influence of the left was responsible for overcoming the intra-party resistance to policy change and a move towards the political centre.

The SPD changed its employment policy concepts twice: first, it introduced environmentalist concerns to the 1990 manifesto without giving up its traditional Keynesian approach. Analysis of the elections in the 1980s advocated the party responding to the challenges from the Green Party but also those from the CDU/CSU. In this context, the party reacted to the challenges from the Green Party. The second change in the 1994 manifesto towards supply-side policy can be characterised as adaptation to the neo-liberal supply-side mainstream and as a signal to the CDU/CSU voters. But this shift only constituted one policy element; the party also maintained demand side policy and a macro-economic approach designed to strengthen consumer-buying power.

The employment conceptions of the SPD represented the division of the party between old left, new left, and modernisers trying to move the party to the middle. As a consequence of the party's frequent leadership change the party lacked the necessary cohesion for wholesale party policy change. The dilemma of the party, aiming at responding to the new social movements of the left but also to the voters of the centre triggered permanent conflicts within the party. The new generation of politicians that grew out of the Land level kept a certain distance from the party and followed their own policy goals. The federal structure of Germany caused disintegration of the party. But as pointed out earlier, the SPD introduced two new issues in the 1990s albeit lacking party cohesion. These policy changes can be seen as reaction to the SPD's poor electoral performance. Because the internal power balance was very fragile and unstable, German Social Democrats trying to gain office through reacting to voter preferences only agreed on modest changes.

From this analysis it is possible to conclude that electoral defeat had direct impact on the SPD and Labour's policy change and can be considered an important factor leading to the observed changes. The SPD and Labour's adaptation to supply-side policies preceded poor electoral performance in the 1980s. The Labour Party, with only one leader from 1983 to 1992, carried out a radical change of its employment concepts. In contrast, the SPD's policy shifts were not complete but half-hearted. This difference results from an instable and frequently changing SPD party leadership and missing party discipline. Thus, party change depends on the party leadership's ability to control power resources within the party and overcome internal resistance against proposed changes. When the SPÖ changed its employment concepts in 1986 while being in office, the chancellor Franz Vranitzky disposed of the necessary conditions to do so. Thus, a cohesive party and the party leadership that has the power over the party's internal life might be considered as decisive for the extent of party policy change.

References

Bell, D. and Shaw, E. (eds) (1994) *Conflict and Cohesion in Western European Social Democratic Parties*, London: Pinter.

Bieling, H.-J. and Deppe, F. (eds) (1997) *Arbeitslosigkeit und Wohlfahrts*staat, Opladen: Leske + Budrich.

Blair, T. (1998) *The Third Way: New Politics for the New Century*, London: Fabian Society.

Blair, T. and Schröder, G. (1999) *Europe: The Third Way – die Neue Mitte*, London/Berlin: Labour Party/SPD.

Boix, C. (1998) *Political Parties, Growth and Equality. Conservative and Social Democratic Economic Strategies in the World Economy*, Cambridge: Cambridge University Press.

Borchert, J. (1995) *Die konservative Transformation des Wohlfahrtsstaates. Großbritannien, Kanada, die USA und Deutschland im Vergleich*, Frankfurt/Main: Campus.

Budge, I., Robertson, D. and Hearl, D. (eds) (1987) *Ideology, Strategy and Party Change. Spatial Analysis of Post-War Election Programmes in Nineteen Democracies*, Cambridge: Cambridge University Press.

Campbell, D. F. J. (1995) 'Fred Sinowatz', in H. Dachs, P. Gerlich and W. C. Müller (eds) *Die Politiker. Karrieren und Wirken bedeutender Repräsentanten der Zweiten Republik*, Vienna: Manz, 520–31.

Cressey, P. (1999) 'New Labour and Employment, Training and Employee Relations', in M. Powell (ed.) *New Labour, New Welfare State? The 'Third Way' in British Social Policy*, Bristol: Policy Press, 171–90.

Dachs, H. (1996) 'Von der "Sanierungspartnerschaft" zur konfliktgeladenen Unübersichtlichkeit. Entwicklungen und Verschiebungen während der Großen Koalition 1986 bis 1994', in R. Sieder, H. Steinert and E. Tálos (eds), *Österreich 1945–1995*, Vienna (second edition): Manz, 286–301.

Ginsberg, B. (1982) *The Consequences of Consent, Elections, Citizen Control and Popular Acquiescence*, New York: Random House.

Gohr, A. (2001) 'Eine Sozialstaatspartei in der Opposition. Die Sozialpolitik der SPD in den 80er Jahren', in M. G. Schmidt (ed.), *Wohlfahrtsstaatliche Politik. Institutionen, politische Prozesse und Leistungsprofil*, Opladen: Leske + Budrich, 262–93.

Harmel, R. and Janda, K. (1992) 'Environment, Performance, and Leadership as Factors in Party Change' (paper presented at the Workshop on Democracies and the Organization of Political Parties, ECPR Joint Sessions, University of Limerick, 30 March – 4 April, 1992).

Harmel, R. and Janda, K. (1994) 'An Integrated Theory of Party Goals and Party Change' *Journal of Theoretical Politics* 6(3) 259–87.

Heath, A. F., Jowell, R. M. and Curtice, J. K. (2001) *The Rise of New Labour. Party Policies and Voter Choices*, Oxford: Oxford University Press.

Held, D., McGrew, A., Goldblatt, D. and Perraton, J. (1999) *Global Transformations. Politics, Economics and Culture*, Cambridge: Polity Press.

Kitschelt, H. (1999) 'European Social Democracy between Political Economy and Electoral Competition', in H. Kitschelt, P. Lange, P. Mark and J. D. Stephens (eds) *Continuity and Change in Contemporary Capitalism, Cambridge,* Cambridge University Press, 317–45.

Kitschelt, H., Lange, P., Marks, P. and Stephens, J. D. (eds) (1999) *Continuity and Change in Contemporary Capitalism*, Cambridge: Cambridge University Press.

Labour Party (1979) *The Labour Way Is the Better Way* (election manifesto).

Labour Party (1983) *The New Hope for Britain* (election manifesto), London: Labour Party.

Labour Party (1987) *Britain Will Win* (election manifesto), London: Labour Party.

Labour Party (1992) *Time to Get Britain Working Again* (election manifesto), London: Labour Party.

Labour Party (1996) *New Labour, New Life for Britain*, London: Labour Party.

Labour Party (1997) *New Labour: Because Britain Deserves Better* (election manifesto), London: Labour Party.

Leif, T. and Raschke, J. (1994) *Rudolf Scharping, die SPD und die Macht*, Hamburg: rororo.

Lösche, P. and Walter, F. (1992) *Die SPD: Klassenpartei, Volkspartei, Quotenpartei*, Darmstadt: Wissenschaftliche Buchgesellschaft.

Luther, K. R. (1987) 'Austria's Future and Waldheim's Past. The Significance of the 1986 Elections', *West European Politics* 10(3): 376–99.

Lutz, B. (1984) *Der kurze Traum immerwährender Prosperität*, München: Campus Verlag.

P. Mair, W. C. Müller and F. Plasser (eds) (1999) *Parteien auf komplexen Wählermärkten. Reaktionsstrategien politischer Parteien in Westeuropa*, Vienna: Signum.

Merkel, W. (1993) *Ende der Sozialdemokratie? Machtressourcen und Regierungspolitik im westeuropäischen Vergleich*, Frankfurt/New York: Campus Verlag.

Meth-Cohn, D. and Müller, W. C. (1994) 'Looking Reality in the Eye. The Politics of Privatization in Austria', in V. Wright (ed.), *Privatization in Western Europe*, London: Pinter, 160–79.

Müller, W. C. (1988) 'Privatising in a Corporatist Economy: the Politics of Privatisation in Austria', *West European Politics*, 11(4): 101–116.

Müller, W. C. (1997) 'Inside the Black Box', *Party Politics* vol. 3, no. 3, 293–313.

Müller, W. C., Plasser, F. and Ulram, P. A. (1999) 'Schwäche als Vorteil, Stärke als Nachteil. Die Reaktion der Parteien auf den Rückgang der Wählerbindung in Österreich', in P. Mair, W.C. Müller and F. Plasser (eds) *Parteien auf komplexen Wählermärkten. Reaktionsstrategien politischer Parteien in Westeuropa*, Vienna: Signum, 201–45.

Padgett, S. (1987) 'The West German Social Democrats in Opposition 1982–86', *West European Politics*, 10(3): 333–56.

Padgett, S. (1993) 'The German Social Democrats. A Redefinition of Social Democracy or Bad Godesberg Mark II', *West European Politics* 16(1): 20–38.

Padgett, S. (1994) 'The German Social Democratic Party: Between Old and New Left', in D. Bell and E. Shaw (eds) *Conflict and Cohesion in Western European Social Democratic Parties*, London: Pinter, 10–30.

Powell, M. (ed.) (1999) *New Labour, New Welfare State? The 'Third Way' in British Social Policy*, Bristol: Policy Press.

Rallings, C. (1987) 'The Influence of Election Programmes. Britain and Canada, 1945–1979', in I. Budge, D. Robertson and D. Hearl (eds), *Ideology, Strategy and Party Change. Spatial Analysis of Post-War Election Programmes in Nineteen Democracies*, Cambridge: Cambridge University Press, 1–14.

Scarrow, S. E. (1999) 'Der Rückgang von Parteibindungen aus der Sicht der deutschen Parteien: Chance oder Gefahr?', in P. Mair, W. C. Müller and F. Plasser (eds) *Parteien auf komplexen Wählermärkten. Reaktionsstrategien politischer Parteien in Westeuropa*, Vienna: Signum, 71–102.

Scharpf, F. W. (1987) *Sozialdemokratische Krisenpolitik in Europa*, Frankfurt/Main: Campus.

Scharpf, F. W. and Schmidt, V. A. (eds) (2000a) *Welfare and Work in the Open Economy. Volume I: From Vulnerability to Competitiveness*, Oxford: Oxford University Press.

Scharpf, F. W. and Schmidt, V. A. (2000b) 'Introduction', in F. W. Scharpf and V. A. Schmidt (eds), *Welfare and Work in the Open Economy. Volume I: From Vulnerability to Competitiveness*, Oxford: Oxford University Press, 1–20.

Schmidt, M. G. (ed.) (2001) *Wohlfahrtsstaatliche Politik. Institutionen, politische Prozesse und Leistungsprofil*, Opladen: Leske + Budrich, 262–93.

Schmucker, R. (1997) 'Großbritannien: Das Ende der "konservativen Revolution"?', in H.-J. Bieling and F. DEPPE (eds) *Arbeitslosigkeit und Wohlfahrtsstaat*, Opladen: Leske + Budrich, 55–87.

Shaw, E. (1993) 'Towards Renewal? The British Labour Party's Policy Review', *West European Politics* 16(1): 112–32.

Shaw, E. (1994a) *The Labour Party since 1979. Crisis and Transformation*, London: Routledge.

Shaw, E. (1994b) 'Conflict and Cohesion in the British Labour Party', in D. Bell and E. Shaw (eds) *Conflict and Cohesion in Western European Social Democratic Parties*, London: Pinter, 151–67.

Shaw, E. (1996) 'Von "Old Labour" zu ‚New Labour': Die Transformation der britischen Sozialdemokratie', in J. Borchert, L. Golsch, U. Jun and P. Lösche (eds), *Das sozialdemokratische Modell*, Opladen: Leske + Budrich, 185–212.

Sieder, R., Steinert, H. and Tálos, E. (eds) (1996) *Österreich 1945–1995*, Vienna (second edition): Manz.

SPD (1983) *Das Regierungsmanifesto der SPD 1983–1987* (election manifesto).

SPD (1987) *Zukunft für alle – arbeiten für soziale Gerechtigkeit und Frieden* (election manifesto).

SPD (1990) *Der neue Weg – ökologisch, sozial, wirtschaftlich stark* (election manifesto).

SPD (1994) *Reformen für Deutschland* (election manifesto).

SPD (1998) *Arbeit, Innovation und Gerechtigkeit* (election manifesto).

SPÖ (1983) *Für Österreich und seine Menschen* (election manifesto).

SPÖ (1986) *Vor uns liegt das neue Österreich* (election manifesto).

SPÖ (1990) *Das Österreich von Morgen* (election manifesto).

SPÖ (1994) *Es geht um viel, es geht um Österreich* (election manifesto).

SPÖ (1999) *Der richtige Weg für Österreich* (election manifesto).

Talos, E. (1987) 'Arbeitslosigkeit und beschäftigungspolitische Steuerung: Problemwahrnehmung/Problemartikulation, Zielsetzungen, Strategien und Maßnahmen in Österreich seit Mitte der siebziger Jahre', in E. Tàlos and M. Wiederschwinger (eds) *Arbeitslosigkeit. Österreichs Vollbeschäftigungspolitik am Ende?*, Vienna: Verlag für Gesellschaftskritik, 91–166.

Talos, E. and Wiederschwinger, M. (eds) (1987) *Arbeitslosigkeit. Österreichs Vollbeschäftigungspolitik am Ende?*, Vienna: Verlag für Gesellschaftskritik.

Walter, Franz (1998) *Die Bonner Parteien auf dem Weg in die Berliner Republik. Politische Kolumnen*, Hamburg: Dr Kovac.

Webb, P. D. (1999) 'Die Reaktion der britischen Parteien auf die Erosion der Wählerloyalität', in P. Mair, W. C. Müller and F. Plasser (eds), *Parteien auf komplexen Wählermärkten. Reaktionsstrategien politischer Parteien in Westeuropa*, Vienna: Signum, 31–70.

Wright, V. (ed.) (1994) *Privatization in Western Europe*, London: Pinter.

10 From 'Eurokeynesianism' to the 'Third Way'

The Party of European Socialists (PES) and European employment policies

Andreas Aust

Introduction

Social democratic parties were traditionally the political representatives of the working class. It was the social cleavage between capital and labour that formed the background of their creation and growth in the late 19th century. As labour parties grew, they faced several issues they had to decide upon: (1) whether to integrate into the existing national sets of institutions in order to reform them from within or to stay outside, (2) whether to remain the agent of working class interests or to look for multi- or non-class support and (3) whether to concentrate on social reform or on revolution (Przeworski 1985: 3). The family of Social Democratic parties in Europe can be defined along the lines of the decisions made: the distinctive feature of Social Democracy is that it decided to take 'the hard road to power' within the existing political and social order (Sassoon 1997). The Social Democratic parties became part of the national political systems and tried to reform the capitalist system in a way that promoted the interests of their supporters. The guiding idea of Social Democracy was that it was possible to use political power to control the development of capitalist economy. After World War II Keynesian thoughts began to influence Social Democracy and the commitments to full employment and an expansion of the welfare state became the core values of Social Democracy (Prezowski 1985; Scharpf 1991; Borchert 1996). Of vital importance to the Social Democratic project was the capacity of the national governments to manage mixed economies. This precondition is said to be undermined by the processes of Europeanisation (Scharpf 1999, 2000; Ladrech 2000; Streeck 2000). If this is true, then the following questions should be asked: How did Social Democracy in Europe respond to the Single European Act and the Maastricht Treaty which were part of a predominantly neoliberal project? Did it develop alternative or complementary strategies, and if so, what kind? Finally, did it succeed in influencing the EU agenda? These are the main questions I intend to analyse in this chapter. Following the classical concept of Hirschman, I would like to distinguish between three broadly defined alternative strategies which Social Democracy might pursue to handle the challenge of European integration: exit, voice and loyality.

Exit

Social democratic parties could reject the whole idea of European integration as reducing the national capacities towards an autonomous 'socialist path'. This idea, for example, prevailed within the 'old' Labour party (UK) in the 1970s and early 1980s when it called for a withdrawal of British membership. By the mid-1980s, a consensus appeared among the socialist parties to accept membership (Featherstone 1988: 3). However, it is worth recalling that countries like Sweden, Finland and Austria, where Social Democratic parties have been particularly strong preferred to remain outside the European Union. These countries joined the EU only in 1995. By now, it seems clear that 'exit' has disappeared as a feasible policy option for Social Democracy.

Voice

The strategy 'voice' is based on the argument that the economy operates on a transnational level and that the national capacity to influence economic processes is therefore restricted. The only way to regain a Social Democratic primacy of politics over economy and to regulate the behaviour of economic actors is to strengthen the cooperation of political actors at a supranational level of governance. The strategy 'voice' accepts European integration, but calls for a reorientation of its policies in order to increase the possibility to pursue *traditional* Social Democratic policies – full employment and welfare state expansion – at both the European and at the national level (see Kesselman 1996). This strategic choice may be called '*Eurokeynesianism*'. As will be shown in the chapter such a strategy was proposed by the European organisation of the Social Democratic parties, the Confederation and later on the PES, throughout the 1980s and 1990s, but was never fully implemented.

Loyalty

The third strategic approach of Social Democratic parties accepts that the challenge of globalisation leaves no alternative but to *adapt the means for achieving Social Democratic values* to the new politico-economic framework. New policies need to be developed to ensure that economic growth can still be combined with social progress and inclusion. This approach argues that traditional Social Democratic instruments need to be rethought (see Giddens 1998): the market is no longer regarded as the structural foundation of a capitalist economy which is inherently irrational and unjust

(Marx and Keynes), but as an effective and efficient way to allocate scarce resources; Keynesian macroeconomic policy is seen to be no longer possible in a world of open markets and the welfare state in its traditional form is criticised for being too passive and bureaucratic, reproducing outdated gender relations, failing in their attempt to eliminate poverty and generating a culture of 'dependency' among welfare recipients. Accepting the new framework of 'states embedded in markets' means putting the issue of competitiveness at the centre of the new Social Democratic strategy and reforming the welfare state towards a 'social investment state'. In that approach the European Union is perceived as an instrument to promote modernisation rather than as an instrument to re-regulate capitalism. Obviously, this strategic choice is informed by the thinking of the so-called 'Third Way' (Giddens 1998; Streeck 2000).

This chapter shows that there has been a gradual transition of Social Democratic European policy from a 'Eurokeynesian' approach to some kind of 'Third Way' strategy in the course of the past two decades. The analysis will build on documents of the Confederation of the Social Democratic Parties in the European Community (CSPEC) with a particular focus on the Party Leaders Meetings. The CSPEC, which was transformed in 1992 into the Party of European Socialists (PES), has developed into an organization that is increasingly trying to coordinate the European policies of Social Democratic actors in the EU. (Hix 1995; Hix and Lord 1997; Ladrech 2000).

A Social Democratic alternative to the single European market?

In the early 1980s, European integration underwent a period of crisis. 'Eurosclerosis' summarised the general feeling. The response to the crisis was the revitalisation of Europe through the White Paper on the Single European Market (SEM) and the Single European Act (SEA) (cf. Moravcisk 1991; Bornschier 2000). The main idea of the SEM project was to finally implement the (old) idea of an integrated liberal internal market until 1992. Therefore, the Treaty of Rome was changed for the first time by the SEA to allow for majority voting in the Council of Ministers in policy areas that were related to the implementation of the SEM. The driving force behind this project was a political coalition between parts of the Commission and big business in Europe; national governments or political parties have been of minor importance (Bornschier 2000).

Social democracy experienced a period of crisis, too. In a number of countries like Germany and the UK, efforts to use macroeconomic policies to achieve economic growth and higher employment failed. Nevertheless, the crucial event for Social Democracy in Europe was the failure of the French government under Mitterand after 1981 to boost the economy against a background of international recession by using a Keynesian reflation strategy (Sassoon 1997: 534ff.). It was regarded as the final proof that Keynesianism in one country was no longer possible. This experience left Social Democratic parties in an intellectual void. Neither to the problems of rising unemployment and inflation nor to the ideological challenges of Reagan and Thatcher did they manage to provide a convincing answer (Scharpf 1991; Borchert 1996; Ladrech 2000). Where in government, Social Democrats turned to restrictive policies 'claiming that there was no alternative ... due to external constraints' (Ladrech 2000: 49).

Parts of Social Democracy turned to the European level in search of a new solution to the problems of economic management. The 12th congress of the Confederation of Socialist Parties in the European Community in November 1982 in Paris tried to give a socialist answer to the crisis (CSPEC 1982) and a working group of the CSPEC developed later on a more comprehensive strategy that could be used in the election campaigns 1984 (CSPEC 1984). Taking a closer look at the contents (CSPEC 1982, 1984), the socialist alternative may be called 'Eurokeynesianism' because of its emphasis on cooperation amongst European countries and on expansionary policy. The overall priority of the strategy was the fight against unemployment by using traditional macroeconomic policies. The headline of the first paragraph revealed the core of a so-called 'better-my-neighbour strategy': 'It pays to cooperate'. The Confederation called for a coordinated economic strategy to fight unemployment along three lines of action:

1 *Recovery*: Public investments were to play a major role in recovery. The Manifesto, therefore, supported the proposal of the ETUC in favour of a coordinated public investment programme that should amount to 1 per cent of GNP. Furthermore, the monetary policy of the member states was called to reinforce this expansionary policy. The Manifesto argued that a strengthened and reformed European Monetary System would be useful to gain more manoeuvrability and independence from the US monetary policy – a clause that was not supported by the UK.
2 *Restructuring*: With regard to structural policies, the Manifesto called for increased cooperation and more resources in the fields of research policy, industrial planning at the national and European level, a common European strategy for a more efficient use of energy, a substantial increase in the resources devoted to regional policy and for industrial democracy.
3 *Redistribution*: Under the heading of redistribution, the CSPEC called for an active employment policy and the maintenance of the welfare state. With regard to employment policy, the socialists argued that economic growth alone was not enough to reach full employment. Thus, they promoted a 'radical redistribution of work' and the 35-hour working week as a common target for the European

Community. Specific labour market policies were demanded for the young as well as for women and legal migrant workers.

Obviously, the Confederation propagated an alternative economic strategy to the neoliberal SEM-project of market liberalisation. However, it seems that the SEM project itself was never regarded as a threat for European Social Democracy. In the 1984 manifesto, the Single European Market was not even mentioned. But already in 1985, the SEM was accepted as a crucial element of European revival. The resolution of the 14th congress in Madrid (April 1985) called for 'the realisation of the great internal market with the aim of abolishing all internal frontiers within the Common Market by 1992' as a 'cardinal point' for economic recovery (CSPEC 1985: 2). After the political decision at the Intergovernmental Conference to implement the SEM, the CSPEC stressed the need to complement the Single Market with a regional and social dimension. Although it rarely put forward own proposals, it backed the initiatives put forward by Jacques Delors as president of the EC Commission such as the Delors I package and the call for a legally binding charter of fundamental rights (CSPEC 1989). Thus, Delors became one of the crucial actors of European Social Democracy: he was able to use his office to implement at least parts of a Social Democratic agenda (see Ross 1995). Against the strong position of Delors, the CSPEC remained of marginal importance to the European decision making process and even to the work of its member parties (Featherstone 1988: 333).[1]

Towards Maastricht: accepting a neoliberal European monetary union

In the mid-1980s, the CSPEC – with the exception of the British Labour Party – called for a strengthened European Monetary System (EMS) in order to stabilise the financial system and to gain more independence from US monetary policy. However, it did not aim at the creation of a Monetary Union. On the contrary, several reforms were proposed to change the functioning of the EMS (CSPEC 1984: 18): the burden of adjustment was to be shared more equally between all partners, the potential of loans was to be used for increasing investments, a European Monetary Fund should be established, and the ECU was to be given a 'clearer role to act as monetary focal point in the constitution of a new international monetary order'. This approach to monetary policy was more or less repeated in the election manifesto of 1989, while the Delors Committee was already working on a strategy for a Monetary Union in the EC.

The leaders of the national Social Democratic parties realized the need to formulate their opinion on a Monetary Union and met several times to discuss the issue. Just a few months after the 16th congress, in June 1989, the leaders met in Paris and declared that they – without exceptions –

'supported the objectives of the Delors Report on the creation of Economic and Monetary Union' and called for a new IGC as early as possible. For the first time the British Labour Party supported closer monetary integration and even a Monetary Union. The idea of the EMU was attractive to the leaders for several reasons:

1 The EMU was seen as the logical next step of European integration after the Single European Market. The leaders welcomed its positive effects of eliminating internal exchange rate fluctuations and reducing transaction costs.
2 It strengthened the role of Europe on the global financial markets. A common currency would thus eventually be less vulnerable.
3 Finally, the existing EMS was dominated by the German Bundesbank and had already left only small margins of manoeuvrability to the other nations.

However, the conditions for a EMU were contested. Following their summit in Madrid in December 1990, the leaders published their main document on the IGCs on Political Union and Economic and Monetary Union (CSPEC 1990). They stressed that both conferences were closely related and that monetary integration needed to be complemented by a deepening of the democratic legitimation of the EC institutions. They accepted the proposed transition to a EMU with an operationally independent European Central Bank. However, they stressed that a major condition for a functioning Monetary Union was real economic convergence. Therefore, monetary integration needed to be complemented by several other economic measures:

- cohesion policies should be strengthened (regional, social and environmental policy);
- although the need for a stability oriented monetary policy was accepted in order to achieve a strong currency, it was to be stressed in the Treaty that the ultimate purpose was the creation of employment;
- some kind of democratic accountability of the European monetary system (unfortunately without any further explanations);
- the Council should have the responsibility for the external value of the currency;
- fixed limits for national debts were rejected though it was accepted that some guidelines for national fiscal policies are needed to guarantee monetary stability;
- the establishment of a system of multilateral surveillance with regard to economic policy was called for;
- instruments needed to be developed which allowed for anticyclical fiscal policy;

- provisions against tax dumping; and
- a stable worldwide financial system was to be re-established.

In addition, the leaders called for majority voting in the fields of social policy to allow for the implementation of the Social Charter and the Social Action Programme of 1989 (except for social security and income policy). In the end, the Social Democratic leaders succeeded only with few of their demands (Ross 1995; Dyson and Featherstone 1999). The success was almost exclusively restricted to the strengthening of the cohesion provisions in the Maastricht Treaty that was mainly due to the bargaining power of the governments of the less developed member states. With regard to the contents of the Monetary Union itself, the leaders had to accept a neoliberal economic constitution. The ECB was to become completely independent of political – and democratic – control. Its purpose was the achievement of price stability and there were only very indirect references to a responsibility for economic growth and employment. The convergence criteria which had to be fulfilled in order to become a member of the EMU were oriented towards monetary convergence only, but not towards any real economic convergence. The primary role of fiscal policy was to avoid inflation: the national debts and the national budget deficits had to be reduced. In spite of its limited impact on the contents and conditions of the EMU, the leaders supported the project and called for its ratification.

Scharpf (1999: 84f.) argued that the Maastricht Treaty institutionally ruled out the possibility of pursuing Keynesian full employment policies. Furthermore, the convergence criteria were quite successful in steering national fiscal policies: all member states were guided by the political will to achieve the Maastricht convergence criteria. Donald Sassoon therefore called the acceptance of the Maastricht Treaty one of the major components of the Social Democratic 'new revisionism' of the late 1980s and early 1990s:

> The Maastricht Treaty had decreed that inflation, and not unemployment, was the main enemy. This was now fully accepted by the Labour Party and by all other European socialist parties. A national road to Social Democracy – or even modernization – was no longer possible. Here lies the authentic neo-revisionism of the 1990s.
>
> (Sassoon 1997: 739)

The post-Maastricht crisis: searching for a European social democratic strategy

As in the early 1990s parts of European Social Democracy considered 'a national road to Social Democracy' no longer possible, efforts to elaborate a European strategy became even more important. This insight got politically relevant when the Danish people refused to ratify the Maastricht Treaty and the French government achieved only a very small majority in a referendum. European integration was trapped in a crisis of legitimation (the 'Post-Maastricht crisis'). For Social Democrats, this crisis was closely related to the policies of the European Union, since it did not contribute in an active and visible way to the fight against unemployment and social disintegration (PES 1993, 1995). This perception was shared by the Commission, the European Parliament and, increasingly, by national governments. The issue of unemployment moved up on the agenda of the European Union and became one of the most important issues.

In this situation, Jacques Delors was commissioned by the European Council to prepare a White Paper on Growth, Competitiveness and Employment (European Commission 1993; see also Ross 1995; Tidow 1998). Delors proposed to reduce unemployment by 50 per cent until the end of the decade and called for a strategy with three main elements:

1 a huge Keynes-like investment programme of 250 bn ECU in European infrastructure (energy, transport and telecommunication) until 2000 to be financed by private investors, national and European contributions;
2 a European 'social pact' which provided means for investments in order to create more jobs to be financed by wage restraint and
3 a reform of the labour market to increase the employment intensity of economic growth. The last element implied a restructuring of the welfare state towards a more employment-friendly system.

Even though the White Paper could be regarded as the most elaborated Social Democratic strategy for Europe up to that time, the PES leaders decided to set up their own working group under the chair of Allan Larsson, a former Swedish finance minister, to present a 'European Employment Initiative' (PES 1993; see also Hix 1995, 26f.; Johannsen 1999, 88–92; Ladrech 2000, 120ff). The European Employment Initiative was presented to the public at a party leaders meeting in Brussels in December 1993. The Larsson report shared with the Delors White Paper the overall aims to reduce unemployment by 50 per cent until 2000, to avoid long-term unemployment and maintain the 'European Social Model' while at the same time adhering to the Maastricht convergence criteria. The PES document stressed that the economic crisis is not due to external factors but 'results in essence from conditions within Europe'. Therefore, a common strategy may solve the problems. According to the PES, Europe suffered mainly from two problems: (1) a missing balance between savings and investments and (2) a 'two-speed labour market' that is characterised by 'a gap between skill requirements and skill formation.' The report argued for 'a new re-employment policy: a new direction': Europe should pursue a 'two-pillar strategy' consisting of an 'investment-led' growth strategy and a labour market policy combining reduced working time, flexibility and skills formation. The proposals to labour market policies were quite similar to those of the Delors White Paper: job guarantees for the youth, active labour market policies instead of passive financial transfers; a new flexible work organisation with reduced working hours and promotion of gender equality. It is remarkable that, for the first time and implicitly, the existing welfare state had been seen as a problem for the creation of additional employment:

> We will establish a . . . new productive balance between security and change. Therefore we will uphold justice and security – the purpose of the welfare society – and reform welfare policy so that it gives good incentives for work and employment. Social protection, taxation and unemployment insurance have to be made coherent to open doors to jobs opportunities and ways out of poverty.
>
> (PES 1993: 8)

However, it was the focus on macroeconomic policies with an emphasis on monetary policy that distinguished the Larsson report from the Delors White Paper. Under the heading of 'put money to work' the crucial element of the strategy to rebalance savings and investments was 'to seek a concerted action to reduce interest rates' (PES 1993). Additional measures were again similar to Delors' and included more investments in Trans-European Networks (TEN), social infrastructure, research and development (an increase from 2 to 3 per cent of GDP was proposed), an ecological tax reform and regional development policies. Larrson summarized his 'investment-led growth' the following way:

> Public policies play a crucial role in creating confidence by stimulating economic activity. We want as much stimulus as possible from monetary measures and as much as necessary from fiscal measures. Interest rates are the key issue both for private and public finances, together with investment in human resources and measures to improve the functioning of the labour market.
>
> (PES 1993: 18)

Both the White Paper and the Larsson Report, can be seen as efforts towards a coherent Social Democratic strategy against recession and unemployment which would not question the only recently ratified Maastricht Treaty. However, it is impossible to say whether they would have been effective as neither of them ever got implemented. The main practical effects of the new focus on employment issues in the EU were the allocation of some more resources to the TEN and the creation of the so-called Essen process, which created a mechanism of coordinated action in labour market policies (Tidow 1998). However, the Social Democratic parties had agreed upon a far-reaching reform strategy.

Governing the European Union

During the 1990s, the voice of the Social Democratic parties became increasingly important. The 'magical return of Social Democracy' (Cuperus and Kandel 1998) reached its climax in the years 1998 to 2000 when Social Democratic parties were in office in all member states but Ireland, Spain and Luxemburg. With regard to European integration, this meant that Social Democratic governments controlled the most important institutions of the EU: the European Council and the Council of Ministers (Dyson 1999; Aust 2000; Dauderstädt 2000; Teló 2001). A historically new 'window of opportunity' to influence the course of the European integration had opened. Using this opportunity depended on a common strategy. The discussions and the documents of the second half of the 1990s, however, reveal that between the Social Democrats there had been a process of *convergence* as well as *divergence*. With regard to convergence, Social Democrats agreed that 'a united Europe is our response to the challenge globalisation poses to old nation state policies. In European cooperation between nations, we develop new transnational initiatives that alone are strong enough to guide and regulate global forces' (PES 1998a: 8).

A first sign of these transnational initiatives with some effects became obvious at the negotiations leading to the Treaty of Amsterdam (Aust 1997; Tidow 1998; Johansson 1999; Ladrech 2000; Pollack 2000). At a meeting in Madrid in 1995, the party leaders called for a strengthening of the measures against unemployment as the top priority of the IGC 1996/97 (PES 1995). Therefore, a commitment to high employment levels was to be included in the treaty as well as a European coordination of labour market policies. This was to be complemented by a 'charter of civil rights'. The introduction of the chapter on employment and its specific contents became one of the most important issues for Social Democrats in the negotiations. However, even the actors who most strongly advocated the introduction of an employment chapter – Sweden and Austria – stressed that it should neither change the rules concerning the EMU, nor increase financial transfers via the EU budget nor change the existing division of competences in the field of employment policies (Aust 1997: 758; Tidow 1998: 35). The provisions of the Maastricht Treaty with regard to the EMU were taboo. Despite those restrictions, a chapter on employment was opposed by the British, the German and the French governments. It was only after the electoral victories of Blair and Jospin shortly before the Amsterdam summit that the German government finally agreed to a new chapter if it was limited to the incorporation of the Essen-process into the Treaty. This process consisted of a commonly agreed set of targets and policies that were to be implemented autonomously by each member state. The implementation was to be supervised by both the national governments and the European Commission. The chapter did not provide any sanctions but relied on public blaming in the case of not achieving the targets and benchmarking procedures in order to allow diffusion processes for best practices. The overall aim of the employment policies was to increase the 'employablity' of the workforce (Article 125 EC Treaty). Additionally, the Maastricht Treaty provided for extended Community competences in the areas of social policy, equal opportunities, environmental protection, public health and human rights.

With regard to the contents of the European Employment Strategy (EES) there has been a growing consensus that there needed to be a strengthening of the human capital building efforts and a reform of the welfare state. The criticism of the traditional welfare state, as formulated by 'Third Way' thinking (cf. Giddens 1998), was increasingly shared within European Social Democracy. The Delors White Paper as well as the Larsson report already called for reforms, and the analysis of Vandenbroucke (1998: 130–1; cf. the contributions in this volume) revealed a growing convergence between European Social Democratic parties in this respect. A paper of the PES EcoFin Group, which proclaimed a 'new European Way', called for a 'new social contract', and argued that 'investing in people' is 'the distinctive response of Socialists and Social-Democrats to globalization' (PES 1998a: 5). The emphasis on strengthening the 'employability' of people and on the functioning of the labour markets is clearly reflected in the European Employment Strategy that was agreed upon at the extraordinary Luxemburg summit of the European Council in 1997. The European Employment Strategy consists of about twenty guidelines that the member states committed themselves to implement within the next five years. The guidelines are presented under the following headlines: (1) improving employability, (2) developing entrepreneurship, (3) encouraging adaptability in business and of employees and (4) strengthening the policies for equal opportunities. An internal evaluation of the PES secretariat by Tuytens and Hughes (PES 1999a; Ladrech 2000: 113–15) showed that most of the specific labour market proposals of the Larsson report found their way into the employment guidelines.

The paper by the PES EcoFin Group was initiated by the British government and the paper therefore stressed 'Third Way' thinking. It accepted the assumption that globalization leaves no strategic alternative but to adapt ('We must work with change not against it') and the necessity of the stability and growth pact. However, there were also elements of a 'Eurokeynesian' approach[2] and therefore the EcoFin Group report represented a compromise. The 'Third Way' strategy was more clearly articulated by the so-called Blair–Schröder paper (1999). The document reduced the 'two-pillar strategy' of the Larsson report to a one-pillar strategy consisting of investment in human capital, increased competition and structural adaptation. This represents the strategic variant that I have called 'loyality'.

Divergence with regard to European policies became visible when the necessary extent of regulation at the European level and macroeconomic policies were discussed. The second strategic variant of European Social Democracy, 'Eurokeynesianism', largely agreed to the necessity of a welfare state reform towards a more activating state, but adhered to the second pillar of the Larrson strategy. It put its emphasis on 'traditional' Social Democratic thought and was articulated, in particular, by the French government and the former German party leader Lafontaine (PS France 1999; Lafontaine and Müller 1998). The Jospin paper, which was the French response to the Blair–Schröder document, stated that Social Democracy still needed to fight for the primacy of politics over the economy since politics was the democratic expression of the will of the people. The major instrument for its implementation remained the state and its agencies. Furthermore, Jospin argued that Social Democracy had to keep its critical attitude towards capitalism as being essentially unjust and irrational. Capitalism still needed to be regulated at the different political levels, from the nation state to the global level.

With regard to the European level, the issue of an appropriate tax policy and how to use macroeconomic policies to achieve full employment had been the subject of two further PES working groups. Both revealed that a large section within European Social Democracy still adhered to 'traditional' Social Democratic policies that were refused by the reformed British Labour Party, 'New Labour'. The Busquin working group called for a regulation and harmonisation of tax policies at the European level (PES 1998b). However, the British Labour party refused to sign as the proposed policies contradicted UK government policies.[3] The Guterres working group presented a report on a European Employment Pact. The main focus of the report was how to implement the second pillar of the Larsson strategy: what kind of macroeconomic strategy was needed to allow the European Central Bank to pursue an expansionary monetary policy? The final proposal was to organise a pact between the ECB, the national governments and the social partners to agree on a common strategy. The overall goal of that strategy was to support economic growth and full employment (1) through reduced interest rates while at the same time maintaining price stability through (2) wage increases in accordance with productivity increases and (3) fiscal consolidation by the national governments. Faster economic growth and reduced interest rates would finally contribute to the fiscal consolidation of the national budgets (PES 1999b). The main argument of Guterres was that the ECB was obliged by the EC Treaty (Art. 2 and 105) to support the general economic policy when possible without hurting the goal of price stability. The Guterres report was finally adopted by the fourth congress in Milan as the official policy approach of the PES. It is interesting to note in this context that the

British government participated as Labour Party in the Guterres working group, but preferred to join the conservative Spanish government in the intergovernmental negotiations. The overall focus of the common Spanish–British contribution is on flexibility, liberalisation and modernisation of the welfare systems. A European strategy using macroeconomic policies – the second 'Larsson-pillar' – is not even mentioned (Council of Ministers 1999).

At the Council Summit in Cologne (1999), the 'European Employment Pact' was agreed upon. The new element was a macroeconomic dialogue, which meant a regular meeting of the ECB, the national governments and the social partners. The ECB and the social partners consented to participation but stressed at the same time that their autonomy was left untouched by these dialogues. This macroeconomic dialogue was called Cologne-process and together with the so-called Luxemburg-process – the implementation of the employment guidelines – and the so-called Cardiff-process – which called for a further deepening of the Single European Market – it was labelled the 'European Employment Pact'.

However, after the resignations of Lafontaine in Germany and later Strauss-Kahn in France, the issue of expansionary monetary policy in order to achieve higher growth and employment rates lost its main supporters. Although, at the extraordinary Lisbon Summit (March 2000), the European Council set itself the target of reaching full employment by 2010 (an employment rate of 70 per cent) and finally agreed to aim at an average growth rate of 3 per cent per annum, the means to achieve these goals no longer refer to macroeconomic instruments but to the development of a competitive, dynamic and knowledge-based economy (for details European Council 2000; Telò 2001). The idea of a 'Eurokeynesian' strategy disappeared from the European agenda while the Blairite 'Third Way' strategy had become dominant in the EU modernisation approach (cf. Teló 2001).

Conclusions

The historical review of Social Democratic behaviour towards European integration revealed an ambivalent attitude towards the EU. While, on the one hand, Social Democrats accepted the most important decisions working towards a neoliberal constitution of the EU (SEA and Treaty of Maastricht), they simultaneously called for a kind of 'Eurokeynesian' strategy. This strategy has been most clearly elaborated by the PES reports of Larsson and Guterres. However, when Social Democracy became the dominant force in the EU with the chance to modify the course of European integration a division between two opposing strategies emerged. 'Eurokeynesianists' called for a Keynesian macroeconomic growth strategy against unemployment and argued that the European Union should be used as an instrument to regulate the Single European Market. The main idea is to revitalise the traditional Social Democratic project of redistribution and state intervention through closer cooperation at the European level. As this strategy implies a change in the course of European integration, I called it 'voice'. The supporters of the 'Third Way' strategy agreed to the need of cooperation at a European level. However, they had 'adapted' their strategy to the given structure of the European Union – the strategic orientation I called 'loyalty'. The 'two-pillar strategy' of the Larrson report consisting of a macroeconomic strategy and a reform of the welfare state had been reduced to a one pillar strategy of modernisation of the welfare state by transforming it to an 'activating state'. The means to achieve social integration – which is still the policy goal – had changed. The main task of the state was no longer to provide employment itself or redistribute financial resources but to enhance the capabilities of the individuals to compete successfully in the market economy. The main strategy was therefore 'investments in people' or increasing 'human capital'. After the resignations of the Ministers of Finance Lafontaine and Strauss-Kahn, the most important advocates of a Eurokeynesian approach disappeared from the stage. This led a to shift within European Social Democracy towards a strategy of modernising the European social model through 'Third Way' policies. The ten-year strategy approach of the Lisbon Summit clearly reflected this shift (Telò 2001).

The shift in European Social Democratic strategy can be explained as a process of adaptation to the political–institutional setting of the EU. The regulations of the Maastricht Treaty (independence of the European Central Bank; the primary orientation towards price stability etc.) and the stability and growth pact militate against a Keynesian growth strategy (Scharpf 1999). The requirement of unanimous decision-making in crucial policy areas such as taxation or social policy builds up further barriers against a re-regulation of the markets. Just one actor is needed to veto relevant decisions. Therefore the politico-institutional conditions for a Eurokeynesian strategy are rather weak. One – given the prominence of Tony Blair – attractive strategy for European Social Democracy to try to reconcile economic efficiency and social progress – which is the essence of the so-called European social model all Social Democrats adhere to – was to move to some kind of Europeanised Third Way, which includes further market integration, supply-side economic polices and a modernisation of the welfare state. However, whether such a strategy is sufficient to achieve traditional Social Democratic policy goals such as full employment and a socially integrated and just society is open to question.

Notes

1 Two major institutional reforms of the transnational party followed from this experience: the party leaders meeting became institutionalised (meetings should be held twice a year in advance of the EC summits) and the reform of

the confederation finally led to the foundation of the Party of European Socialists in 1992.

2 These are 'a commitment to an increase of disposable incomes that is compatible with price stability' involving 'wage-developments oriented towards productivity growth' and 'public investments in infrastructure'.

3 In their common contribution to the European Employment Pact, the Spanish and British governments state: 'However, we see no need for the harmonisation of corporate taxes across the EU. . . . We will not agree to measures that damage competitiveness or damage jobs.' (Council of Ministers 1999).

References

Aust, A. (1997) 'Der Amsterdamer Vertrag: Vertrag der sozialen Balance'? Sozial- und Beschäftigungspolitik in der Regierungskonferenz 1996/97', *Zeitschrift für Sozialreform* 43, 10: 748–77.

Aust, A. (2000) 'Dritter Weg oder Eurokeynesianismus?: Zur Entwicklung der Europäischen Beschäftigungspolitik seit dem Amsterdamer Vertrag', *Österreichische Zeitschrift für Politikwissenschaft* 29, 3: 269–83.

Blair, T. and Schröder, G. (1999) *Europe: the Third Way/die Neue Mitte*, London: Labour Party.

Borchert, J. (1996) 'Alte Träume und neue Realitäten. Das Ende der Sozialdemokratie', in Borchert, J., Golsch, L., Jun, U. and Losche, P. (eds), *Das sozialdemokratische Modell. Organisationsstrukturen und Politikinhalte im Wandel*, Opladen: Leske + Budrich, 39–80.

Bornschier, V. (ed.) (2000) *State-building in Europe: the Revitalisation of Western European Integration*, Cambridge: Cambridge University Press.

Confederation of Socialist Parties in the European Community (CSPEC) (1982) *Die Krise in Europa und die sozialistische Antwort. Resolution des 12. Kongresses*, Brüssel: CSPEC.

CSPEC (1984) *Manifesto*, Luxemburg: CSPEC.

CSPEC (1985) *An Independent and Democratic Europe. Final Resolution of the 14th Congress*, Madrid: CSPEC.

CSPEC (1989) *Manifesto*, Brussels: CSPEC.

CSPEC (1990) Erklärung der Parteivorsitzenden zu den Regierungskonferenzen, Madrid: CSPEC.

Council of Ministers (1999) *European Employment Pact – Member States Contributions*, Brussels: document 8906/99.

Cuperus, R. and Kandel, J. (eds) (1998) *European Social Democracy: Transformation in Progress*, Amsterdam: Wiardi Beckman Stichting and Friedrich Ebert Stiftung.

Dauderstädt, M. (2000) *Wege, Umwege und Dritte Wege zu einem sozialen und demokratischen Europa*, Bonn: Friedrich Ebert Stiftung (Eurokolleg 44).

Dyson, K. (1999) (eds) 'Benign or malevolent leviathan? Social democratic governments in a neo-liberal Euro Area', *Political Quarterly* 70(2): 195–209.

Dyson, K. and Featherstone, K. (1999) *The Road to Maastricht. Negotiating Economic and Monetary Union*, Oxford: Oxford University Press.

European Commission (1993) *White Paper on Growth, Competitiveness and Employment*, Brussels, COM(93) 700 final.

European Council (2000) 'Presidency conclusions. Lisbon European Council 23 and 24 March", Press release SN 100/00.

Featherstone, K (1988) *Socialist Parties and European Integration: a Comparative History*, Manchester: Manchester University Press.

Giddens, A. (1998) *The Third Way: the Renewal of Social Democracy*, Cambridge: Polity Press.

Hix, S. (1995) *A History of the PES*, Brussels: PES Research Series No.1.

Hix, S. and Lord, C. (1997) *Political Parties in the European Union*, London: Macmillan Press.

Johannson, K. M. (1999) 'Tracing the employment title in the Amsterdam Treaty: uncovering transnational coalitions', *Journal of European Public Policy* 6(1): 85–101.

Kesselman, M. (1996) 'Sozialdemokratische Wirtschaftstheorie nach dem Ende des Keynesianismus', in Borchert, J., Golsch, L., Jun, U. and Losche, P. (eds), *Das sozialdemokratische Modell. Organisationsstrukturen und Politikinhalte im Wandel*, Opladen: Leske + Budrich, 135–67.

Kitschelt, H. (1999) 'European Social Democracy between political economy and electoral competition', in Kitschelt, H., Lange, P., Marks, G. and Stephens, J. D. (eds), *Continuity and Change in Contemporary Capitalism*, Cambridge: Cambridge University Press, 317–45.

Ladrech, R. (2000) *Social Democracy and the Challenge of European Union*, London: Lynn Rienner Publishers.

Lafontaine, O. and Müller, C. (1998) *Keine Angst vor der Globalisierung. Wohlstand und Arbeit für alle*, Bonn: Dietz Verlag.

Moravcsik, A. (1991) 'Negotiating the Single European Act: National Interests and Conventional Statecraft in the European Community', *International Organization* 5(1): 19–56.

PES (Party of European Socialists) (1993) *The European Employment Initiative ('Larsson-report')*, Brussels: PES.

PES (1995) *Die Europäische Union ins Gleichgewicht bringen. Erklärung der Konferenz der Parteivorsitzenden*, Madrid: PES.

PES (1998a) 'The New European Way – Economic Reform in the Framework of EMU', a paper by the PES EcoFin Group, Brussels: PES.

PES (1998b) *A Strategy for Solidarity: Report on Taxation ('Busquin-report')*, Brussels: PES.

PES (1999a) *Putting Europe to Work 1994–1999: a review: What Has Been Achieved in the Last Five Years?*, Brussels: PES.

PES (1999b) *A European Employment Pact. For a new European Way*, Brussels: PES.

Pollack, M. (2000) 'A Blairite Treaty: Neo-Liberalism and Regulated Capitalism in the Treaty of Amsterdam', in K. Neunreither and A. Wiener (eds), *European Integration after Amsterdam. Institutional Dynamics and Prospects for Democracy*, Oxford: Oxford University Press.

Przeworski, A. (1985) *Capitalism and Social Democracy*, Cambridge: Cambridge University Press.

PS France (1999) 'Das Jospin-Papier. Beitrag der Sozialistischen Partei Frankreichs zum 21. Kongreß der Sozialistischen Internationale', *Blätter für deutsche und internationale Politik* 44, 11: 1391–402.

Ross, G. (1995) *Jacques Delors and European Integration*, New York: Oxford University Press.

Sassoon, D. (1997) *One Hundred Years of Socialism: the West European Left in the 20th Century*, London: Fontana Press.

Scharpf, F. (1991) *Crisis and Choice in European Social Democracy*, Ithaca, NY: Cornell University Press.

Scharpf, F. (1999) *Governing in Europe. Effective and Democratic?*, Oxford: Oxford University Press.

Scharpf, F. (2000) 'Economic changes, vulnerabilities, and institutional capabilities', in F. Scharpf and V. Schmidt (eds) *Welfare and Work in the Open Economy: From Vulnerability to Competitiveness, Vol. I*, Oxford: Oxford University Press, 21–124.

Schröder, G. and T. Blair (1999) 'Der Weg nach vorne für Europas Sozialdemokraten', *Blätter für deutsche und internationale Politik* 44(7): 887–96.

Streeck, W. (2000) 'Competitive Solidarity: Rethinking the "European Social Model" ', in Hinrichs, K., Kitschelt, H. and Wiesenthal, H. (eds) *Kontingenz und Krise. Institutionenpolitik in kapitalistischen und postsozialistischen Ländern*, Frankfurt/Main: Campus Verlag, 245–62.

Teló, M. (2001) 'The European dimension of the Third Way', in R. Cuperus, K. Duffek and J. Kandel (eds), *Multiple Third Ways*, Amsterdam, Wien and Berlin: Friedrich Ebert Stiftung, Wiardi Beckman Stichting and Karl Renner Institut, 171–85.

Tidow, S. (1998) *Europäische Beschäftigungspolitik. Die Entstehung eines neuen Politikfeldes: Ursachen, Hintergründe und Verlauf des politischen Prozesses*, Marburg: Forschungsgruppe Europäische Gemeinschaften.

Vandenbroucke, F. (1998) 'Globalization, inequality and Social Democracy', in R. Cuperus and J. Kandel (eds), *European Social Democracy. Tranformation in Progress*, Amsterdam: Wiardi Beckman Stichting and Friedrich Ebert Stiftung, 93–146.

11 Social Democratic party policies in Europe

Towards a Third Way?

Giuliano Bonoli

Introduction

The late 1990s witnessed the return to power of Social Democratic parties in a majority of western European countries. For a period of time, eleven of the fifteen EU Member-states were ruled by left-of-centre governments. This situation did not last very long, as by the early 2000s Social Democrats had been forced out of office in several countries, but it represents a unique opportunity to assess and rethink the left's role in western European politics. As a matter of fact, the brief spell of Social Democratic hegemony did result in widespread and sustained debate on the future of the left, the orientation it should take and its prospects as a political force.

Much of the debate on the future of Social Democracy has revolved around the notion of the Third Way, or the claim that Social Democratic governments have adopted a new political orientation that is different from both neo-liberalism and traditional Social Democracy. The Third Way is clearly a centrist ideology, and even though many would claim that it lacks the stature and the coherence of previous political projects, it is indisputable that in the late 1990s and early 2000s the Third Way has acquired a central place in west European politics. For the most part, the debate has focused on the level of ideas, dealing with questions such the position of the Third Way in western political thought, or its suitability as a progressive political discourse (see Powell, Chapter 1, this volume).

As the debate unfolded, Social Democratic parties in power had to deal with the practical problems that governments face all over the world: to arbitrate among conflicting interests, to stimulate economic growth, to deal with social problems and so forth. How did they fare in the day-to-day management of political power? Did they develop distinctive and innovative solutions? Did the ideas circulating in international political and academic circles have any influence on what they have done?

These questions were behind our collective effort and they have been dealt with in the various contributions at the level of individual countries or policy sectors. The objective of this final chapter is to bring together the evidence presented in the book and provide a wider picture of what

Social Democrats in power have been doing in the late 1990s/early 2000s. It addresses two key questions: whether there is convergence in social and economic policy-making among European countries ruled by Social Democrats, and second, to the extent that there is convergence, whether the emerging new approach is distinctive. The chapter starts with a summary account of policy-making in Social Democratic Europe. It distinguishes between two components of policy: first it looks at the discourse in which government policies are embedded, and second at the actual rules that are adopted. The results of this survey of policy are presented next. Finally, the chapter concludes with a short and tentative analysis of the electoral consequences of the Third Way.

Policy developments in Social Democratic Europe

This section reviews key policy developments across Social Democratic Europe in the late 1990s and early 2000s. Its main objective is to assess the extent to which left-of-centre governments are developing a common and distinctive approach in economic and social policies. The presentation of policy follows the distinction drawn in Chapter 1 between rhetoric, values, goals and mechanisms. Public policies are understood as consisting of an ideational dimension as well as a factual, legislative component (see e.g. Jobert and Muller 1987; Sabatier 1993). The two dimensions are not necessarily tightly coupled, and can generate different conclusions as far as convergence is concerned.

Discourse: rhetoric and values

When discussing the transformation of Social Democratic discourse it is helpful to distinguish between two important components of that discourse: the rhetoric, or the choice of words that are used, and the values, or the normative content of the discourse. To say that the choice of words is important is not to subscribe to a nominalistic understanding of politics. The labels that are used to designate political projects and policy goals carry meanings that clearly go beyond their simple denotative value. For example, as a result of the centrality in international debates of Giddens' and Blair's writings, the 'Third Way' has become the reference label for all renewed Social Democratic parties, but in many countries there is reluctance to explicitly referring to the term 'Third Way' to describe the new political orientation of Social Democratic parties.

This is understandable. First, in many European countries the label 'Third Way' is often associated with Britain, (post)-Thatcherism and neo-liberalism. It is thus regarded as inappropriate terrain for the left, however modern it aspires to be. Second, to openly adopt the 'Third Way' label may be perceived as some form of acknowledgement of a leadership role for the UK and the British Labour Party in the international Social Democratic movement. This can make Social Democrats, proud of their own achievements in their respective countries, feel uneasy. It seems thus reasonable not to expect European Social Democratic parties to rush into explicitly adopting the Third Way label.

As a matter of fact, explicit attempts to adopt the Third Way label or to identify with the political movement it represents are rare. Beside the British Labour party, few other Social Democratic parties have openly embraced the Third Way label. The German SPD, with the publication of the Blair–Schröder paper in 1999, has taken some steps in that direction. However, the reactions in Germany, to the paper were so negative, that they have discouraged the party leader from insisting in stressing its intellectual affinity with the Third Way. The Italian DS (reformed communists) under the leadership of the then Prime Minister Massimo D'Alema briefly played with the idea of joining the 'Third Way' club in Europe, including by hosting a meeting in Florence in 1999. But this did not pay off, as D'Alema was forced to resign after a poor performance in regional elections.

It is intriguing that one of very few governments that makes open reference to the Third Way movement is the Belgian purple coalition government, lead not by a Social-Democrat but by a Liberal, Guy Verhofstadt (Hoop, Chapter 4, this volume). Similarly, in Germany, the Blair-Schroeder paper was greeted with much more approval by the liberal FDP than by any other political party, including of course Schröders'own SPD (FDP 1999). The Third Way label does not seem to attract the interest of Social-Democrats as much as it does of Liberals.

Other Social Democratic parties tend to avoid open declarations of affinity with the Third Way movement. The various chapters in this volume show how reluctant most European Social-Democrats are to openly declare themselves part of the Third Way political project. Parties like the Dutch PvdA or the Portuguese PS, in spite of being clearly at the forefront of the process of Social Democratic renewal in Europe, carefully avoid any hint of association with the Third Way movement (Hoop, Chapter 4; Costa Lobo and Magahles, Chapter 5, this volume). The Swedish SAP has supported many key Third Way policies for several years (active labour market policies, gender equality, etc.) but to join the Third Way movement would mean failing to acknowledge the contribution that the party has made to develop such policy ideas in the first place (Svensson 2001: 221). And finally, the French Socialist leader Lionel Jospin has probably been the most vociferous critic of the 'Third Way', taking position against it publicly on several occasions (Clift, Chapter 7, this volume).

Lack of explicit, visible convergence in political discourses under a common label, however, does not mean that there cannot be a convergence in the normative content of the discourses adopted. Values like entrepreneurship, equality of opportunity, no rights without responsibilities may be stressed in national political discourses even without mentioning an affinity to Giddens and Blair's teachings. As a matter of fact, these values made their appearance in western political thought long before the emergence of the Third Way debate, at least if taken individually. It is thus not surprising that if instead of looking at labels and at declared affiliations, one focuses on the content of discourse and on the values that are put forward, things look rather different. In the 1990s, key 'Third Way' values featured prominently in Social Democrats' election manifestoes throughout the continent, but especially, in Spain, The Netherlands, Germany, Belgium, and Portugal. According to Volkens' content analyses of party manifestoes, Social Democratic parties in all the countries above score higher than the British Labour Party in the extent to which they conform to Third Way values (Volkens, Chapter 2, this volume).

The case studies presented in this volume as well as other analyses of the evolution of Social Democratic political discourse confirm this finding. In the Netherlands, even though there is no explicit mention of the Third Way as a guiding principle of policy, the government discourse is characterised by a strong emphasis on work for all and the idea that the policies they put forward goes beyond traditional cleavages between labour and capital (Braun and Girod, this volume; Hoop, Chapter 4, this volume). In Germany, the Schröder government had troubles developing a coherent discourse. Initially, internal divisions, most notably between Schröder himself and Oscar Lafontaine, prevented the government from speaking with one voice. After Lafontaine's resignation in early 1999, came the Blair-Schröder paper, a clumsy attempt to introduce the political discourse of the Third Way in the German context. More recently, German Social Democrats seem to have abandoned the ambition of developing grand political ideas, and have resorted to a more pragmatic discourse, justifying policy with reference not so much to values and notions of social justice, but more to expected benefits in dealing with widely recognised problems. In Portugal, the Socialists have swapped equality with solidarity and equity as the fundamental goals of the party. Election manifestoes in the 1990s put substantial emphasis on employment promotion as an anti-poverty policy and on the acceptance of a role for the private sector in the delivery of public services (Costa-Lobo and Magalhaes, Chapter 5, this volume).

Typical Third Way values like equality of opportunity, entrepreneurship, or social justice understood as equity rather than equality have featured in the political discourse of other Social Democratic parties in government. In Italy, leaders of the left-leaning Olive-tree coalition insisted that the country's current level of social expenditure is about right, but that it needs to be reoriented towards more productive ends: away from old age and disability pensions and towards training and family policies. There was an attempt to put forward a new conception of social justice, summed up by the slogan 'More to the children, less to the fathers', (*Più ai figli meno ai padri*), and also by the rejection of the clientelistic system of political intermediation inherited from the previous governments (Ferrera and Gualmini 1999; Schmidt 2000: 300). In Austria, already in the mid-1980s the SPÖ abandons Keynesian demand management as its key policy preference and embraces supply side-based employment promotion and privatisation of public enterprises as major policy objectives. (Feigl-Heihs, Chapter 9, this volume).

It is probably in the Nordic countries that traditional Social Democratic values of equality of outcomes and universality of welfare provision remain most influential. In Sweden the dominant discourse has focused on how to preserve the Swedish model in an international economic context characterised by tight constraints, but there has not been, on the Social Democratic side, any deep questioning of the desirability and adequacy of such a model. The Danish Social Democrats have maintained a similar position, but have also incorporated typically liberal values like efficiency in the management of public services and equity in the welfare state (Braun and Girod, Chapter 3, this volume; Schmidt 2000: 259–67). Finally, the French Socialists have also been very reluctant to adopt Third Way values in their political discourse. In the late 1990s and early 2000s Lionel Jospin has insisted on traditional Social Democratic themes such as the superior status of politics over markets in Democratic societies, and duties of solidarity towards the most disadvantaged in society.

Overall it seems that the values and the principles that Third Way advocates have adopted and popularised under the Third Way label are having considerable more success than the label itself. Very few Social Democratic parties maintain a traditional discourse emphasising equality of outcomes, vertical redistribution, and the vision of capitalism as an inherently evil entity that needs to be controlled. The French socialists and the Swedish Social Democrats are probably the parties that have so far less distanced themselves from these traditional Social-Democratic values. Everywhere else, however, Social Democratic parties seem to be recasting their discourses in a way that resonates the writings of Blair and Giddens. This, however, should not necessarily be seen as proof of influence of the Third Way movement in Europe. Many social Democratic parties reoriented their discourses in a more liberal, centrist, and post- industrial direction, but many did so long before these ideas were attributed the label of 'Third way' (see Volkens, Chapter 2, this volume).

Policy goals and mechanisms

Moving from discourse to policy one can identify a number of themes that describe what Social Democratic government have been doing over the last few years or so. Our focus here is limited to social and economic (particularly employment) policies. These are central policy areas both in relation to how Social Democratic parties define themselves and to what citizens tend to regard as crucial aspects of their lives. However, it is clear that other areas of public policies have been central to governments' activities in many European countries. Among these the most important are law and order, European integration, the environment, and immigration. Common themes like those we identify in relation to social and economic policies may well exist in these areas as well.

Taking a broad perspective on developments in social and economic policy, one can identify three salient themes in policy making in Social Democratic European countries: to maximise employment, to contain public expenditure, and to strengthen the social investment component of welfare states. Virtually all left-of-centre government have in the late 1990s and early 2000s adopted policies that clearly fall under these different rubrics.

Maximise employment

At first sight, this policy objective may resemble the more traditional Social Democratic goal of full employment, but in fact there are substantial differences between the two. First, full-employment was about guaranteeing a job to anyone who wanted one, essentially able-bodied, working-age male breadwinners. Today, maximisation of employment is less concerned with the fulfilment of aspirations, and tends to target all citizens, including people that in the past were not expected to take up paid employment (single parents, older people, partially disabled people). Second, the instruments used to achieve the two goals are very different. During the golden age of traditional Social Democracy, full employment was maintained thanks to demand management and state financed job creation or preservation. Today, the maximisation of employment takes place through a mix of positive and negative incentives that are expected to push as many non-working individuals as it is reasonably possible into the labour market.

In practical terms, the maximisation of employment relies on a large number of policy instruments. First, several countries have introduced or tightened conditions attached to cash benefits for unemployed people. In general, in order to continue receiving a benefit, recipients must demonstrate efforts to obtain work. This may involve participation in labour market programmes, availability to attend a meeting with a social worker to evaluate work prospects, or simply to accept a job offer. Non compliance may result in sanctions such as benefit suspensions or reductions. This has been the standard approach in the Nordic countries for several years, even though work requirements are now being enforced more strictly than in the past (Goul Andersen 2000). Most other countries have moved in this direction during the 1990s under Social Democratic rule. The UK and the Netherlands have developed policies that target non-working people, including older workers, single parents and disabled people, and encourage them to (re-) enter the labour market, although benefit conditionality is generally not enforced for these social groups.

With the exception of the Netherlands and possibly Belgium,[1] continental European countries have been less inclined to introduce employment promotion mechanisms in their unemployment compensation systems. In France, the main income support programme (RMI – *Revenu Minimum d'Insertion*), introduced by the Socialists already in 1988, does contain obligations for recipients, but this is seldom interpreted as an obligation to re-enter the labour market. Germany has not seen any significant expansion in work requirements and benefit conditionality over the last few years, but this seems to be to a large extent a result of the institutional structure of the German unemployment compensation system, which includes a strong entitlement-based contributory component, and is based on shared responsibilities between different levels of government (Clasen 2000).

Southern European countries have not made significant moves in this direction, but they generally lack developed unemployment compensation systems so that the issue of benefit conditionality is not as pressing as in other parts of Europe. Where new income support schemes have been introduced, however, these incorporate many of the employment promotion features that have been developed in Northern Europe. Beneficiaries of the Portuguese '*Rendimento Minimo Garantido*' are expected to be available for work, and to attend vocational training (Costa-Lobo and Magalhães, Chapter 5, this volume). In Italy and in Spain, similar minimum income programmes have also been introduced.

Second, a number left-of-centre governments have introduced subsidies for low wage employment, with the double objective of encouraging job creation in this segment of the labour market and create incentives for non-workers to take up the jobs that are thus created. The Netherlands, Portugal, France and Belgium have introduced social insurance contribution reductions/exemptions for low paid workers. In Germany the Schröder government considered this option, but has long been unable to implement it essentially because of strong opposition from the social partners. More recently, following a relatively successful experiment in the town of Mainz, the government has introduced a nation wide scheme that provides subsidies covering part of the social contributions paid by low income workers. The size of the programme, however, remains limited in comparison to those existing in other EU countries (D'Alessandro 2002).

France and the UK have also introduced cash benefits that supplement the wages of low paid workers. This instrument provides an additional incentive to take up employment for non-working people, but can also be seen as redistributive social policy measures, insofar as it boosts low income people's purchasing power. The British version, the Working Families Tax Credit, was adopted soon after the 1997 general election and was part and parcel of a wider employment promotion policy package which included also a national minimum wage. In France, the *prime pour l'emploi* is paid to workers at a variable rate that is highest for a full-time worker at the minimum wage level.

Employment maximisation has been pursued also in the field of labour legislation, often through the relaxation of employment protection laws. In the 1990s Italy has taken some limited steps in this direction by relaxing restrictions of employment agencies, and on temporary and part-time employment. It has also introduced incentives for the social partners to agree on regional or local employment pacts that have the objective of generating employment in economically depressed areas (Ferrera and Gualmini 1999). In the Netherlands, a reduction in employment protection for stable workers has been traded with an improvement for marginal temporary employees (Hemerjck *et al.* 2000). A similar course has been followed by Portugal and Spain. Apparent outliers here are Britain and the Nordic countries. However, in this part of Europe employment protection legislation was never particularly strong, so that a relaxation of the modest existing provision is not seen as necessary. Germany and France are more exceptional in this respect, although previous French governments had already somewhat reduced the extent of job protection.

Employment maximisation, a policy goal that is qualitatively different from full employment, seems to be included in the policy repertoire of virtually every Social Democratic government in Europe. The exception seems to be Germany here, but this may not be as a result of a different orientation of the Schröder government. In fact, many of the initiatives adopted in other EU countries have been subject to intense debate and negotiation in Germany as well, but did not result in major policy reform because of the successful opposition of non-governmental actors, like in the case of contribution exemptions for low paid workers. It should also be noted that Germany has adopted an important tax reform that has significantly reduced corporate taxes. In a way, this can be seen as an alternative to employers' contribution exemptions or reductions in an effort to reduce fiscal pressure on business. If countries have been developing policies in this field to different extents, this seems to be more related to the obstacles (institutional, political), or to differences in starting points, than to possible differences in government's political orientation.

The challenge for German Social Democratic leaders is to find polices that allow them to pursue their modernisation agenda and that at the same time prove politically feasible in an institutional context characterised by multiple veto players. The decision taken recently to allow individuals who have been taking care of a child for three years to draw unemployment benefit could be an example of how this can be done. It is a measure that encourages (re-) entry into the labour market of individuals (mostly women) who have been inactive, and in this respect reflects well the goal of employment maximisation, but at the same time does not undermine established vested interests.

Contain public expenditure

A second ubiquitous theme in current Social Democratic policy-making is that of containing public spending. Arguably under pressure from international constraints, Social Democratic parties have accepted fiscal discipline as an unavoidable constraint over policy making (Aust, Chapter 10, this volume). Under such circumstance, European Social Democrats have been left with no option but to adopt public expenditure cuts in the core areas of the welfare state, like pensions, unemployment or disability insurance. These programmes (especially pensions) are generally the largest items of expenditure in public budgets, and in this respect they constitute an obvious target for cost containment initiatives. At the same time, however, retrenchment in these policy areas is notoriously a politically treacherous exercise (see e.g. Pierson 1994).

Pension reforms have been adopted in a number of countries, with the objective of containing the expected increase in public spending on old age pensions. Germany, Italy and Sweden, under left of centre majorities, have adopted similar policy measures in this field. In all three countries, benefit formulas for public pensions have been modified so as to result in lower benefits. Often, this has been done in a rather obscure way, and presented as an inevitable development to electorates. Together with these measures, however, all three countries have introduced a 2nd private pillar of pension provision that is supposed to supplement the diminished state pensions. The acceptance of a role for the private sector is certainly something that distinguishes today's Social Democrats from their predecessors, to whom such measure would most likely have sounded like anathema. However, it should be noted that the regulatory framework of the new private pensions is particularly stringent (especially in Sweden) and clearly geared towards social objectives, so that, for example, in Germany, individuals who are not working because they are performing caring tasks full-time, can see their private pensions subsidised by the state (Anderson and Meyer, Chapter 8, this volume).

In France, cuts in public pensions were adopted by the right-wing coalition government headed by Edouard Balladur in 1993, although he simply implemented a blueprint prepared by his Socialist predecessors (Bonoli 2000: ch. 5). More recently, the Jospin Government has also introduced a form of employment-based long term saving provision, called *épargne salariale* (wage earners' saving funds). The government has been adamant that this has nothing to do with private pensions, an instrument that is openly opposed by the Socialist leadership. The time horizon of *épargne salariale* in fact is ten years, but whether it will turn out to be an instrument for the provision of retirement income depends on the use that employees are going to make of it (Clift, Chapter 7, this volume).

Social Democratic pension policies reveal an interesting and innovative approach in this area, which combines liberal ideas of public spending containment, preference for the private sector, with Social Democratic goals like equality of access and vertical redistribution. It seems qualitatively different from both the standard liberal approach followed by Thatcher in the 1980s and, the traditional Social Democratic policy of crowding out the market from pension provision (Anderson and Meyer, Chapter 8, this volume).

The choice of targets for expenditure cuts has differed according to individual countries' welfare state structures. For instance, countries like the Netherlands or the UK, who had in the past been exceptional in the European context because of their large private pension sectors, did not take steps towards increasing private pension provision. Both countries, however, took initiatives aimed at improving the 'social performance' of private pensions in terms of universality and benefit adequacy for low income and atypical workers.

Cuts in public expenditure have tended to fall on income transfer programmes, or 'passive' expenditure, and within these programmes on those that seemed to be abused or those that provided benefits seen as over-generous. This was particularly the case in Italy with early retirement pensions and in the Netherlands with invalidity insurance. If cost containment is being pursued by Social Democratic governments, it seems not to be guided merely by expenditure consideration, but to incorporate social concerns, as testified by the choice of the targets for cost containment and by the inclination to regulate private alternatives with the objective of making them more suitable to those whose position in the labour market is weakest. Of course, whether this strategy will be successful in achieving the standard social policy objectives of poverty prevention and universality of coverage, remains to be seen.

Strengthen the social investment component of welfare states

Cuts in public expenditure on passive welfare benefits have sometimes been instrumental in freeing funds to be used for welfare programmes with a stronger social investment dimension, an approach that Jonah Levy has insightfully termed 'turning vice into virtue' (Levy 1999). More in general, even though the 1990s are considered to be a decade of 'hard times' for European welfares states, there are some social programmes that have prospered in those years, as we have seen the development in several European countries, of policies that have a strong social investment dimension. These distinguish themselves from the more traditional forms of social intervention, which basically have the objective of providing income security and protection against market risks. Social investment policies are those that make individuals more successful in the labour market. Typical social investment polices are training, particularly when related to employment policy, measures that help parents reconcile work and family life, and of course the emphasis that Social Democrats have been putting on education policies.

The UK is probably the country that has taken the most substantial steps in this direction, considering the degree of underdevelopment of these policies before the accession to power of New Labour in 1997. In that country, a significant effort has been made in active labour market policies that include training, job placements, or socially useful activities. Various 'New Deals' are targeted at different groups of the population, like for example, youth unemployed people, the long term unemployed, single parents or the disabled. Child care vouchers have also been made available to low income parents, so that they can more easily participate in the labour market, and finally a wage supplement for low paid workers has been introduced in the shape of a tax credit (Millar 2002).

Some of these measures have been adopted in several other countries, generally under Social Democratic leadership (e.g. the Netherlands, Italy, France, Germany). Active labour market policies have been introduced or strengthened throughout the continent, although in some countries, the focus on reintegrating the labour market is less strong than in other ones. For example, the French RMI includes a reinsertion component that is generally interpreted in terms of 'social insertion' rather the (re-) integration of the labour market. As a result, the sorts of measures that are offered to RMI recipients do not necessarily improve opportunities in the labour market. There are however in France other schemes that include a more work-oriented dimension.

Policies that aim at reconciling work and family life are also being stepped up in a number of countries. In Germany new legislation on parental leave and benefits promised in the 1998 election campaign has been adopted in 2000 by the Schröder government, with the result of increasing child benefit levels and introducing the right to part-time employment for young parents, though with some exceptions. The Netherlands has also introduced a legal right to ask employers to work part-time for parents. In Italy, the duration of parental leave has been extended to up to 11 months. But these developments are not found only in countries ruled by the Social Democrats. In Austria, the ÖVP/FPÖ coalition government, has introduced in 2001, a child care voucher for low income parents, and Spain has also recently improved parental leave coverage (Bertelsmann Foundation 2000; 2001). If the idea of a 'social investment' welfare state originated in Social Democratic thinking (Giddens 1998), it seems that today Social Democrats are not the only political force that is pursuing this course of policy.

Towards a Third Way?

The objective of this chapter, and of this whole book project, was to examine the policies adopted by the Social Democratic governments that were in power in Europe in the late 1990s and early 2000s. We wanted to ascertain whether the impressive production of political ideas, and discourse taking place under the 'Third Way' label is being matched by a corresponding development on the more mundane level of government's policy-making. We were particularly interested in establishing whether there is some convergence in Social Democratic approaches to social and economic policy in Western Europe, and the extent to which the possibly emerging model is distinctive in relation to previous progressive and liberal approaches.

In relation to the first question, our review of policy has shown a substantial degree of convergence among Social Democratic government policies. Policies falling under any of the three rubrics identified above have been adopted and developed, consistently, by virtually all Social Democratic governments. Often, where this has been less the case (e.g. in Germany in relation to employment maximisation), this was not as a result of a different orientation of the government in power. Lack of convergence seems to be more easily explainable with reference to institutional obstacles, and the presence in a political system of powerful veto players, who can effectively prevent the adoption of policy measures that run against their interest. In Germany, Schröder's ambitions to move policy in the direction of the 'Third Way' have often been frustrated by the influential trade unions. However, on occasions with skilful policy making strategies, the German government has managed to introduce policies that have a distinctive Third Way flavour, like in the field of pensions (see Hering this volume). Similarly in Italy the failure of the centre-left government of 1996–2001 to take a more centrist stance in labour market deregulation and in the containment of public spending may also be explained with reference to the presence of an important veto player in the ruling coalition: the left Socialist party (first *Rifondazione Comunista* and subsequently *I Comunisti Italiani*).

What is particularly striking, is that such convergence takes place more on the level of actual policies than on the level of discourse and, especially, labels. There is much more similarity in what Social Democrats are doing than in what they say they are doing. With the exception of Britain and possibly Germany, the Third Way label is generally rejected by Social Democratic leaders. There is somewhat more similarity if analysis moves beyond labels and focuses on the values that are defended by Social Democrats. Here we do find some convergence on values like 'equality of opportunity' on the positive role that the private sector can make in the production and in the delivery of public services, in the importance of having a competitive economy, etc. But we also find, in Sweden and France, a stronger attachment to traditional Social Democratic values.

Discourse needs to be adapted to the political context and traditions of individual countries. In this respect, it is not so surprising that there is variation in it. The most striking example in this respect is probably the famous Blair-Schröder paper, published in 1999 in English and in German (Blair and Schröder 1999). A quick comparison of the two versions reveals a number of not-so-innocent discrepancies between them and omissions. For example, the German version contains a sentence of praise for the labour movement,[2] which is totally absent form the English version. Other differences refer to the role of the social partners in promoting economic change,[3] and the fact that the Third Way should address the concerns of both winners and losers (only in the English version). These differences illustrate the difficulties involved in transposing political discourses from one country to another. As a matter of fact, in spite of them, the document was still sharply criticized in Germany, while in the UK it was virtually ignored.

Turning to our second question, whether the approach to social and economic policy developed by the new Social Democratic governments is distinctive, it is clear that Social Democratic parties have experienced a clear break with their past. Some of them have rewritten their statutes, abandoning the few remaining Marxist elements (Britain, Portugal). In Italy the transformation was underlined by a change of name of the main party of the left (the 'Communist party' was renamed 'Democratic Party of the Left'). However, what is probably more important, is the abandonment of some key policy objectives like the commitment to full-employment via demand-management and to vertical redistribution. The political orientation of the new Social Democratic governments in economic and social policy seems to be qualitatively different from that of their predecessors.

But is it substantively different from what their opponents are doing where they are in government? This question is somewhat more difficult to answer for want of cases. In the late 1990s and early 2000s very few European countries were ruled by right-of-centre governments. Where this is the case, in Spain and in Austria, the approach to social and economic policy does not seem to be very different from what Social Democratic government are doing in the rest of the continent. The typical Third Way policies discussed above seem to be equally common currency in Social Democratic and right-of-centre Europe. If anything, right-of-centre government may, in some instances, be more effective in imposing Third Way policies that generate opposition form vested interest. The comparison of Spain and Italy in relation to employment protection legislation is instructive in this respect. Both countries have a traditionally high level of protection against dismissal, which is widely seen as a key obstacle to job creation in the service sector, and is associated with higher unemployment rates for young people and women (Esping-Andersen 2000). In Italy, the centre-left governments of the 1990s tried on several occasions to spark a debate on how to relax job protection rules, but the fierce opposition of the trade unions and of left-wing coalition partners has not allowed them to take any significant step in that direction. In Spain, in contrast, the right-wing *Partido Popular* government was able to trade a reduction in the protection for core workers with an improvement of employment rights for atypical employees: a typical Third Way approach not so dissimilar from the one adopted in the Netherlands (Moreno 2000).

Differences exist also on the level of discourse, but in a rather unexpected direction. Today in Europe, the political leaders who seem to be most comfortable with the 'Third Way' label, are not Social Democrats, but Liberals. The claim to be pursuing a 'Third Way' political project is put forward much more forcefully in Spain (*via media*, see Moreno 2000) or in Belgium (by a Liberal Prime Minister) than in most of the countries ruled by left-of centre governments.

Overall, it seems that relatively little variation in policy can be ascribed to the government's political and ideological orientation. The factors that have been identified above as responsible for the variation in policy outcomes such as country specific institutional structures and differences in starting points seem much more relevant than politics in accounting for difference. This view is supported by Huber and Stephens' quantitative analysis of nearly half a century of social policy making, which shows that there has been first a reduction and then the disappearance of partisan effects on welfare effort (Huber and Stephens 2001: 321). These conclusions suggest that the 'Third Way' rather than a renewed form of Social democracy, can best be seen as an emerging new consensus that draws support from across party lines and replaces previous 'consensuses' (Keynesianism, neoliberalism) as the dominant paradigm in economic and social policies.

Postcript: the electoral failures of the third way

One of the most recurring critiques made against the centrist reorientation of Social Democratic parties, has been that of electoral opportunism, and in this respect it is somewhat ironic that many of the left-of-centre governments that were in power in the late 1990s, lost elections in the early 2000s. How can we explain this reversal of fortune for European Social Democrats? A spatial interpretation of the electoral failures of centrist left-wing parties, would have it that the move towards the right has created an empty space on their left which has either been filled by a left-wing competitor or resulted in voter disaffection and low turnout among those on the far left. While theoretically convincing, such an explanation is not confirmed by election results. In fact, in most of the Western European countries that have held elections in the early 2000s, Social Democratic parties have suffered electoral losses. The winners, however, have not been left Socialist parties, but their right-wing competitors. As table 1 shows, in a majority of the countries that were ruled by left-of-centre governments in the 1990s and that have had elections in the early 2000s, the decline in the vote for Social Democratic parties has been accompanied by losses among their left wing competitors and by gains for centre-right parties.

Table 11.1 Election results of selected European Social Democratic parties*

	Main Social Democratic party		*Main left-wing competitor*		*Main right-wing competitor*	
	Late 1990s	*Early 2000s*	*Late 1990s*	*Early 2000s*	*Late 1990s*	*Early 2000s*
Denmark	35.9	29.1	7.6	6.3	24.0	31.2
Francc	25.2	24.1	9.9	4.8	19.8	33.3**
Germany	40.9	38.5	5.1	4.0	35.2	38.5
Italy	21.1	16.6	8.6	5.0	20.6	29.4
Netherlands	29.0	15.1	7.3	7.0	18.4	27.9
Portugal	43.8	38.5	8.9	7.1	32.2	40.9
Sweden	36.3	39.8	11.9	8.3	22.9	15.2
UK	43.2	40.7	–	–	30.1	31.7

Sources: Data obtained from individual parliaments

Notes
* Results are for the lower chambers . In France, first round; in Germany second vote, in Italy, proportional representation vote.
** in 1997: RPR, in 2002 UMP, which includes also part of UDF.

To explain the reversal in the electoral fortunes of Social Democratic parties in the early 2000s is a task that clearly falls beyond the scope of this book. However, the conclusions presented in this last chapter can help us generate a hypothesis to this end. It is possible that the Third Way has been a victim of its own success. In the mid-1990s, the values and the policies that had been popularised under this label were strongly associated with Social Democratic parties. Voters who liked this new approach had no choice but to vote left-of-centre. In the early 2000s, however, these values and policies have become much more pervasive, and are now common currency in the programmes of most mainstream political parties. With Social Democrats being unable to offer a distinctive product, voting behaviour is more likely to be determined by non-policy-related factors, such as party identities, personality of candidates, and so forth. This would allow us to understand the contrasting fortunes of left wing leaders and parties in the early 2000s, while in the 1990s electoral success seemed to be within reach for all.

Notes

1 The Christian–Social governments that have ruled Belgium during most of the 1990s, did not develop such employment promotion policies to any significant extent (Hemerijck *et al.* 2000). However, the new Liberal–social purple coalition government seems considerably more oriented towards an 'activation' approach in policy towards non-working people (Hoop, Chapter 4, this volume).
2 "Wir wollen, dass die Gewerkschaften in der Moderner Welt verankert bleiben" (We want the trade unions to remain embedded in the modern world).
3 The English version says that: 'we will strive to pursue an ongoing dialog with

the social partners that supports, *not hinders*, necessary economic change'. The phrase '*not hinders*' is absent in the German version.

References

Bertelsmann Foundation (ed.) (2000) *International Reform Monitor. Social Policy, Labour Market Policy, Industrial Relations*, Issue 3, October.

Blair, A. and Schröder G. (1999) *Europe: the Third Way – die Neue Mitte*, London/Berlin, Labour Party/SPD.

Bonoli, G. (2000) *The Politics of Pension Reform. Institutions and Policy Change in Western Europe*, Cambridge: Cambridge University Press.

Clasen. J. (2000) 'Motives, means and opportunities. Reforming unemployment compensation in the 1990s', *West European Politics*, 23(2): 89–112.

D'Alessandro, P. (2002) 'La Terza Via nella politica occupazionale tedesca. Cambiamento programmatico o strategia elettorale?', unpublished manuscript, Institute of Political Science, University of Berne, Switzerland.

Esping-Andersen, G. (2000) 'Who is harmed by labour market regulations?: quantitative evidence', in G. Esping-Andersen and M. Regini (eds), *Why Deregulate Labour Markets?*, Oxford: Oxford University Press, 66–98.

FDP (1999) *Gerhardt Schröders Wendepapier – auch ein Wendepunkt fuer die SPD?*, Bonn, Press release, 9 June.

Ferrera M. and Gualmini E. (1999) *Salvati dall'Europa?*, Bologna, Il Mulino.

Giddens, A. (1998) *The Third Way: the Renewal of Social Democracy*, Cambridge, Polity Press.

Goul Andersen, J. (2000) 'Welfare crisis and beyond: Danish welfare policies in the 1980s and in the 1990s' in S. Kuhnle (ed.), *Survival of the European Welfare State*, London, Routledge, 69–87.

Hemerijck, A., Unger B. and Visser, J. (2000) 'How small countries negotiate change: twenty-five years of policy adjustment in Austria, the Netherlands and Belgium, in Scharpf, F. and Schmidt, V. (eds), *From Vulnerability to Competitiveness: Welfare and Work in the Open Economy*. Oxford: Oxford University Press.

Huber, E. and Stephens, J. (2001) *Development and Crisis of the Welfare State: Parties and Policies in Global Markets*, Chicago, University of Chicago Press.

Jobert, B and Muller, P. (1987) *L'Etat en action*, Paris, PUF.

Levy, J. D. (1999) 'Vice into virtue? Progressive politics of welfare reform in continental Europe', *Politics and Society* 27: 239–73.

Levy, J. D. (2000) 'France: Directing Adjustment?' in Scharpf, F. and Schmidt, V. (eds), *From Vulnerability to Competitiveness: Welfare and Work in the Open Economy*. Oxford: Oxford University Press.

Millar, J. (2002) 'Adjusting welfare policies to stimulate job entry: the example of the United Kingdom', in H. Srfati and G. Bonoli (eds) *Labour Market and Social Protection Reforms in International Perspective*, Aldershot, Ashgate, 266–84.

Moreno, L. (2000) 'The Spanish development of Southern European Welfare', in S. Kuhnle (ed.), *Survival of the European Welfare State*, London, Routledge, 140–65.

Pierson, P. (1994) *Dismantling the Welfare State? Reagan, Thatcher and The Politics of Retrenchment*, Cambridge, Cambridge University Press.

Sabatier, P. (1993) 'Policy change over a decade or more', in P. Sabatier and H. Jenkins-Smith (eds), *Policy Change and Learning. An advocacy Coalition Approach*, Boulder, Westview Press, 13–39.

Schmidt, V. (2000) 'Values and discourse in the politics of adjustment' in F. Schaprf and V. Schmidt (eds), *Welfare and Work in the Open Economy: Diverse Responses to Common Challenges, Volume 1,* Oxford: Oxford University Press, 229–309.

Svensson, C. (2001) 'Swedish Social Democracy and the Third Way: a delicate affair', in R. Cuperus, K. Duffek and J. Kandel, (eds), *Multiple Third Ways: European Social Democracy Facing the Twin Revolution of Globalisation and the Knowledge Society,* Amsterdam/Berlin/Vienna, Friedrich-Ebert-Stiftung/Wiardi Beckman Stichting/Renner Institut, 217–26.

Index

References to figures and tables are in *italic.*

For Product Safety Concerns and Information please contact our EU representative GPSR@taylorandfrancis.com
Taylor & Francis Verlag GmbH, Kaufingerstraße 24, 80331 München, Germany

www.ingramcontent.com/pod-product-compliance
Ingram Content Group UK Ltd.
Pitfield, Milton Keynes, MK11 3LW, UK
UKHW020159200926
475702UK00004B/527
* 9 7 8 0 4 1 5 3 0 4 2 5 2 *